Translation Ethics

Translation Ethics introduces the topic of ethics for students, researchers, and professional translators. Based on a successful course and written by an experienced instructor, the Introduction and nine core chapters offer an accessible examination of a wide range of interlocking topic areas, which combine to form a cohesive whole, guiding students through the key debates.

Built upon a theoretical background founded in philosophy and moral theory, it outlines the main contributions in the area and traces the development of thought on ethics from absolutism to relativism, or, from staunchly argued textual viewpoints to current lines of thought placing the translator as agent and an active – even interventionary – mediator. The textbook then examines the place of ethical enquiry in the context of professional translation, critiquing provision such as codes of ethics. Each chapter includes key discussion points, suggested topics for essays, presentations, or in-class debates, and an array of contextualised examples and case studies. Additional resources, including videos, weblinks, online activities, and PowerPoint slide presentations on the Routledge Translation studies portal provide valuable extra pedagogical support.

This wide-ranging and accessible textbook has been carefully designed to be key reading for a wide range of courses, including distance-learning courses, from translation and interpreting ethics to translation theory and practice.

Joseph Lambert is a Lecturer in Translation Studies at Cardiff University. His research focuses on translation ethics and the translation profession, and he teaches both undergraduate and postgraduate sessions on translation ethics. Recent publications include a chapter on Professional Translator Ethics in the *Routledge Handbook of Translation and Ethics*.

Routledge Introductions to Translation and Interpreting
Series Editor:
Sergey Tyulenev is the Director of the MA in Translation and Russian Studies at the School of Modern Languages and Cultures, Durham University, UK.

Advisory Board
Luise von Flotow, University of Ottawa, Canada
Ricardo Munoz Martin, University of Bologna, Italy
Kobus Marais, University of the Free State, South Africa
Nike K. Pokorn, University of Ljubljana, Slovenia
James St André, Chinese University of Hong Kong, China
Michaela Wolf, University of Graz, Austria

Routledge Introductions to Translation and Interpreting is a series of textbooks, designed to meet the need for teaching materials for translator/interpreter training. Accessible and aimed at beginning students but also useful for instructors designing and teaching courses, the series covers a broad range of topics, many of which are already core courses while others cover new directions of translator/interpreter teaching.

The series reflects the standards of the translator/interpreter training and professional practice set out by national and international competence frameworks and codes of translation/language service provision and are aimed at a global readership.

All topics combine both practical and theoretical aspects so as to ensure a bridging of the gap between the academic and professional world and all titles include a range of pedagogical support: activities, case studies etc.

Most recent titles in the series:

Translation Project Management
Callum Walker

Translation Tools and Technologies
Andrew Rothwell, Joss Moorkens, Maria Fernández Parra, Joanna Drugan and Frank Austermuehl

For more information on any of these and other titles, or to order, please go to https://www.routledge.com/Routledge-Introductions-to-Translation-and-Interpreting/book-series/RITI

Additional resources for Translation and Interpreting Studies are available on the Routledge Translation Studies Portal: http://cw.routledge.com/textbooks/translationstudies

Translation Ethics

Joseph Lambert

LONDON AND NEW YORK

Designed cover image: Getty Images | wildpixel

First published 2023
by Routledge
4 Park Square, Milton Park, Abingdon, Oxon OX14 4RN

and by Routledge
605 Third Avenue, New York, NY 10158

Routledge is an imprint of the Taylor & Francis Group, an informa business

© 2023 Joseph Lambert

The right of Joseph Lambert to be identified as author of this work has been asserted in accordance with sections 77 and 78 of the Copyright, Designs and Patents Act 1988.

All rights reserved. No part of this book may be reprinted or reproduced or utilised in any form or by any electronic, mechanical, or other means, now known or hereafter invented, including photocopying and recording, or in any information storage or retrieval system, without permission in writing from the publishers.

Trademark notice: Product or corporate names may be trademarks or registered trademarks, and are used only for identification and explanation without intent to infringe.

British Library Cataloguing-in-Publication Data
A catalogue record for this book is available from the British Library

Library of Congress Cataloging-in-Publication Data
Names: Lambert, Joseph (Lecturer in translation studies), author.
Title: Translation ethics / Joseph Lambert.
Description: Abingdon, Oxon ; New York, NY : Routledge, 2023. |
Series: Routledge introductions to translation and interpreting |
Includes bibliographical references and index.
Identifiers: LCCN 2022041923 | ISBN 9780367708528 (paperback) |
ISBN 9780367708535 (hardback) | ISBN 9781003148265 (ebook)
Subjects: LCSH: Translating and interpreting–Moral and ethical aspects.
Classification: LCC P306.97.M67 L36 2023 |
DDC 174/.941802–dc23/eng/20221221
LC record available at https://lccn.loc.gov/2022041923

ISBN: 978-0-367-70853-5 (hbk)
ISBN: 978-0-367-70852-8 (pbk)
ISBN: 978-1-003-14826-5 (ebk)

DOI: 10.4324/9781003148265

Typeset in Sabon
by Newgen Publishing UK

Access the Support Material: http://routledgetranslationstudiesportal.com/

Contents

	List of Figures	vi
	List of Boxes	vii
	Acknowledgements	viii
	About the Author	x
	Series Editor's Foreword	xi
	Introduction	1
1	Philosophical Foundations	11
2	Translation Ethics	29
3	Truth	43
4	Responsibility	58
5	Justice	75
6	Commitment	93
7	Standards	116
8	Ethical Professionals	136
9	Other Viewpoints	161
	Bibliography	175
	Index	187

Figures

0.1	Translation and interpreting ethics "levels"	3
4.1	Functionalist model of communication	60
4.2	Areas of responsibility in Pym's ethics of cooperation	66
6.1	The continuum of agency	99
8.1	Gender Bias in Google Translate	157
9.1	Potential reflections on responsibility in translation and interpreting	171

Boxes

1.1	Starting out: A problem to ponder	11
1.2	Deontology in practice: A thought experiment	20
1.3	Consequentialism	23
1.4	Alive, but at what cost? A test of ethical stances	25
2.1	The link to virtue ethics	32
2.2	Kimigayo	36
2.3	The Chinese tradition	40
3.1	Berman's twelve deforming tendencies	48
3.2	Translating idioms: An example	52
4.1	How to achieve loyalty?	63
4.2	Cooperation in action	67
4.3	A case study on loyalty and cooperation	71
5.1	Ethics and subjectivity	77
5.2	Foreignisation in practice	82
5.3	A critique of cultural mediators	89
6.1	"I'm just the translator"	97
6.2	Activism, accountability, and conflicts of interest	106
6.3	*Telos* and accountability in action	109
6.4	Unbridled relativism: The fake sign language interpreter	112
7.1	The ATA Code of Ethics and professional practice	119
7.2	A case study: Confidentiality	130
7.3	A case study: Neutrality	132
8.1	Environmental sustainability	141
8.2	The Railway Man – Ethical stress in T&I	145
8.3	How much should you charge?	149
8.4	Technology, money, and ethics	158
9.1	How far do questions of ethics extend? Gender-inclusive language and ethics	164
9.2	Enlightened egoism	167
9.3	A case study: Amanda Gorman's Dutch translator	169

Acknowledgements

There are so many people who have contributed both directly and indirectly to the drafting of this textbook over the course of the last few years, and it feels a somewhat futile task to fully thank them all here. Nevertheless, I'll give it a try.

Above all, thank you to the series editor Dr Sergey Tyulenev (Durham University) for having the trust and confidence in me to write one of the first books in this fantastic new series. Thank you for always being such a generous colleague, a patient editor, and a constant supportive presence, from drafting the initial proposal through to final submission.

Thanks, too, to colleagues at Cardiff for regularly sharing ideas and suggestions, pointing out potentially interesting avenues of exploration, resources, and cases studies, and – importantly – allowing me to develop ideas in the classroom, having free reign over sessions on ethics. Of course, I must also thank our students – the primary target audience for this book – for their willingness to engage with all of these ideas and to share their personal perspectives and examples.

Huge thanks go to the reviewers of the textbook, who provided a wealth of invaluable suggestions that have improved the shape, structure, and content of the book considerably. I only hope that the final content is able to reflect your vision for the project.

I also owe a debt of gratitude to Dr Callum Walker (University of Leeds) for assistance with pretty much everything along the way. It has been a huge help to work on this book "in parallel" to your own wonderful contribution to the series, and my work has benefitted no end from your input. Our regular chats over the years about all things translation (and much more besides) have provided countless insights, new perspectives, and laughs while your invaluable comments on chapter drafts, help with content structure, and willingness to try out these ideas with your own cohorts are all very much appreciated.

Thanks too to Evie Elliott for her reader's perspective on chapter drafts, general editorial wizardry, and unrivalled attention to detail. Your thoughts, ideas, and suggestions were all hugely helpful.

A special mention goes to Louisa Semlyen, Talitha Duncan-Todd, and Eleni Steck at Routledge, whose support, guidance, patience, and understanding were extremely welcome throughout the process.

Finally, thank you to my family and friends for the much-needed support and distraction, and to little Tobias as a constant smiling presence.

Any omissions, inaccuracies, or other errors are my own.

About the Author

Dr Joseph Lambert is a Lecturer in Translation Studies at Cardiff University, having joined in September 2020. He teaches and convenes a range of modules on both the MA Translation Studies and the BA Translation. His current teaching includes a considerable focus on translation ethics as well as sessions on computer-assisted translation technology, pathways into the translation profession, general and specialised translation (French to English), and translation theory more generally, as well as supervising translation projects and dissertations at both UG and PG levels. He has previously taught at Durham University (2019–2020), University of Birmingham (2018–2019), and University of Hull (2014–2018).

His primary area of research interest is the ethics of translation, and, like his teaching, this work sits at the interface between translation theory and practice. He has authored and co-authored a number of articles and book chapters relating to translation ethics, including several articles on codes of ethics, a chapter on "Professional Translator Ethics" in *The Routledge Handbook of Translation and Ethics* (2021, Kaisa Koskinen and Nike Pokorn, eds.), and work exploring the complex relationship between translation rates of pay, status, and regulation.

Much of his research is designed with the aim of eliciting tangible impacts upon working practices and bridging the gap between academia and the translation industry, a link that is concretised by a background in professional translation. He set up his own freelance translation business in 2012 and has accumulated a wealth of real-life experience in the translation industry, *working* from French and Italian into English. Though he works primarily in the contexts of sports and social media translation, this work has spanned a wide range of text and practice types, from app localisation to academic translation, and has ranged in scale from standalone projects with individual clients to long-standing partnerships with global institutions.

Series Editor's Foreword

Translator and interpreter training programmes have become an integral feature of the present-day professional educational landscape all over the world. There are at least two good reasons for that. On the one hand, it has been realised that to work as a translator or interpreter, one needs more than to speak a couple of languages; a special training in translation and interpreting is a must. On the other hand, translator/interpreter training programmes are seen as a practical way to start a career in the language-service provision industry or to earn a degree as a Translation/Interpreting Studies scholar. These programmes may be part of the university curriculum or stand-alone courses in various formats of continuing studies or qualification upgrading.

Yet there is still a dearth of teaching materials geared at novices in translation or interpreting. In every class, students are either given sheaves of handouts which, by the end of the course, build up into a pile of paper or referred to a small library of publications for a chapter here and a chapter there. As a result, the student struggles to imagine the subject area as a coherent whole and there is no helpful textbook for references while in the course or after.

The lack of coursebooks makes life little easier for translator/interpreter trainers. Even if they find a suitable book or monograph, a great deal of adaptation must be done. The instructor would have to adjust the book to the length of the course and individual teaching sessions, to add exercises and assignments, questions and topics for presentations to facilitate students' engagement with the materials and to help them go beyond the 'read-only' mode of working with the recommended book(s).

The purport of the series *Routledge Introductions to Translation and Interpreting* is to put into the hands of the translator/interpreter trainee and trainer ready-made textbooks. Each textbook is written by an expert or a team of experts in the subject area under discussion; moreover each author has vast experience of teaching the subject of their textbook. The series reflects what has already become staple courses and modules in the translator/interpreter training – but it also introduces new areas of teaching and research. The series is meant as a kind of library of textbooks – all books present various aspects of a translation and interpreting training programme viewed as a whole. They can be taken as a basis for developing new programmes and courses or reinforcing the existing ones.

Translation ethics, the theme of the present textbook, is still a relatively new subject in translator and interpreter training. Every profession has its ethical standards. Translation and interpreting are no exception. Nowadays translators and interpreters pay more and more attention to the moral choices they face and to the ethical aspects of their relationship with clients and colleagues. Today the professional translator and interpreter is required to perform not only as a skilled expert but also as an ethical person.

While there are numerous publications on various aspects of translator/interpreter ethics, few of them are adapted as a (self-)taught course. This is exactly what this textbook does. It offers an in-depth theoretical discussion of the most fundamental aspects of translation/interpreting ethics and at the same time it invites the reader to consider practical applications of the learned theories.

The textbook has global appeal. It is written with the international readership in mind. It considers the ethics of both translation and interpreting. It is suitable for the budding translator/interpreter and the seasoned professional alike.

Translation/interpreting ethics is Dr Joseph Lambert's academic specialism. He has published on the topic, and he has been teaching it for several years in translator/interpreting training programmes. All this makes him an ideal guide into the multifaceted and vital world of ethics.

Sergey Tyulenev

Introduction

What is the 'right' way to translate a text? How should a 'professional' interpreter act? What has been the ethical impact of technological developments in the language industry? Who can or should translate in a particular context? All of these questions (and many more!) fall under the far-reaching domain of translation and interpreting ethics, a topic that has now long occupied scholars and practitioners and represents an ever-broadening area of focus within the field.

While sporadic works on ethics within Translation and Interpreting Studies (TIS) can be found prior to the 1990s, it was at the end of the twentieth century when a number of influential scholars really began to tackle the subject in earnest. Since then, its increased relevance in the last two decades has been exemplified by the efforts of scholars such as Mona Baker and Christiane Nord to incorporate ethics into updated editions of their previously published works and the proliferation of an ever-expanding catalogue of publications on ethics, which is constantly pushing in new directions as we seek to keep on top of such a dynamic, fast-changing, and crucial topic. In the last five years, scholars have sought to tackle issues including social responsibility (Drugan and Tipton 2017), representativeness (Kotze and Strowe 2021), sustainable Machine Translation (e.g. Moorkens, Kenny, and do Carmo 2020), and ethical stress (Hubscher-Davidson 2021). On the professional side, meanwhile, while codes of ethics have long been a feature of discourse on ethics, they are not without their shortcomings, and emerging conversations in relation to technological developments, industry disruptors, and issues of pay (among others) have highlighted a number of gaps. Despite a history steeped in neutrality and invisibility, as explored at length in this textbook, translators and interpreters are inevitably, and perhaps increasingly, both politically and ethically engaged.

And yet, beyond this explicit engagement with ethics, there is also a more implicit undercurrent within research dating back centuries. Indeed, there is an underlying assumption that ethics is relevant to all translation, with the very act necessitating "an account (explicit or implicit) of how the encounter with the 'other' human being should be conducted" (Goodwin 2010:26). Unsurprisingly, this level of generality leaves a vast area to be

DOI: 10.4324/9781003148265-1

covered, which can be approached from a number of different perspectives. This scope means that there is little to no consensus on what ethics requires of us, and this partly stems from differing understandings of key terms and ideas. As Inghilleri and Maier put it:

> [d]espite growing commitment amongst groups of translation scholars and practitioners to address such questions [pertaining to ethics] [...] we have not by any means reached a clear understanding of or agreement about what an 'ethical' approach actually means in the context of translation theory or practice, or the construction of the field itself.
> (Inghilleri and Maier 2011, in Baker 2011a: 100)

And though Koskinen convincingly argues that "conclusive historical charting of the ethics of translation is, if not impossible, an enormous task" (Koskinen 2000: 16), this textbook intends to bring together a wide range of ideas in an accessible format and provide a basis for further explorations in the area.

Chapter Content and Design

As alluded to above, the "ethical" conundrum of how exactly we should act when we translate or interpret, where we should/can place our loyalties, or how we should engage with the world is by no means a straightforward matter. Until now, it has been a particularly complex landscape to navigate for those entering the field. This textbook represents a first attempt to bring together key ethical questions and guidance in a manner accessible to students, educators, and professionals alike, establishing a grounding from which to delve further into the vast array of contributions in the field.[1] Given the vast range of perspectives on ethics, the task of bringing contributions together in a logical, meaningful way is a tricky one. Thankfully, however, there are a number of overarching frameworks developed in recent years to facilitate the process. Chesterman (2016: 168), a leading voice on ethical issues in translation, makes a productive distinction between micro- and macro- levels to ethics, which offers a useful starting point for trying to group these far-reaching conceptions. For him, **macro-ethical** matters

> concern broad social questions such as the role and rights of translators in society, conditions of work, financial rewards and the client's profit motive, the general aims of translation as intercultural action, power relations between translators and clients, the relation between translation and state politics: in short, the relation between the translator and the world.

Micro-ethical matters, meanwhile

concern the translator's action during the translation process itself, questions dealing with specific textual matters, translation strategies and the like: in short, the relation between the translator and the words on the page.

While Chesterman rightly notes that the lines are blurred between these two categories, which mutually impact each other, the divide remains a useful one to begin to categorise the mass of contributions into more manageable groups. We will return to this micro/macro distinction at multiple points.

Another slightly more nuanced division is made in the field of interpreting by Phelan et al (2020: 62), who use the illustration in Figure 0.1 to conceptualise concerns with ethics as three circles expanding from a centre. Commenting on the diagram, the authors explain that while "the intrinsic ST-TT (source text-target text bond is the nucleus of translational ethics at a textual level, it is embedded in other levels or spheres of professional ethics" (Phelan et al. 2020: 61). These levels are labelled as the interpersonal and the social (or the "community sphere") and correspond to Chesterman's conception of macro-ethical considerations. With these models firmly in mind, I follow a path from micro- to macro-ethical matters (to use Chesterman's terminology) or from the centre of the diagram to the outer edges (Figure 0.1), gradually expanding the scale of our enquiry. However, I also recognise the need to provide some underlying context before diving into the challenges of translation and interpreting specifically.

In Chapter 1, I begin by exploring slippery definitions of ethics and covering fundamental **philosophical foundations** that (often implicitly) underlie the translation theories covered in this textbook. This brief general

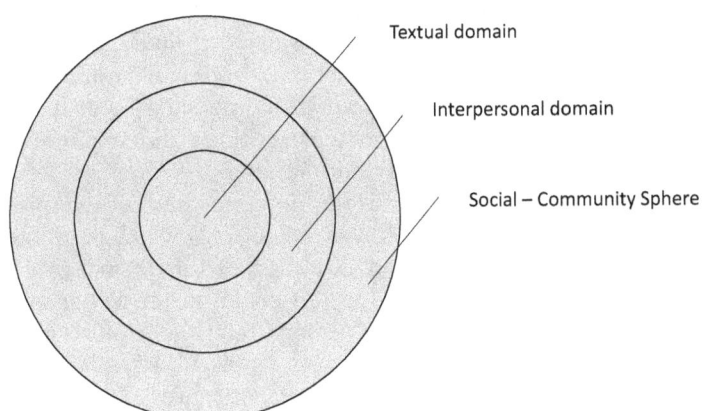

Figure 0.1 Translation and interpreting ethics "levels" – adapted from Phelan et al. 2020: 62.

overview enables readers to meaningfully engage with ideas in TIS, defining key concepts and outlining three of the most prominent schools of thought within moral theory – deontology, consequentialism, and virtue ethics – which all feature in theories of translation ethics.

Next, I turn to the context of **translation ethics** specifically, exploring some fundamental ethical ideas in Chapter 2. This chapter outlines four key areas of focus on translation ethics and explores the vital question of fidelity. This leads to a foregrounding of the textual domain, which is explored at length in Chapter 3 in relation to questions of **truth**. Discussions in this chapter simultaneously bring deontology squarely into focus and question whether there is a universally 'right' way to translate, considering the ideas of influential translation scholar Antoine Berman. His passionately defended cause draws our attention to a key range of textual features to consider when translating, though some important limitations force us to extend our enquiry elsewhere. This is where Chapters 4, 5, and 6 come in, moving to the interpersonal domain, where we no longer simply focus on our relationship with texts, but rather start to consider the wide range of agents involved in the translation industry. While all three chapters can be loosely grouped under a wider theme of **agency**, exploring varying degrees of active engagement among translators and interpreters, each with their own advantages and disadvantages, there is a gradual outward expansion across the chapters as the interpersonal subtly transforms into the social.

Chapter 4 initiates an ongoing problematisation of the complex issue of **responsibility** – first from a functionalist perspective, exploring Nord's powerful concept of loyalty, and then in relation to Pym's fascinating and evolving concepts of cooperation, risk, and trust. These ideas place the human beings involved at the heart of our thinking and challenge us to consider where our responsibility lies, as well as alluding to the context-based, personal, ideologically charged dimensions of ethics. This final range of themes is accentuated in Chapter 5, which is based around the question of **justice**. As well as consolidating the non-neutral, subjective nature of ethics, this chapter categorically posits the translator and interpreter as active agents in shaping knowledge transfer. It achieves this via an exploration of Venuti's ubiquitous work on visibility and an ethics of difference, as well as Inghilleri's powerful critique of neutrality in the context of interpreting, and marks a decisive shift to the wider social context in which practitioners work. Chapter 6 is, in some ways, an extension of this theme, exploring the limits of agency under an overall label of **commitment**. Discussions in this chapter blur the lines between the personal and the professional and expand the translator and interpreter's roles from cultural mediators to advocates and even activists who champion certain causes. I explore these ideas through close engagement with Baker's thought in particular, which eventually leads us to consider the importance of being accountable for our choices and actions and the perils of moral relativism.

Chapters 7 and 8, meanwhile, represent something of a shift in focus, turning our attention squarely to the professional context. Chapter 7 explores **standards** that professional translators and interpreters are expected to abide by via an in-depth examination of the content, construction, and shortcomings of codes of ethics in the area. It explains key principles as well as exposing gaps, blindspots, and contradictions, encouraging readers to engage critically with these documents. Chapter 8, meanwhile, considers other key concerns facing today's **ethical professionals**. This wide-ranging chapter covers topics as diverse as rates of pay and environmental sustainability, and proposes both outward and inward reflections, where the question of responsibility once again rears its head. Outwardly, we must consider social responsibility, while inwardly we must also reflect on the need to prioritise our own mental and physical (and arguably financial) health. The fast-changing nature of the language industry also dictates that we consider emerging ethical challenges that have accompanied technological developments. These sweeping changes have, in some cases, revolutionised the way we need to think about translation – notably in terms of practice types, quality, fidelity, and privacy.

Finally, Chapter 9 brings proceedings to a close by considering **other viewpoints** – combining sets of ideas that were not explored elsewhere (whether due to space constraints or as a means of maximising the overall cohesion of the textbook) and emerging ideas that demonstrate new, innovative, and challenging ways that we can continue to reflect on how we conceptualise ethics and how we should treat Others. The central 'case studies' in treating otherness touch upon themes of selfhood, representation, and representativeness, before I return one final time to the ever-present issue of responsibility. This time, armed with knowledge gleaned from the wide range of theories, thought, and frameworks explored over the course of the textbook, readers are encouraged to reflect on potential paths forward, and suggestions are provided for potential essay, discussion, and research topics in many of the domains covered.

At this point, a quick note on the inclusion of both translation and interpreting is in order. Though the term 'translation' is often used as a hypernym to cover both practices, I have endeavoured to explore the distinct challenges raised by both oral and written modes of translation. It is worth noting that while there are many challenges that are shared across and beyond these modes, the range of practices that fall under the umbrella of translation is so diverse that it is impossible to cover every context. For instance, this textbook offers no in-depth, specific coverage of subtitling or localisation despite the current prominence of these practices, and this is reflective of the wider focus of research in TIS. Readers are encouraged to reflect on how the ideas covered will apply to the specific contexts in which they work, which also reflects the wider design of this textbook and the relevance both to the academic and professional contexts.

About this Book

Audience and features

As an introductory textbook, it is not possible (nor desirable) to cover every theory, framework, or idea in detail. Instead, this book is designed to provide a balanced, wide-ranging grounding in translation ethics while also inviting readers to reflect and engage with ideas beyond those that are explicitly presented here. I place considerable focus on encouraging readers to explore additional sources and to consider the applicability of core ideas in their specific professional domain, language area, or cultural setting, for instance. Indeed, a core objective throughout the book lies in encouraging the reader to be reflective and to critically consider what they read. Each chapter asks key questions and opens up space for critical engagement with ideas covered, commenting upon strengths and potential weaknesses or gaps where appropriate. Above all, this textbook is designed to be an accessible entry point to a complex and multifaceted topic that has long been prominent in TIS and continues to gain attention in both academic and professional contexts.

While primarily written with a postgraduate student of interpreting or translation in mind, this book is designed to be used by a broad audience of students, trainers, scholars, professionals, and interested readers in parallel domains. An accessible tone is adopted throughout and insights are designed to be practically relevant and contextualised in relation to the practices they describe. Given the nature of typical translation cohorts, which may be at undergraduate or postgraduate level and often include non-native speakers of English, content is designed to be user-friendly, breaking down often tricky ideas in an easily understandable manner. This book can act as a basis for independent study in ethics, a complement, companion, or a counterpoint to studies in translation and interpreting, a source of inspiration for ideas or examples, and an underlying framework for a key area of professional concern. Given the textbook leaves a number of unanswered and underexplored topics in relation to ethics, the talking points provided throughout could also provide the blueprint for dissertations and even PhD study. Finally, professionals too will benefit from this textbook, exposing them to many ideas that have rarely entered the professional domain, and which may inform practice or challenge current understandings.

Each chapter opens with a rundown of three key questions tackled, and this is intended to act as a point of orientation for readers, priming them for the discussions to come and concretising central themes. In each chapter key concepts are bolded, and there are a series of questions interspersed between discussions to encourage readers to pause and reflect on the ideas covered. At times these questions are rather simple and straightforward. At others, they can be more complex or even deliberately provocative. This range is designed to reflect the scope of discussions that can be sparked when covering what are often dense, challenging topics. At the end of each chapter, there are also three 'Discussion, Presentation, and Assignment Topics', which (as the name suggests) variously invite readers to consider lines of enquiry that may open up new discussions or could be used for assessments – from group and individual presentations to opinion pieces, blog entries, and academic essays and dissertations. Finally, this book is also complemented by additional learning materials on the Routledge Translation Studies Portal ('TS Portal' at http://routledgetranslationstudiesportal.com), including additional assignment tasks, discussion points, and case studies. Future updates will also include slide templates for each chapter. To find the relevant resources for this textbook, readers should click on *Resources* and *View by Book*, before navigating to the link for this book.

A case study-based approach

More widely, the textbook reflects a now long-standing call for further coverage of ethics in translator training, arising on the back of the recognition of its undeniable importance to both translators and contemporary TIS scholars.[2] Zhou (2022: 1) contends that ethics is now an "explicit and integrative component of translator education" and that the goal of teaching ethics has moved from "preaching abstract, universalistic translator codes of ethics to training translation students' ethical sensitivity and reflexive moral judgement (i.e. ethical decision-making)." Central to this aim of encouraging reflexive, sensitive judgement in this textbook is the use of numerous case studies throughout. This follows Drugan and Megone's recommendation for an integrated approach to ethics, which does not reduce ethics to a single session within a larger "theory" module (prevalent on many courses in translation), thus stymying links to actual practice (2011: 207), but rather seeks to embed ethics within the wider context of translator training, by slotting key themes in with existing concerns, both professional and theoretical in nature.

As such, the case studies I use do not just apply to practical, "real life" scenarios, but also to the theoretical explorations in each chapter, where scholars' ideas are selected as representing a key idea or development of thought that advances our thinking or introduces a new perspective. Elsewhere, case studies expose the travails of the translator and interpreter in terms of individual decision-making and in the wider context of industry workflows, drawing attention to the complex networks and power relations at work. While the profession is not explicitly our central focus until Chapter 7, it is a crucial implicit theme throughout, and the use of practical case studies reinforces this focus.

In line with the goal of fostering curiosity outlined above, readers are also encouraged to seek out their own case studies in languages or personal areas of interest to apply the ideas covered in this book in a concrete, independent manner and open up additional channels of dialogue either in the classroom, between friends and family or colleagues, or personal study. Case studies may appear in local news publications, on social media (translator and interpreter groups often involve discussions of ethical issues), via Internet searches for keywords such as "translation confidentiality", or via translation profession-specific websites such as ProZ.com and TranslatorsCafe.com, which have dedicated forums with specific sub-sections for ethics-related cases. For the instructor, these cases work well as both whole-group exercises, with the instructor presenting a case and then inviting responses, or small-group exercises, with students discussing a case as a team before feeding back to a larger discussion, which will usually highlight illuminating points of commonality and contrast around the classroom. While I have sought to avoid prescriptiveness as much as possible, there are also several suggested responses to discussions to provide a starting point for further debates and perspectives to be shared.

For both students and trainers looking for realistic case studies, Drugan and Megone's (2011) article is another invaluable resource. Not only does their paper include five fascinating scenarios based on key challenges that translators are likely to face in their work (194–204), but it also includes eight suggested headings under which ethical issues in translation could be classified (205–206). The five full scenarios cover **rates of pay, ownership of resources** (see Chapter 8 for coverage of both of these areas), **refusing work** (covered briefly in Chapter 6), **the limits of confidentiality** (Chapters 6 and 7), and **specific translational choices** (see Chapter 3 for a perspective on this). Their additional suggested areas, meanwhile, are **client relations, etiquette, collegiality, the standing of the profession, visibility, competition, accountability,** and **power structures**.

These areas are well worth mentioning here as they pre-empt a whole host of pertinent points of discussion that will be raised in this textbook and, as Drugan and Megone put it, are "indicative of the variety of areas in which ethical issues may be raised within a curriculum" (2011: 206). Analysis is necessarily formed on a case-by-case basis, with the context-dependent nature of ethics problematising one-size-fits-all solutions, as we will see. And, when using these cases, it is worth noting that discussions can be applied to many different theorists' ideas, allowing us to compare and contrast these approaches and to critically engage with their strengths and weaknesses.

In the classroom

All of these features – the theoretical and practical case studies, in-text questions, essay titles, and discussion topics – can be carried through to training settings. Indeed, the content of this book has been developed on the back of creating successful sessions, modules, and assessments on translation ethics in a range of UK-based universities, at both undergraduate and postgraduate levels. Therefore, for teachers of translation and/or interpreting, the materials can be easily adapted to the classroom, whether setting up new modules or bolstering existing content. Specifically, this textbook has been structured with a one-semester course in mind (typical of specialist MA modules in translation and interpreting), with each chapter roughly corresponding to a teaching week.[3] Each chapter provides content that neatly corresponds to the common lecture plus seminar approach, using lectures to explore theoretical ideas and seminars either to discuss key texts in detail or to explore a range of pre-prepared case studies that problematise the themes discussed in the lecture. The aforementioned features provide abundant platforms for dynamic teaching sessions and further reading suggestions and bibliography entries facilitate more in-depth engagement or allow for a flipped approach, with students reading a text before a session (in particular, individual papers provide a manageable and digestible amount of reading material).

Of course, within this framework there is considerable scope for flexibility. In my own teaching, I have often dedicated entire series of lectures to scholarly thought that only fills a sub-section in the current textbook, such as Venuti's thought on ethics, narrative theory, or technology and ethics. This allows trainers to tailor the content to their specific needs and resources. Understandably, many courses do not have space for an entire optional module on ethics, and so the range of content can also be embedded within existing modules. While Zhou (2022: 10) proposes an illuminating approach to teaching ethics that works best as a standalone course, and contends that simply setting aside "twenty minutes each class [to] talk about ethics is not enough", the realities of course design limit such possibilities and developing underlying expertise on the part of trainers is key – applying relevant insights from translation ethics to the teaching of other content when pertinent. The beauty of ethics is that it touches upon a vast range of key themes: through the lens of ethics, students can become acquainted with linguistic debates around fidelity and equivalence, explore differing degrees of agency, consider the impact of technological developments, and critique current and emerging issues with prevalent industry workflows.

Conclusion

Ultimately, the writing of this textbook has been undertaken with a spirit of openness in mind – an openness to other readings, other viewpoints, other languages, and other cultures. Readers must make up their own mind on issues and delve further into the topics that interest them. While the content offers the basic building blocks for understanding key debates in relation to ethics, there is also a strong focus on providing material that will provoke ideas, responses, and – hopefully – critical reflection on your own and others' stances. As will be explored in later chapters, our own views and beliefs necessarily seep into our actions and I must readily acknowledge that my own limited, partial, and situated viewpoint has inevitably impacted the construction and delivery of each chapter. My own position as a specialist in written translation and my linguistic and cultural limitations risk causing me to default towards the familiar, though I have endeavoured to be attentive to a range of other practices, languages, and cultures, in keeping with the general ethos of the series. This same spirit of openness is something that should be present in the classroom: ethical discussions require a willingness to listen, learn, and engage with challenging ideas in a humble manner. While ethics permits no easy answers, it can also be comforting that there are often no categorically right or wrong answers.

Notes

1 There are two other publications with similar aims that should be mentioned here. Firstly, *The Routledge Handbook of Translation and Ethics* (Koskinen and Pokorn, 2021, eds.) represents a wonderful, comprehensive collection of thought in the area, though one that is less accessible for those new to the debate. However, the depth on offer in that publication marks it out as an ideal next step for readers interested in exploring particular topics in more detail, hence the multitude of references to the collection throughout this textbook. Secondly, Phelan et al.'s (2020) *Ethics in Public Service Interpreting* is a rich, informative, and accessible source, one which adopts an approach to ethics that is in some ways similar to that of this textbook. However, as the name suggests, it is focused more narrowly on the field of Public Service Interpreting.
2 In the European context, for instance, ethical skills are included in the influential list of competences that European Master's in Translation (EMT)-accredited institutions are expected to teach. In China, meanwhile, there is a similar expectation that ethical concerns will become increasingly central in the near future. Wang and Li comment on the current situation in China and argue that, in spite of the consensus that "translator professionalism and ethical training go hand in hand", "[v]ery few, if any, training programmes incorporate explicit teaching on ethics in Chinese translation curricula" (2019: 165), asserting a need for understandings of ethics to move beyond perceived qualities of loyalty or fidelity to the source text.
3 An 11-week format I have used is as follows: an introductory session; a session for each of the nine chapters; plus, a final week where students present and discuss their own case studies or deliver group presentations. Armed with a range of theories and ideas, this final session allows students to reflect upon how those ideas help (or not) with a concrete practical situation. These sessions lead to exciting, dynamic, and challenging discussions. Furthermore, given that students of translation and interpreting are often from a hugely diverse range of geographical, linguistic, cultural, and educational backgrounds, cohorts are often neatly set up for an exchange of a vast range of viewpoints.

1 Philosophical Foundations

> **Key questions**
> - What is ethics and what are the fundamental ethical questions?
> - How has ethics been studied?
> - What are the key ethical schools of thought that we can apply in the context of translation and interpreting?

This opening chapter offers a brief general overview of some key ethical building blocks, particularly those provided by philosophy. It introduces a range of underlying conceptual tools, defines key terms, and raises fundamental ethical questions and approaches to studying ethics to allow readers to meaningfully engage with ethics in general and later in both TIS and the professional contexts of translation and interpreting. At a more granular level, the chapter outlines three of the most prominent schools of thought within moral theory – deontology, consequentialism, and virtue ethics – anticipating discussions in the coming chapters, where these ideas are rearticulated in the contexts of translation and interpreting specifically. Finally, the chapter asks why we should study ethics, discussing the benefits and pitfalls of exploring this area on a wider scale.

> **Box 1.1 Starting out: A problem to ponder**
> What is the difference between the following terms?
>
> - Ethic(s)
> - Moral(s) and morality
> - Etiquette
>
> If possible, discuss in small groups or note down some ideas relating to the three terms. Then, check how they are defined in a dictionary. Also

DOI: 10.4324/9781003148265-2

> check the etymology of the words, as this research into the original meaning of the word or its components always helps us to understand why they were chosen to mean the things they mean.
>
> ? What do these words have in common and in what way(s) are they different from one another?

What is Ethics?

A useful first step when starting to study or discuss a new area is to define the key terms and concepts and this is one of the central aims of this chapter. It makes sense to start by defining our most fundamental concept – ethics – but this is no mean feat. It is easy to be overwhelmed by the amount of material written on the subject. Browsing a university's library catalogue on ethics, for instance, the number of titles available is likely to leave any newcomer to the area dismayed. Similarly, searching for the word "ethics" online is even more disorienting. For this reason, perhaps the best starting point is to look up its definition in an established, trustworthy dictionary. *The Oxford Dictionary of English*, defines ethics as follows:

> **1** *[usually treated as plural]* **moral principles that govern a person's behaviour or the conducting of an activity**: *medical ethics also enter into the question | a code of ethics.*
>
> the moral correctness of specified conduct: *many scientists question the ethics of cruel experiments.*
>
> **2** *[usually treated as singular]* **the branch of knowledge that deals with moral principles**: *neither metaphysics nor ethics is the home of religion.*

This definition brings up a key distinction between two different usages: one relating to **behaviour,** and a second relating to **the scholarly discipline** studying that type of behaviour. The second important point to note is that in both instances, ethics is defined further in relation to the word "moral". What exactly does this word mean? What are "morals"? Based on the mini research project you were invited to conduct in Box 1.1, you will have probably found that the word "moral" comes from the Latin word "mos/mores" meaning "custom(s)", "habit(s)". Some of you may recall the exclamation used by Cicero "O tempora! O mores," which means something like "What a time! What customs!". Cicero used the phrase to express his disgust with the low mores of the Roman society of his time, for instance in his famous speech against his political adversary Lucis Sergius Catilina. In English (again, according to the *Oxford Dictionary of English*), the word "moral" can be used to mean "right" or "good" or to refer to the study of what is good and what is bad:

1 concerned with the principles of **right and wrong behaviour:** *the moral dimensions of medical intervention* | *a moral judgement*.

concerned with or derived from **the code of behaviour that is considered right or acceptable** in a particular society: *they have a moral obligation to pay the money back.*

[attributive] examining the nature of ethics and **the foundations of good and bad character and conduct:** *moral philosophers.*

2 holding or manifesting **high principles for proper conduct:** *he prides himself on being a highly moral and ethical person* | *he is a caring, moral man.*

Somewhat confusingly, we have now gone full circle. Indeed, "ethical" and "moral" can mean, in essence and according to dictionary definitions alone, the same thing and just come from two different languages (Greek and Latin): defining "ethics" and "ethical" through "moral" is as good as defining "moral" through "ethical". For Rudvin, however, despite this tendency to use the terms interchangeably in both academic literature and everyday discourse, there is a generally accepted distinction. For her, ethics can be seen as "belonging to a public, collective domain, about which there is at least some degree of consensus in any given social group or community of practice" (in Phelan et al. 2020: 35). Morality, meanwhile, refers to an individual's own principles of right and wrong, pertaining to "a more private, personal, inner-oriented and more subjective behavioural and belief domain" (ibid.). It is worth noting that this distinction risks establishing a separation that is not always borne out in TIS, where we discuss both personal and professional ethics (not professional ethics and morals, for instance) and significant attention has been paid to problematising that divide (see Chapter 6 in particular). Nevertheless, it is as helpful a distinction as we can find and is widely accepted. Far from being a futile exercise, this process of defining and deliberating over definitions has drawn our attention to a vast range of key concerns (as illustrated by the bolding in the definitions). Whatever differences exist, both terms relate to "customs", "habits", or "principles", which can be described as "good" or "bad", "right" or "wrong". This is what we are exploring in this book: what is good or bad in the context of translation and interpreting, in simple terms at least.

At this point, it is helpful to take into consideration the place that the study of ethics occupies among other disciplines that explore social aspects of human existence. Ethics is one of the branches of Western philosophy which, since Aristotle (384–322 BCE), has been divided as follows:

1. ontology (studying what the world as it is, from the Greek words 'ont-' *being* + 'logos' *study*);
2. epistemology (studying methods we use when we study the world as it is, from the Greek words 'episteme' *knowledge* + 'logos' *study*);

3. politics (studying society as it is, from the Greek word 'polis' *city*);
4. ethics (studying society as it should be rather than as it is, from the Greek 'ethos' meaning *custom, disposition*);
5. aesthetics (studying what we would call today arts, that is, things of beauty and the nature of beauty, from the Greek 'aestheta', *things perceived*).

For us here, the most important juxtaposition is perhaps that of ethics with politics. Following this division, politics focuses on human relations in a group from the point of view of their actual state, both their good points and their imperfections, problems, issues. Ethics, in contrast, is about how we would like to see our society and our relations within it. One might say, politics is about what *is* or *was* while ethics is about what *should be* or what *should have been*. Politics is about the actual state of human relations while ethics is about a desirable state of human relations. However, as will become abundantly clear in the chapters that follow, these lines become blurred and at numerous points we will examine works that cross the borders between the supposedly ethical and political.

Before we go on to explore a range of fundamental ethical questions, a caveat is in order. In the present discussion of ethics, we will draw primarily on Western teachings of ethics. This does not mean to say, however, that these teachings are the most authoritative or the most sophisticated. Our choice is prompted by my own upbringing and education, the space constraints in this textbook, and the fact that these underpinnings are reflective of the starting point of much of the exploration of ethics in TIS. I invite readers to explore their national traditions in studying and practicing ethics, and it is undeniable that TIS research on ethics would benefit from further engagement with other ethical systems. As Rudvin puts it in the context of public service interpreting specifically, this "could profoundly change the landscape and scope of investigation in our discipline and profession" (in Phelan et al. 2020: 34). These changes stem from the fact that other national systems of ethics often prioritise different values, perhaps the prioritisation of compassion and charity in the Islamic tradition, or the value assigned to group harmony in the ancient Chinese philosophical tradition, and such work could form the basis for a fascinating research project or classroom presentation. Indeed, the underlying knowledge developed by studying other national traditions of ethics and other cultural and linguistic perspectives, could lay a foundation for invaluable research into the applicability of those ideas to translation/interpreting and translators and interpreters.

? What does ethics mean to you?
? What is your take on the separation of ethics and politics?

The Fundamental Ethical Questions

Our tentative separation between branches of philosophy suggests that by ethics we mean not just any custom, habit, or character, but a desirable one.

Now, we turn to the challenging question of what kind of behaviour is desirable, which once again invites us to move beyond the somewhat circular definitions uncovered above. To say that moral behaviour is desirable is not too enlightening because then we still must ask what is meant by "moral" (or 'ethical'). Instead, we must delve into identifying the criteria of distinguishing between right and wrong/good and evil. This is a daunting question, and one that finds its origins well before the philosophical thought briefly mentioned above. Many of the earliest formulations of this guidance were linked to religion, with traces dating back to ancient Egypt and Babylonia. Elsewhere, the oldest Indian ethics are found in the Vedas (c. 1500–800 BCE) while key Chinese philosophers Laozi and Confucius developed their influential ethical thought a few centuries later (c. 500–600 BCE) (Koskinen and Pokorn 2021: 2). Christianity, Judaism, and Islam developed their thought later, and it is here that we take our starting point before turning away from religious perspectives.

Take, for instance, the following verses from the Old Testament of the Bible, the foundational book of Judaism and Christianity, and a book that is taken as a life guide for many people, including for the ethical/moral aspects of life. Here, we see that the question of distinguishing between right and wrong was deemed so daunting that the question is not even considered worth asking. In the Book of Genesis (chapter 2, verse 17), we read that the first humans created by God, when they were place in the Garden of Eden, or Paradise, could partake of any of the many trees planted there, "but of the tree of the knowledge of good and evil, thou shalt not eat of it: for in the day that thou eatest thereof thou shalt surely die" (King James Version). In other words, this "collective" human being, Adam plus Eve, was prohibited from considering what is good and what is evil. They were created naked but, until the day they did eat from the forbidden tree of good and evil, they did not have shame. Once they had eaten of the tree of knowledge of good and evil, they realised that they were naked and became ashamed of that and made coverings for themselves from fig leaves. While before they had walked in the presence of God, now they lost it and eventually, as we know, they lost their place in the Paradise of God. All as the result of learning what was good and what was evil. Thankfully for us, however, there is considerably less risk involved in studying ethics.

In these verses we see that distinguishing between good and evil was not supposed to be a question humans should try and answer for themselves and, consequently, apply to their behaviour. Yet throughout history humans have considered a wide range of sources of ethical behaviour beyond divine commands and have developed numerous sophisticated frameworks to allow us to ponder the right and wrong or good and evil in their own behaviour and in the behaviour of others around them. The issues subsumed in ethics include

- how to live a good life and what a good life is/a good person is;
- how to speak about moral issues and how to define concepts of ethics;

- what are moral decisions and how we choose between good and bad/right and wrong;
- our rights and responsibilities/duties in society.

Here another caveat is in order. It is important to make a clear point that the goal of a course in translation/interpreting ethics is not to give definitive answers to how to translate and how not to translate or how translators or interpreters should act under various circumstances. Rather the goal is to make the budding translator/interpreter aware of the complexity and sometimes of the controversial nature of ethical questions and to encourage them to reason about these matters in a knowing and informed fashion.

? What does being "good" mean to you?
? What are some key rights that you have in society and, in turn, what are your responsibilities? Where does this information come from?

Approaches to Studying Ethics

Ethics is a societal matter. When talking about ethics, we are forced to consider how we are dealing with the Other, how we can respect the choices of the Other, how we can (or if we can) balance not only our own concerns and interests but also concerns and interests of the society in which we live – or, in the case of translators/interpreters, the societies, cultures, languages that we are a part of or representing. For some, as we have seen above, ethics implies going even "higher" and considering gods' or God's interests. As our initial definitions demonstrated, ethics is about fundamental values, such as honesty, kindness, respect, and so forth. All of these matters bring us inevitably to desirable relationships with the other in a shared social space. Below, I turn to a range of philosophical explorations of ethics in an attempt to shed further light on ways in which we can seek to answer these pressing questions of "right", "wrong", "good", and "evil". These discussions move from overarching contemporary frameworks to specific schools of thought and introduce a range of key terminology or metalanguage – the language of right and wrong, and how to speak about moral issues – which will be useful to internalise ahead of the translation and interpreting-specific discussions of later chapters.

Metaethics, Normative and Applied Ethics

Ethical philosophy (also known as moral philosophy, perhaps unsurprisingly!) is one of the most fruitful avenues of enhancing understandings of translation ethics. This sub-domain of philosophy offers a nuanced and well-developed basis to inform discussions and contextualise our explorations moving forwards. Employing this more systematic basis is also useful to try to tame what is an incredibly broad, and sometimes unwieldy area. Indeed, ethics touches upon or informs debates ranging from human or even animal rights to professional conduct, from self-care – prioritising your own physical and mental wellbeing – to concern for future generations. From the previous sections it should be clear by now that the crux of the matter when ethics is discussed is the difference between right and wrong, or what is considered "right" and what is considered "wrong" and coming up with ideas or, perhaps, recommendations of what ethical translation or interpreting *should be* like (as opposed to what they *are* like). Yet despite the clarity of the fundamental questions, answers and approaches to answers represent a big pool of ideas, which often contradict each other, often inherited from various religious beliefs, philosophies, cultures, and worldviews.

According to many contemporary understandings of ethics, philosophers nowadays tend to divide ethical theories into three areas: metaethics, normative ethics, and applied ethics. These three areas in some ways mark a move from the general to the specific. **Metaethics** ("meta-" is a Greek prefix meaning here *beyond* or *behind*) invites us to ask questions about the nature of moral judgement and the ideas behind moral judgement. Metaethically, we are searching for the origins and meaning of (a given set of) ethical principles. For instance, in a religion such as Judaism or Christianity, as is obvious from the fragment from the Bible discussed above, the ultimate source of all ethics in that case is one's belief in God and in this God's guidance in terms of what that person should do and what moral decisions to make. In some other cultures, other deities are responsible for instructing their believers, but the general conclusion would be the same: behind all moral judgments and codes of ethics in religious cultures it is likely that the final say lies with deities, and it is they who are believed to have communicated to humans the ethical principles that the latter should apply in their lives. It is different in atheistic cultures where humans are responsible for their decisions and the codes applicable to their behaviour are believed to be formulated over history as a result of complex interactions between people. Another key potential source for metaethics could be a virtuous person to emulate, something we explore further below in relation to virtue ethics.

Normative ethics, meanwhile, looks into the content of moral judgements. Normative ethics studies the criteria for deciding what is viewed as the opposition "right vs. wrong". When talking about the Bible above, for instance, we concluded that the right for a follower of Judaism or Christianity is to do what God requires of them. Using religion as the source of ethics, we may come up with normative guidelines such as "thou shalt not murder", though many non-religious legal bases in ethics of course reach similar normative conclusions! **Applied ethics** is even more focussed. While normative ethics looks at codes of ethics and rules of behaviour in general, applied ethics attempts to put our moral knowledge into practice by analysing specific, controversial issues in private and public life such as war, animal rights, and capital punishment.

So, which category does translation or translator ethics fall into? While sources of ethics in translation and interpreting can be both academic or professional in nature and offer invaluable guidance in wide-ranging contexts, they always relate specifically to what translators do. As Koskinen and Pokorn neatly put it, "[w]ithin Translation Studies, ethics is the subfield that aims to understand what is good and bad, right and wrong in *translatorial praxis*" (Koskinen and Pokorn 2021: 3), concretising this link to the way in which theories, lessons, or skills are enacted, applied, or embodied in actual practice. This practical leaning alludes to the *applied* nature of translation ethics, which is typical of wider trends in ethics, that is, rather than reflecting on the nature of good and bad in itself (theoretical metaethical questions), there is a pragmatic focus in mind in many domains.

Thinking carefully, however, it becomes clear that when we discuss translation and the translator from the point of view of their ethics, we need to analyse them from all the three angles – meta-, normative, and applied ethics – and, particularly on the scholarly side, there are strong metaethical strands. What is more, the complexity of translation and interpreting problematises any neat definitions. Consider, for instance, the translation of sacred texts. Here, translators must inevitably engage with "correctly" representing the authoritative message of God – a considerable complication given that, for instance, the Qur'an is "routinely claimed to be inimitable and untranslatable" (Israel 2021: 442). The translator may be a follower of a "competing" religion with its own normative ethics and, at the very least, they are an enculturated social being raised within a particular ethical system which consciously or subconsciously is bound to manifest itself to a greater or smaller degree. Even if the translator tries to resist his or her "home" ethics, they are still engaging with it, if only subconsciously, and, hence, the analysis of their behaviour would have to take that into consideration. This is just a glimpse of discussions to come.

Beyond the metaethics of the translator's acts, there is also considerable scope to apply normative ethics in this context. Whether explicit or implicit, there are often clear rules that the translator observes in their behaviour. And here we can find principles and convictions that the translator applies both in their private life and in their job (this divide between personal and professional ethics is explored in more detail in Chapter 6 in particular). For instance, a translator may consider themselves to be anti-abortion and refuse to take on translation work that argues for the legality of abortion. Yet, while there is a normative strand here – the belief that abortion is wrong, which requires that they have thought of many important normative ethical issues, such as the rights of the involved human beings and, perhaps, their ultimate existential responsibilities (a belief in the life after death and answering to a god in a judgment), there is an overlap here with applied ethics in that debates about abortion are one of the focused controversial issues. Ultimately, these three labels are excellent guides in attuning our minds to the different levels of ethics (just as the illustrations in the introduction did), but it is also clear that all three are connected in complex ways. Sometimes they agree but sometimes they may clash in one and the same person or that person's private and professional behaviour, and the addition of translation and interpreting complicates these relationships even further. While we could continue to ponder the origins of good and evil, the high-level (and often abstract) nature of these discussions means that the most productive way to proceed at this point lies in normative ethics, which allow us to form an overarching basis that can later relate ideas to the specific context of translation and interpreting more easily. In the next section, we consider three of the most important normative theories.

? Can you think of examples of contradictions on the level of metaethics, on the level of normative ethics, or on the level of applied ethics that the translator or interpreter has to negotiate?
? Have you experienced or have you witnessed somebody else experiencing conflicts between their private convictions and the requirements they had to meet professionally?
? Are there any unchanging moral rules that apply in all cultures and at all times?

Deontological Ethics

Deontology is a normative ethical theory that has come to (implicitly) shape much of the thought on ethics in TIS and remains one of the most commonly used notions of ethics in general. It is sometimes also known as nonconsequentialism as it is concerned with the actions themselves and not with the consequences. Etymologically, it comes from the Greek *deon*, meaning "obligation, or duty" plus *-logy*, meaning "the study of". It teaches that some acts are right or wrong in themselves, whatever the consequences, and people should act accordingly. Ultimately, it is the theory that people are using when they refer to "the principle of the thing."

Deontologists believe that certain actions are intrinsically right or wrong and that we can therefore pinpoint certain guidelines to be followed at all costs. Immanuel Kant, the most famous defender of a deontological ethics, believed that moral rules can be drawn from reason alone. Furthermore, because he deemed reason to be universal, these rules must also be universal and consistent. This is the *categorical imperative*, a rule that categorically applies to all individuals. We are to ask ourselves "what if everybody did X?". Yet we also need the will to put these imperatives into practice, which will lead us to carry out certain actions, or to do our "duty", for its own sake, that is, because that action is right in itself. From early childhood, we are taught rulings such as do not lie, do not steal, or respect your elders, yet these rulings are not universally practised; the will is not always there even if we agree upon the basis of the rule itself.

While Kant places the universals of moral law with the rational man, others place this responsibility elsewhere. One potential alternative is the so-called divine command, as explored above, which places this moral "rightness" within the decrees of a God. This implies that we should act in a certain way because that is what our God commands, the "rightness" of the act sitting within the command, not any good that it causes (this idea of ends over means will be considered below and in Chapter 4).

The appeal of a deontological method is immediately apparent. It offers a neat, universal message that applies to the entire possible range of contexts. However, there are a few potential drawbacks that have received attention within moral theory. While the origin and the content of rulings can vary considerably – *what* we have to do and *why* – the very nature of these rulings, or the question of *how* we go about following them once we have established them, can prove to be equally problematic. Indeed, there is a major paradox that exists within deontology. While few would argue that it is "right" to intentionally kill innocent people – a claim that a deontological ethics could well put forward – even a seemingly clear-cut case such as this is not as simple as one would perhaps assume. As Robert Nozick points out in his 1974 paper "The Rationality of Side Constraints", we must question *why* an action should be forbidden if its very performance would help prevent the act that it forbids. The classic example here is being able to go back in time to meet a figure who would go on to kill multiple people. Would it be right to kill them in order to prevent other deaths? As Shafer-Landau asks: "[i]f the value [of whatever it is that we hold as a deontological requirement] is so important as to generate a deontological requirement, then why isn't the value so important as to license a violation of that requirement if such violation would better protect the relevant value?" (Shafer-Landau 2013: 482) The examples in Box 1.2 and Box 1.3 offer further insight into this paradox and bring together these ideas of the content, origin, and practice of rules. These three elements are important to consider in the discussions below – *what* our rulings prescribe, *why* they are prescribed, and *how* we are to follow them.

? What deontological principles do you follow on a daily basis? What is the source of these principles?
? How universal are the principles that you follow?
? Can you justify breaking these principles? In what contexts?

Box 1.2 Deontology in practice: A thought experiment

Consider the following adaptation of a famous example used in ethical training (itself adapted from Awad et al. 2018). Imagine that you are a programmer behind the manufacture of autonomous vehicles and are anticipating a range of tricky scenarios once your vehicles are on the road:

One of your self-driving vehicles, carrying three elderly passengers, is travelling at speed and is about to crash. The vehicle can either continue along its course, ending the lives of the passengers, or can veer across the road where it will hit and kill a young woman who is jaywalking. There is no course of action that can result in all lives being saved. What would your choice of action be? Where would you look for guidance with your moral reasoning? Would it be a case of following your own intuition? Would you ask a moral guide for advice? Or would you look to theories of ethics or documentation to concretise or support your thinking? (We will cover all of these eventualities in the context of translation in subsequent chapters.)

One logical course of action could be to consult widely used deontological guidelines. One such famous attempt at developing guidelines to inform our decision-making when programming AI comes from science fiction author Isaac Asimov, who in 1942 dreamed up three laws of robotics that have since been employed in numerous novels, films, and academic articles:

- A robot may not injure a human being or, through inaction, allow a human being to come to harm.
- A robot must obey the orders given to it by human beings except where such orders would conflict with the First Law.
- A robot must protect its own existence as long as such protection does not conflict with the First or Second Laws.

(Asimov 1950: 40)

Clearly, we cannot reach a satisfactory answer to our dilemma based on these basic normative ethical principles alone, with the situation inevitably causing the first rule to be broken. So, at that stage, where do we look for guidance? Do we accept that injury by inaction is better than actively causing that injury? Does causing one death to save three permit us to deviate from our guidelines? We build upon these themes in Box 1.3. For now, it is simply a thought experiment designed to introduce some potential issues that we may run into with deontological rulings, and is something to bear in mind as we turn to the context of translation.

Consequentialism

As the name suggests, when it comes to consequentialism, **our emphasis is on the consequences of human actions and not on the actions themselves,** as was the case with deontology. It is, at its core, a family of theories that assesses the ethical rightness of an action or rule solely based on the amount of good that it causes, or the amount of bad that it helps us avoid. The theory can be divided into two branches: **act consequentialism** and **rule consequentialism**. Act consequentialism posits that morally right actions are those that are expected to achieve the best results (or sufficiently good results) of all the potential actions available to a person at a specific time. Rule consequentialism, meanwhile, sees morally right actions as following optimal social rules, which themselves ensure that the best possible results are reached when they are properly followed. While the nature of setting rules in this way is reminiscent of the deontological impositions discussed above, rule consequentialists do not make their demands because they are intrinsically good but rather because they maximise good. They take a stand on what is intrinsically valuable and it is the consequences of actions rather than the actions themselves that represent the ultimate guiding force for conduct. In setting rules to maximise certain end results, rule consequentialism represents something of an intermediary point on the sliding scale from deontology to act consequentialist, or even an attempt to reconcile deontology and consequentialism. In general, act consequentialism is much more popular than rule consequentialism as the imposition of steadfast rulings always runs the risk of inciting an irrational rule worship. Here, agents can be forced to act in a suboptimal manner simply to follow those rules – a criticism that is of course similarly levelled against deontological thought and has been outlined in this chapter.

The most common and well-known forms of consequentialism (and indeed of normative ethics all together) are the various versions of utilitarianism, which favour actions that produce the greatest amount of good. One famous way of putting this is "the greatest good for the greatest number of people." In the context of Western philosophy, these ideas are credited to Jeremy Betham and John Stuart Mill, whose ideas radically overturned the notion that our understanding of things like right and wrong stems from divine intervention, instead arguing that they are in fact down to humans. As humans, we base our decisions on the sensations of pleasure and pain and calculate the amount of each that our actions will cause, thus assessing their "utility", the source of the name utilitarianism. **Utilitarianism** is based around the notion of impartiality and agent-neutrality – everyone's happiness counts the same – important concepts that will be raised at numerous points in the context of translation. Furthermore, in order to avoid the assignment of intrinsic value that destabilises theories such as deontology, consequentialism does not label specific acts as ethical or unethical, and indeed actions can be viewed as right or wrong depending on the context. For instance, while dishonesty would be condemned by many deontological theories, if telling a small white lie would reduce the suffering of the hearers, it could be justified according to utilitarian principles. However, if that same lie caused many others to suffer, it would become immoral.

While a hugely pervasive school of thought, one problem with utilitarianism and consequentialism is that it can lead to the conclusion that some quite dreadful acts are good. Indeed, though in many cases an action that leads to suffering will be viewed as immoral, this is not necessarily always the case and utilitarianism attempts to reorient our traditional notions of justice. Indeed, if my action causes a few people to suffer but results in a great number of people being happy – consider, for instance, the killing of a universally despised figure – then, based on the idea that the consequences of the action are our deciding factor in morality, this act would be viewed as moral. This can be particularly unpalatable. Related to this, it is also incredibly difficult to predict and evaluate the consequences of actions. Indeed, how do we know how much suffering or happiness is caused, and to how many people, can happiness and suffering even be compared?

Box 1.3 Consequentialism

In 2015, *New York Times Magazine* asked readers "if you could go back and kill Hitler as a baby would you do it?" Their response found that 42 per cent of readers said yes, 30 per cent said no, and 28 per cent were not sure.

? Where do you stand on this question?

Of course, the hypothetical nature of the question clouds our decision-making. Do we ignore important considerations such as the Butterfly Effect, which suggest that a change like this in an initial state can cause radical changes in a later state? Of course, there's no guarantee that Hitler's non-existence would have prevented the atrocities of World War II (this act of killing could theoretically even lead to a worse situation). However, the question encapsulates the important distinction between deontology and consequentialism as well as alluding to an important limitation of consequentialist ideas.

Deontological principles stating that you should not kill would dictate your response, while a consequentialist outlook would consider the potential for a greater good being achieved. If killing one person would result in saving the lives of millions, then we should do it. However, calculating the outcome of even simple acts is very difficult and the reality of this act – i.e. killing a baby! – and its very real human, psychological impact is not something we can remove from our calculations.

Virtue Ethics

Ethics deals not only with the morality of actions, but also about the goodness of human beings (as social actors) and what it means to live a good life (in society), and virtue ethics is the branch of ethics that encapsulates this side of matters most clearly. Instead of looking at actions or behaviour, here we look at virtue or moral character. This school of ethical thought concerns itself with a long view of ethical issues, questioning not simply "what should I do?" but more generally "what kind of person should I be?", and committing the individual to a lifelong process of learning and improvement (for an incisive introduction to virtue ethics, see Hursthouse and Pettigrove 2018). In this way, it is more about how individuals live their lives and less concerned with assessing particular actions, and develops the idea of good by looking at the way virtuous people express their inner goodness in the things that they do. Generally, virtue ethicists place emphasis on virtues of character rather than moral rules of conduct and actions are good because they exemplify virtuous character, not because they conform to an already-established moral rule. Their moral rulings advise us to follow the ways in which certain virtuous exemplars would act. Thus, an action is right if and only if it is an action that a virtuous person would do in the same circumstances. Virtues are located between the extremes of vices and have to be learned through experience and habituation.

In virtue ethics we move from the Kantian notion of an objective good and a correct way to lead your life to a subjective good, defining good and happiness with respect to the unique individual. The theory has experienced a recent resurgence inspired by reconsiderations of Aristotle's ethical thought but it is not as well defined as deontology, for example. Aristotle's *Nicomachean Ethics* (1985, 1999) represents a canonical source of virtues and includes both intellectual virtues (theoretical wisdom, practical knowledge, intuitive understanding, practical wisdom, craft knowledge) and moral virtues (courage, temperance, generosity, magnanimity, self-confidence/self-respect, proper ambition, good temper, truthfulness, wittiness, friendship (concern for others), modesty, righteous indignation). In general, virtue ethics often appears to be a more valid choice of ethical theory because of the failings of other schools of thought that emphasise one important element (e.g. happiness for utilitarians, fairness for Kantians, fidelity to one's agreements for contractarians). This provides a more flexible basis for development as importance is assigned to multiple elements, that is, virtue ethicists are not forced to simply follow one overarching ethical ruling but are instead guided by a range of virtues that are bound by the context. On the other hand, however, this rejection of ethical monism (the claim that there is only one right way to decide moral correctness, as opposed to pluralism, which allows for multiple possibilities) also fails to give sufficiently concrete guidance on how we should act – how do these various elements relate to one-another? Is there a fixed hierarchy or are we simply pulled in several directions rather than one? Furthermore, Julia Annas (2004) suggests that the way in which most theories of virtue ethics replace an ethical manual that tells us how to act with a virtuous person for us to copy is an illusory substitution. For her, just as there may be no intrinsic good/right, maybe there are no virtuous people. What, for instance, would mark out a virtuous translator or interpreter?

Based on the explorations above, there are a range of sources for judging ethical behaviour. For instance, if we unite ethics and religion, the only source of moral rules is God. That is, something is good if God says it is and a good life is achieved by doing what God wants. Our ethics could come from human conscience and intuition; we could reason out what is ethical. It could also be derived from a rational moral cost-benefit analysis of actions and their effects: how much good or bad (or happiness, or suffering, or cultural innovation, or cross-cultural cooperation perhaps) will my actions cause? Or finally, it could stem from the example of good human beings who act in a virtuous way. While it is clear from the discussions on this point that there are no easy, one-size-fits-all solutions, these conceptions of ethics play an important role in allowing us to reflect on various ways of pondering ethical dilemmas. The example in Box 1.4 below provides a challenging ethical dilemma to do just that.

> **Box 1.4 Alive, but at what cost? A test of ethical stances**
>
> *Alive* (1974, 2005) tells the harrowing story of a Uruguayan rugby team and a number of friends and family members who were involved in a plane crash in the Andes in late 1972. Out of a total of 45 passengers on the flight, many were killed in the crash, and only sixteen survived the ordeal of living for ten weeks in excruciating sub-zero conditions.
>
> Once their meagre rations ran out, the survivors' situation became even more bleak and, eventually, they decided to eat the bodies of their dead friends, relatives, and teammates in order to survive. When rescued, the few survivors hid the remains and, upon their return to Uruguay, attempted to keep what they had done a secret. Eventually the truth was discovered and, while some still greeted them as heroes who had simply done what was necessary to stay alive, others were repulsed by their actions. Some even believed that the stronger survivors had killed weaker ones and covered it up.
>
> ? What is your take on this situation? Were the survivors right to eat the bodies of the dead?
> ? How can we apply the three schools of thought covered above to this case?

Various rationales were given by the survivors for their decision to eat the dead:

Empathising: They argued it was what the dead would have wanted – if it was the other way around, we would want them to survive.

Religion: All survivors were devout Catholics and some viewed the dead bodies as a gift from God, and even the body of Christ. They believed that the souls had already left the body and that, following their religious teachings, they were justified in eating the bodies.

Survival: Both pure and nuanced – that is, a pure drive to make it home alive and the nuanced need to survive in order to preserve the memory of the dead.

Deontological rulings lie at the heart of what makes this so problematic. While cannibalism is legally and morally prohibited in many societies around the globe, is the extreme nature of the situation enough to override any such rulings? Of course, the dilemma also points to cultural relativism: while some cultures are known to practice cannibalism, in many societies it is perhaps the ultimate taboo. Context undoubtedly counts. In this case, the decision was not taken lightly by any of the survivors, though some were more reluctant than others, waiting almost until the point of their own death to agree to the choice, alluding to the subjective nature of ethics. Is there a certain point at which our values decisively change?

Using consequentialism, meanwhile, they could perhaps argue that the happiness of their surviving, their families being reunited, and the ability to preserve the memory of the dead would override any unhappiness caused, yet how clear-cut is this calculation? And what of the lasting mental toll on the survivors themselves, for instance? Or potential legal ramifications? Many were too ashamed to say what they had done upon their return. In terms of virtue ethics, meanwhile, the survivors considered their parents as virtuous characters and considered what they would think of the decision, but often found their reflections overshadowed by the bleak context they found themselves in.

Why Study Ethics?

Ultimately, despite providing no definitive answers, ethics can help in identifying the source of potential "right" decisions. Most moral issues (killing, capital punishment) evoke strong feelings, and we tend to think about them based on how our "heart" leads us. Ethical philosophy takes another route: it suggests rules and principles that are supposed to guide us to consider these issues. In this sense, ethics offers us a moral map that is there to guide us in difficult and controversial issues. Ethics can also help us to pinpoint the source of disagreement. Using the concepts developed within philosophical ethics, it is easier to put one's finger on what a discussion is about exactly so that constructive efforts may be made to resolve the issue in question.

However, sometimes ethics seems to fail to help when either not all suggested concepts are acceptable to the arguing parties, the bases of ethical disagreements lie "more deeply" (cultural or religious discrepancies), or when, with at least one of the parties involved, there is no real intention to act ethically. In these cases, ethics is felt to fall short of giving the "right" answer to a moral problem and many problems seem to have more than one answer (in different configurations this could be "win-win", "the best" vs. "the least worst"). Especially in the past, it was believed that ethical problems could be solved in one of two ways: either by interpreting correctly a divine design or will or by thinking rigorously about ethical problems. Modern thinkers try to identify what is at stake in a particular (type of) situation and what frameworks may be applicable to handling the situation. The main criterion for selecting this or that course of action tends to be relying on rational choices. It is important to remember that the goal of ethics is not to provide a single right answer. Rather, it is to raise our awareness of an issue or, at most, to offer a set of principles that we need to apply to particular cases (perhaps translation theories), and to feel confident in exercising one's own moral responsibility and making difficult choices in concrete situations.

Conclusion

Despite a somewhat circular pursuit of the definitive meaning of the key terms at work, this chapter has nevertheless narrowed our enquiry and explored a range of key ways in which ideas of good, bad, right, and wrong have been conceptualised in Western history. This coverage provides a foundation for the next chapter and beyond, when we move into the realm of translation and interpreting proper and begin our exploration of the ways in which ethics has been conceptualised in relation to these practices specifically. Virtue ethics lies behind the ethical musings of Andrew Chesterman, whose wide-ranging ideas are covered in Chapter 2 and provide a springboard to further explorations, deontological ethics in translation is covered in more detail in Chapter 3, while consequentialism lies implicitly behind the ideas in Chapter 4.

Discussion, Presentation, and Assignment Topics

1. What do you think are the most and least useful insights into ethics in this chapter, and why?
2. Presentation: select a potentially tricky ethics-related topic (for instance, capital punishment, organ donation, or euthanasia) and present and support your stance. Remember to deal with these topics sensitively and to respect other opinions.

3. Discussion: What is the most important ethical principle that you follow in your daily life, and are there any times that you have gone against it?

Further Reading

Simon Blackburn's *Being Good* remains a hugely accessible and engaging introduction to the world of ethics, with the author covering basic questions of ethics with the support of an array of real-world examples. **Patrick Stefan Kermit and Mette Rudvin's chapters in** *Ethics in Public Service Interpreting* **(in Phelan et al. 2020, Introduction and Chapter 1, respectively)** are a wonderful contribution to the field of interpreting and translation ethics. The authors situate these practices within moral philosophy and address many of the same concerns that are dealt with across this textbook, as well as providing a more detailed history of ethics that is intertwined with practical insights from the worlds of translation and (mostly) interpreting.

2 Translation Ethics

> **Key questions**
> - What different approaches are taken to ethics in TIS?
> - Where can we find the root of ethical enquiry in relation to translation?
> - What is the concept of fidelity and why is it potentially problematic?

Introduction

Having explored the underlying philosophical basis of ethics in the previous chapter, Chapter 2 turns to examining the emergence of ethics in TIS specifically. This chapter does not simply review the literature tackling ethics explicitly, but rather considers the ethical dimension inherent in several core ideas underpinning TIS, looking at how, where, and why ethics was imported into the discipline and how it came to occupy a more central position.

In this chapter, we begin by anchoring ourselves via a set of influential ideas from the contemporary context, employing Andrew Chesterman's 2001 'Proposal for a Hieronymic Oath' in particular to illustrate four key areas of focus in TIS ethical enquiry. These serve to introduce subsequent discussions in this chapter (and indeed throughout the rest of the textbook), revolving around the question of fidelity. Friedrich Schleiermacher's seminal 'On the different methods of translating' (1813) serves as our central theoretical case study and exemplifies a more implicit basis in ethics. These ideas outline the inherent difficulty of translation and in turn uncover a number of key lines of enquiry in an ethical sense, which serve as a basis for ideas from key TIS scholars Antoine Berman, Anthony Pym, and Lawrence Venuti (to be discussed in chapters 3, 4, and 5, respectively). Before reading on, consider the following questions:

? What does fidelity mean to you, both in general and in relation to translation and interpreting?

DOI: 10.4324/9781003148265-3

? If you have explored literature in TIS in the past, can you think of any particular instances of the question of ethics coming up?

A Powerful Theoretical Basis – Andrew Chesterman

In recent decades, the term "ethics" has come to represent something of a buzzword in the professional world and in various domains of academia. Keen to develop and display an increased awareness of their own roles and responsibilities, translation and interpreting scholars and professionals embraced the subject as it came into vogue in the 1990s and subsequently resurfaced with ever more prominence in the post-9/11 era of global politics. However, despite this interest in the topic, the somewhat elusive nature of the term, as explored in Chapter 1, has meant that these scholars and professionals have approached the question of ethics in translation from different angles and through different lenses. Thankfully for us, the ideas below assess what is at stake in a more overarching, comprehensive, and ground-clearing manner and these represent a perfect place to expand our understandings of ethics in translation specifically.

Let us take as our point of departure one of Chesterman's key contributions to ethics (which represents an ongoing preoccupation in his work): his 2001 paper 'Proposal for a Hieronymic Oath' ("Hieronymic" as opposed to a doctor's Hippocratic oath). Here, Chesterman attempted to draw up a professional code of ethics for translators that would surpass many of the codes in force in the translation profession (see Chapter 7 for detailed coverage and a critique of these documents). His aim was to build upon more solid foundations and focus solely on a deontological professional ethics while separating personal ethics from the discussion, a division that comes to the fore in chapters 4–5, and 6 in particular. Here, Chesterman divides ethics into four key areas (**truth, loyalty, understanding,** and **trust**). This represents a slight shift from a prior affiliation to descriptive translation studies in his work (Chesterman 1995), though he has continued to use this basis in norms in more recent work, recalling that etymological link between ethics and customary, "normal" behaviour (Chesterman 2016: 170). He then critiques each of these areas individually and eventually draws up his ultimate oath. We will revisit the immediate context of this Oath in Chapter 7 when we look in detail at codes of ethics, but for now let us focus on the four areas identified by Chesterman, which encapsulate key considerations in translation ethics and indeed throughout this textbook.

Chesterman's four key ethical domains:

1. **Ethics of representation:** this deals with fidelity, accuracy, truth, and how to choose and transmit a good, or the best, interpretation of a source text. This prioritises the value of "being true to the source" and represents the crux of a translation ethics for many translators and

interpreters. As such, this area will be given substantial attention in the remainder of this chapter as well as representing a fundamental basis of both development and criticism in chapters 4 and 5. However, particularly in recent decades, its centrality has been questioned as other factors take precedence. In the context of community interpreting, for instance, the status of fidelity as "the dominant virtue for translators has long been questioned" (Chesterman 2021: 17), with interpreters feeling that they are not simply translating, but rather acting as helpers, mediators, or advocates within a complex interactive process, a position that problematises fidelity and also foregrounds the relationship between personal and professional ethics (explored further in Chapter 5).

2. **Ethics of service**: this falls in line with functionalist models of translation, which are explored in Chapter 4. Here, discussions revolve around providing a service where the "translator is deemed to act ethically if the translation complies with the instructions set by the client and fulfils the aim of the translation as set by the client and accepted or negotiated by the translator" (Chesterman 2001: 140). These last few words are presumably added to ensure that the translator is not blindly bending to the whims of their client but rather enforces their own ideas of what is right and wrong in setting the aims. In line with Nord's ethics (see Chapter 4), Chesterman assigns **loyalty** as the key value in his ethics of service.

3. **Ethics of communication**: this is about "reaching understanding" (Chesterman 2021: 15). It is not about "representing the Other" – which falls under the ethics of representation – but rather "**communicating with others**" (Chesterman 2001: 140-1). This idea of communicating with others is a key underlying principle in Anthony Pym's ethics (see Chapter 4), where long-term cooperation and cross-cultural communication is the goal within both translation and society at large. Ultimately, in light of this model of ethics, **the** "ethical translator is a mediator working to achieve cross-cultural understanding" (ibid. 141) of each other; an idea that we will explore further in Chapter 5.

4. **Norm-based ethics**: this centres around predictability and hence trustworthiness. Essentially, a norm-based ethics says that **if we behave in a predictable manner and state where we have moved away from norms (using prefaces and so forth, when possible) then we can be trusted.** However, inherent in this adherence to norms is the assertion that to follow existing standards is to be ethical, a notion that has been questioned with considerable force (and success) in the work of Venuti (discussed in Chapter 5), who uncovers the supposedly deforming tendencies of commonplace fluent strategies in literary translation.

The number of cross-references in four explanations above clearly demonstrates the inherent links between Chesterman's work and the range of invaluable ideas from scholars across TIS. And yet, simply acknowledging this array of concerns does not mean we can call ourselves ethical translators or interpreters. There is considerable crossover and conflict between these four areas as each has different ethical values. Indeed, the model of truth (representation) is likely to conflict with each of the other values due to the tension that exists between the various demands placed upon the translator. For instance, what if the client requires us to deviate from the source text to represent a particular ideological slant that would forward their cause? In this case, which of these values do we prioritise? Chesterman's work undoubtedly provides a range of very useful tools for thinking through various aspects of translator agency, but the lack of hierarchisation can mean that readers may find the tools and categories difficult to operationalise in practice. After pondering potentially ethical notions such as clarity and readability, Chesterman himself accepts that these models fail to adequately cover ethics and cannot be broken down into a suitable hierarchy (a stumbling block that accompanies many models of ethics) and instead posits that we might instead look to virtues rather than values when discussing ethics in translation (See Box 2.1).

Despite these potential limitations, however, Chesterman clearly identifies the complexity involved in an ethics of translation and asks some intriguing questions while hinting at the potential of a range of ideas from ethical theory. His first model of ethics – the ethics of representation – is now used as the starting point for our in-depth exploration of a range of theoretical explorations of ethics in TIS.

Box 2.1 The link to virtue ethics

In his 2001 article, Chesterman sees virtue ethics as a way of bypassing potential issues of clashes and hierarchisation that accompany the use of ethical values. As we saw in Chapter 1, however, how to assign virtue in the context of translation was a key unanswered question. Chesterman contends that a virtuous translator "can be relied upon to seek ethically justifiable solutions" (and wants to strive for this excellence in their practice) and he includes a value or virtue alongside each clause of his Hieronymic Oath:

- Commitment
- Loyalty to the profession
- Understanding
- Truth
- Clarity
- Trustworthiness
- Truthfulness
- Justice
- Striving for excellence

? What are your thoughts on these virtues? Are they elements that you would have considered as fundamentally important to translators and interpreters? Or are they more general "virtues" applicable to daily life?
? Is it clear what all of these elements would require from you as a translator/interpreter?

The Roots of Ethics in Western Translation Studies: Fidelity

While only recently have we seen regular and explicit engagement with ethics in TIS, the (more implicit) roots of ethical enquiry in the domain date back much further. Indeed, it can be argued that ethics is a "perennial question of translation, be it in written or spoken form" (Koskinen and Pokorn 2021: 1). We now return to a fundamental ethical question posed by the likes of Socrates, Plato, and Aristotle, who ask "how should one live?", but instead think about this question in relation to translation specifically: "how should one translate?"

In the Western world, the core of much discussion of translation – not just in terms of ethics, but more widely – has revolved around the question of fidelity, which continues to be viewed as an essential component of how we conduct ourselves. For many, this question has been reduced to an opposition, or sometimes a continuum, between literal (word-for-word) translation and free (sense-for-sense) translation. A famous example comes from around 19 BCE, when Roman lyric poet Horace referred to a "fidus interpres" [faithful interpreter] in his *Ars Poetica*, which has both been taken as meaning that a faithful translator should take care not to translate word-for-word ("nec verbum verbo") and as a criticism of slavishly translating word-for-word (see, for instance, Kelly 1979). Roman orator Cicero, meanwhile, (106–43 BC) outlined his ideas on translation in *De optimo genere oratorum*, where he presented his own translation of Greek speeches by Demosthenes. He criticised literal (i.e., word-for-word) translation and claimed that he "did not translate them as an interpreter, but as an orator, keeping the same ideas and forms, or as one might say, the 'figures' of thought, but in language which conforms to our usage. And in so doing, [he] did not hold it necessary to render word-for-word, but [he] preserved the general style and force of the language" (Cicero 46 BCE/1960 CE: 364).

These ideas had a profound influence on the "Father of Translators", St Jerome, well-known for his translation of the Bible (*Vulgata*), which was translated from the original Hebrew, rather than from the Classical Greek of the *Septuagint*. In a letter to Pammachius, a Roman senator and friend of St Jerome (the text is nowadays widely known simply as "Letter to Pammachius"), he defended his decisions in the translation process: "Now I not only admit but freely announce that in translating from the

Greek – except of course in the case of the Holy Scripture, where even the syntax contains a mystery – I render not word-for-word, but sense-for-sense" (St Jerome 395 AC/1997: 25), again reasserting this dualistic distinction.

The key idea behind fidelity is that the translation is faithful to, or stands in for, the source text in some way. As we have seen, for Chesterman fidelity is underpinned by the value of truth: "a translation must be true to its original, as a translator must be true to the original author" (Chesterman 2021: 15). And, in the accounts shared above, there is a sense that the method of sense-for-sense translation has allowed the translators to achieve such truth. In extreme cases, this search for truth can even be a life-or-death matter, and there are several famous examples of translators paying the ultimate price following accusations of failing to represent this truth in the "correct" way, particularly in the case of Bible translation where the text itself is the Word of God and deviations are viewed as a sin. William Tyndale, for instance, was executed in 1536 for heresy after translating the New Testament into English. The enduring power of this tenet can be seen within *skopos* theory, introduced into TIS in the 1970s by Hans J. Vermeer (see Chapter 4), in which fidelity remains a core concept. Katharina Reiss and Vermeer (1984: 113) offer a fidelity rule stating that there must be coherence between the information in the source text, the translator's interpretation of that information, and the information encoded in the TT, though there is no detail on what this coherence relationship should be, signalling its elusive nature.

In many other cases, too, this notion of what exactly we are to retain is rather abstract. In a European context, Georges Mounin advocated for translators to replicate a certain "global meaning" (Mounin 1957: 150) while, more recently, Umberto Eco has argued the translator should be faithful to the source text's "guiding spirit" (Eco 2001: 117). In more recent TIS enquiry, meanwhile, Jean-Marc Gouanvic's work on ethics is testament to a lingering concern with these questions in an academic context. Indeed, when considering the act of translation, Gouanvic provides two telling examples that exemplify his conceptions of ethical and unethical translation. Discussing the French translation of John Steinbeck's *The Grapes of Wrath* he argues that, in seeking to fulfil a political orientation towards the interests of Nazi Germany, the translation shows numerous omissions, additions, and modifications, including phrases such as "I lost my land" being translated as "J'ai perdu mon pays" ['I lost my country'] and the names of Marx and Lenin and illusions to the workers' movement all being deleted. According to Gouanvic, in doing so the significance of Steinbeck's text is completely diverted, which should be labelled as unethical. His "ethical" example, meanwhile, explores Boris Vian's French translations of Canadian science fiction author A.E. van Vogt's work. He briefly notes that while Vian reproduces van Vogt's text in a different register, "the significance of the source text is preserved" and "the translator assumes the role of a reviser, correcting the source text while in thorough agreement with the original author's proposal" in a translation that "could not be more ethical"

(Gouanvic 2001: 210). Here, Gouanvic clearly demonstrates his belief that there is something inherently right or wrong in translation, a good or bad way of approaching the task – primarily that we should maintain the "significance" of the source text. This is what a deontological ethics is all about (see Chapter 3). Though Gouanvic does not explicitly state any specific rules or guidelines to follow, his insistence upon the maxim of accuracy/fidelity ("the significance of the source text", the "original author's proposal") implies a belief in an inherently correct way of translating – however abstract and subjective.

Clearly, while for many scholars discussions of fidelity in TIS have given way to wider concerns of the context and the people involved in the process (which we will cover in subsequent chapters), these issues persist. This is particularly true in the profession and, beyond scholarly or classical viewpoints, fidelity also sits at the heart of the way that we teach, mark, and assess translations. Indeed, fidelity is perhaps the most fundamental concept in judging the quality of a translation in the professional world, while in the classroom it is used at all levels. Court interpreting, for instance, is still based upon an insistence on fidelity and accuracy, demanding interpreters render elements including a speaker's hesitations; while at the early stages of language learning, translation is often used to test comprehension and as such translation students can struggle to break away from the idea that adding or taking things away from a text may not necessarily mean that a translator has been 'unfaithful'. At graduate and post-graduate level, meanwhile, the question of how far one can or should deviate from a text is a chief concern, with students grappling with issues of equivalence, fidelity, and accuracy. Finally, in the profession, many codes of ethics contain guidelines stipulating that translations must be "accurate" and "faithful", though thankfully the penalty for perceived deviations is not death.

Of course, it is incredibly difficult to get to the bottom of this question of truth – in daily life and in translation! – and a deeper enquiry sits at the heart of our enquiries in Chapter 3. Unfortunately, translation is not a simple case of swapping terms for perfect equivalents that will work in exactly the same way in another culture/time/place, or for another readership, for instance. This means that the aim of achieving total parity from source to target is simply not possible. As such, what we are looking for is not necessarily perfect sameness, but rather **equivalence**, a term which has too been fiercely contested (see Pym 2014, chapters 2 and 3) but raises a range of questions to consider. Chesterman sums it up best when he asks, "what exactly should a translator be faithful to, and when? Meaning? Form? Style? Spirit? The author's intention? The intended effect? Something else? Lip movements (as in dubbing)? Under what conditions should one aspect be given priority over others?" (Chesterman 2021: 16). This points to a wide range of crucial factors to consider when reflecting on how we go about being faithful (or accurate, or perhaps even ethical […]), and represents a fitting precursor to many of the discussions to come.

Box 2.2 Kimigayo

With questions of fidelity firmly in mind, compare the two translations of the Japanese national anthem below. The first is a poetic English translation by Basil Hall Chamberlain while the second is a more literal English translation used by the Japanese Ministry of Foreign Affairs. I have also included a very literal back translation from the Japanese.

? Which translation is more faithful? How do we decide?

Source text
君が代は
千代に八千代に
細石の
巌と為りて
苔の生すまで

Literal back translation
May the Imperial Reign be
1000 generations, 8000 generations
Until small pebbles
Become a boulder and
Grows moss

Basil Hall Chamberlain (1850–1935)
Thousands of years of happy reign be thine;
Rule on, my lord, until what are pebbles now
By ages united to mighty rocks shall grow
Whose venerable sides the moss doth line.

Japanese Ministry of Foreign Affairs, 2000 (cited in Hood 2001)
May your reign
Continue for a thousand, eight thousand generations
Until the pebbles
Grow into boulders
Lush with moss

Even those of us with no knowledge of Japanese can see that the second translation corresponds much more closely to the source text in terms of length. And, using the back translation, it is seemingly much closer to the source text content, too. But, is this what we are looking for when we talk about fidelity in translation, a simple linguistic equivalence? What about more pragmatic values? For instance, a national anthem is designed to be sung. The rhyme and rhythm of the first translation certainly renders it more singable and it falls in line with our expectations for a national anthem in English. What about more subtle linguistic issues, though, such as the fact that the second line is also an archaic set phrase used to mean 'forever and ever'? Does either translation capture this level of meaning? These considerations highlight a split between source and target orientation as we battle between fidelity to the form, meaning(s), or function(s) of the ST against the TT, its function(s), and its audience.

So, what is the 'right' way to translate? As always in translation, 'it depends' is a powerful answer (and one we will examine more closely in later chapters), but many scholars have contended that we have a moral responsibility to privilege certain elements of a text (Chapter 3) despite the appeal of pluralist viewpoints.

Friedrich Schleiermacher: Problematising Translation and Fidelity

Building upon this basis in fidelity, a pivotal contribution to not only translation ethics but indeed to the development of modern translation theory as a whole was Friedrich Schleiermacher's 1813 lecture 'On the Different Methods of Translating' ('*Über die verschiedenen Methoden des Übersetzens*'). While Schleiermacher is perhaps better known as a theologian and has written on a vast array of topics, his work on translation had a profound influence on the domain and this lecture provides the most sustained coverage of the topic.

Though Schleiermacher's work is more implicitly related to ethics when it comes to translation, ethics was nevertheless a core interest of his. For instance, he planned to translate Aristotle's *Nicomachean Ethics* in the late 1780s at the age of just twenty. His wider thought on ethics often revolved around binary oppositions, and this is a key feature of his (and others'!) thought on translation that has elicited much subsequent reflection in the area – consider the divides between free and literal translation, or word-for-word and sense-for-sense translation mentioned above, for instance. Importantly, the key to many of Schleiermacher's views on translation are embedded within his wider reflections on ethics, dialectics, and – above all, perhaps – hermeneutics. Hermeneutics hinges on understanding as a means of overcoming uncertainty, and moving across languages increases the risk of misunderstanding, as "every language becomes the repository of a particular system of concepts and ways of combining" (2002b:82, 1981: 109, cited in Hermans 2018: 22). Within this search for hermeneutic understanding, we also come across another important principle. For Schleiermacher, hermeneutic effort – an effort to interpret and understand – is not required in all contexts, for instance he cites "common discourse in business matters and in habitual conversation in everyday life" (1998: 7) as areas that do not require such effort. Importantly, he considers that translating texts such as journalism or travel literature fall into this domain as "in these genres the subject-matter is the sole concern, everyone is familiar with the things being referred to, the phrases used are no more than counters determined by law or convention and so speakers are readily understood ('schlechthin verständlich': 2002: 70)" (Hermans 2019: 26). For him, translating these texts is a "mechanical exercise" (2012: 45; 2002: 70) and this fragmentation of ethical enquiry both initiates a discussion of universality (explored further in subsequent chapters), and opens up a channel for subsequent accusations of elitism, which have prompted further discussion in later years.

Along similar lines, Schleiermacher also draws a stark dividing line between the oral interpreter ('Dolmetscher'), which he dismisses as unworthy of discussion, and the 'translator proper' (2012: 44; 'der eigentliche Uebersezer': 2002: 68), which is concerned with written discourse. For him, written discourse prevents the translator from clarifying misunderstandings, whereas speakers can supposedly make use of this resource unproblematically in the context of interpreting. Unfortunately, as we will see in later chapters, this does not reflect the reality of interpreting and interpreter ethics has long focused on issues of fidelity, truth, responsibility, and so forth, as well as battling with other prominent issues that may even be intensified when contrasted with the challenges faced by translators. These potential limitations are important to note as they raise vital ethical questions to be considered later in this textbook.

Returning to the key work at hand, Schleiermacher himself considered the paper to be "a rather trivial piece" (2002: xxxiii), and it is perhaps its subsequent position as the core influence behind pivotal ethical texts in translation by Berman and Venuti (whose ideas are covered in detail in chapters 3 and 5, respectively) that has seen it take on such canonical status in TIS. For Hermans (2019: 25), the lecture is about applying wider hermeneutic principles to translation, which is seemingly simply the "extension of hermeneutic principles from the intralingual to the interlingual" – from working within the same language, to moving between languages. However, there is more to it than meets the eye. Hermans continues by noting that translation is also

> very special, due the irrationality of language being at its most acute here, and to the fact that, in order to articulate their understanding of the foreign text, translators have at their disposal only their own tongue as they address readers unfamiliar with the foreign tongue.
> (Hermans 2019: 25)

In the context of "translation proper" – where substance and expression are inseparable – problems emerge both because of the lack of one-to-one equivalence between languages and because moving from one language to another heightens what is already a difficult task in a monolingual context. i.e. the aim of taking into account both the "discourse to the language as such and to the individual author" (Hermans 2019: 27). Schleiermacher explains as follows in a key passage:

> Now if understanding works of this sort is already difficult even in the same language and involves immersing oneself in both the spirit of the language and the writer's characteristic nature, how much yet nobler an art must it be when we are speaking of the products of a foreign and distant tongue! To be sure, whoever has mastered this art of understanding by studying the language with diligence, acquiring precise knowledge of the entire historical life of a people and picturing keenly before him the individual works and their authors – he, to be sure, and he alone is justified in desiring to bring to his countrymen and contemporaries just this same understanding of these masterworks of art and science.
> (2012: 47)

This passage highlights in no uncertain terms the difficulty of translation. Translators must master the source language with "the greatest diligence", of course, but must also carry out detailed historical study into the works and the people behind them in order to carry out this hermeneutic work of understanding, which they subsequently present to their audience in the target language. Schleiermacher goes on to describe this task of attempting to allow the target audience to understand the author's way of thinking as expressed through the source language with its own distinct feel as "an utterly foolish undertaking" (2012: 47), reasserting this difficulty that hinges on the fact that to "give voice to all this and provide the reader with a vicarious experience similar to his own, the translator has only his own language" (Hermans 2019: 27).

On top of this inherent difficulty of the task that faces us, there is for Schleiermacher a correct way of going about this engagement with our texts. At this point, we come to the central dictum of the lecture and an oft-repeated citation. For Schleiermacher, "[e]ither the translator leaves the author in peace, as much as possible, and moves the reader toward him. Or he leaves the reader in peace, as much as possible, and moves the author toward him" (Schleiermacher 2012: 49), leaving the translator with two separate paths they can follow. Hermans contends that the dichotomy is not real as the second option is "mentioned only to be dismissed" (Hermans 2019: 27) and argues that both poles are impossibilities. Indeed, Schleiermacher again indicates that the irrationality of language – the fact that words do not simply map together as one-to-one equivalents – means that our translations can only be an approximation, a reconstruction, and for us a compromise (we face "the obvious task of balancing out" elements of the languages we are working with in an attempt to make the content similar (1862: 181)). Yet the hermeneutic task, our aspiration to fully understand the foreign and know the "totality of thought in one language" (ibid.), brings us closer to this aim. Translation is all about handling difference and Otherness and, while this acknowledgement that we can only approximate problematises the notion of absolute fidelity, in Chapter 3 we will consider a set of ideas that attempt to flesh out this search for key elements of the foreign, as well as concretising the ethical basis of this search further.

> **Box 2.3 The Chinese tradition**
>
> In the Chinese tradition, we also find that fidelity has been a powerful foundational concept in thought on translation. Yan Fu's translation theory, revolving around the interdependent concepts of "faithfulness, expressiveness, and elegance", sets faithfulness as its most important element, prioritising fidelity to the original text and accessibility to the reader. These concepts are viewed as one of the most important developments in Chinese translation theory, long representing the standards for good translation and "the fundamental tenets of twentieth-century Chinese translation theory" (Chan 2004: 4).
>
> Meanwhile, translation ethics in China has similarly well-established roots. China itself has been described as a society centred on ethics (Liang Shuming [1949] 2011: 78, in Guangqin 2021: 25) and we find translation steeped in the deeply embedded tradition of Confucianism – a combination of normative and virtue-based ethics. Confucian ethics covers key principles including "*xin* [faithfulness], *zhong* [loyalty] or *shuzhong* [reciprocity and faithfulness], *cheng* [sincerity] and *ren* [benevolence]" (Guangqin 2021: 25) and several of these principles are core to understandings of translation ethics.
>
> However, despite a long and closely intertwined relationship between ethics and society in general, and a long history of translation, with translation having been practiced in China for about 3,000 years, a sustained exploration of ethics and translation in the country only emerged alongside the rapid development of TIS at the start of the twenty-first century. Yet within these contributions we find important implicit sketches of historical approaches to ethics in translation. Guangqin (2021) outlines four key issues that persist throughout the history of translation ethics in China in spite of the lack of explicit discourse on these areas. These four areas are **faithfulness, responsibility, the convergence of ethics and politics, and the ethics of difference**, and these four issues closely intertwine with the development of ethics in Western TIS, as we will see in the forthcoming chapters. The final issue in particular was itself heavily influenced by Western ideas as they were imported to China.
>
> As a counterpoint to Schleiermacher's ideas above, here I discuss the issue of faithfulness in particular. This principle has not only been central to Western translation theory, but is also "the very first responsibility on the part of the [Chinese] translator" (Lin Yutang [1933]

2009: 493). And, just like in Western translation theories, this faithfulness has taken on different guises throughout the history of Chinese translation. At various points, translators have been seen to abide by the concepts of *xin* [faithfulness], *zhong* [fidelity], or *zhongshi* [equivalence] (Tan 1999: 27, Zhang 2004: 108), and the former – which refers to a more narrow understanding of accuracy and was used from 220–280 CE until the 1920s–1930s (Guangqin 2021: 28) – has gradually come to be replaced by the latter two, which are "broader and richer ethically" (Wang Dongfeng 2004: 5) – though all three concepts continue to receive attention. Indeed, despite developments in terminological usage, questions of faithfulness continue to arouse discussion, and the distinctions are not clear-cut. For Lan Hongjun, *zhongshi* is synonymous with *xin* and requires the translator to transfer the meaning of the source text "truly and completely to the reader of the target text", while leading TS theorist Xie Tianzhen maintains that "as Chinese culture and literature go global, Chinese stories should be told in a language and manner popular in the receiving context, that is, it is acceptable for some translations to be rewritten or altered for better reception and communication" (Guangqin 2021: 29).

A multiplicity of viewpoints continue to be debated, and there is a clear parallel to the paths discussed in Schleiermacher's seminal paper as well as subsequent Western discussions of the topic, alluding to a certain universality to considerations of ethics in translation. Without doubt, the Chinese perspective strengthens the view that the question of fidelity or faithfulness is not one that permits any easy answers in any context.

Conclusion

Ultimately, despite potential refutations of the possibility of either pole in Schleiermacher's famous dictum, its dualistic nature has been central to discourse on translation and translation ethics. Indeed, many modern understandings of translation take on a similarly dichotomised form, reminiscent of ethics' ultimate dichotomy between good and bad. In Schleiermacher's case, moving the reader to the author would be 'good' translation, and multiple variations on this theme can be seen elsewhere. According to Pym, this trend dates back to at least Cicero and has resurfaced on an alarmingly frequent basis "in more recent pairs such as 'formal' versus 'dynamic' (Nida), 'semantic' versus 'communicative' (Newmark), 'anti-illusory' versus 'illusory' (Levy), 'adequate' versus 'appropriate' [acceptable] (Toury), 'overt' versus 'covert' (House), 'documental' [documentary] versus 'instrumental' (Nord), and 'resistant' versus 'transparent' (Venuti)" (Pym 1997: 2–3). In ethical terms, each of Pym's examples provide us with two opposing paths, one falling in line with what each respective scholar sees as the "correct" way to translate, and the other representing a supposedly erroneous (yet sometimes prevailing) methodology. Ultimately, our starting point for ethical discussions on a simplistic level is a distinction between source and target-oriented approaches to the text. We will continue with this theme of textual ethics in the next chapter, sitting firmly within Chesterman's definition of ethics at a micro-level as well as falling in line with his ethics of representation discussed above.

Discussion, Presentation, and Assignment Topics

1. To what extent do the conceptions of ethics developed by Chesterman match wider understandings of ethics considered in Chapter 1?
2. Presentation topic: To what extent can you separate the labels' faithfulness, fidelity, and equivalence? What do they mean to you in relation to your translation practice? Or, do they have additional specific meaning(s) in other languages you work with?
3. Is fidelity easier to achieve in some language combinations, practices, and/or text types than others? Why?

Further Reading

As an entry point to all things ethics in translation, **Chesterman's 2001 'Proposal for a Hieronymic Oath'** is hard to beat. Though his eventual development of a translator's Oath is more in keeping with discussions in Chapter 7, the initial theoretical explorations and his separation of ethics into four key areas offers a sound framework to explore a wide range of issues. A more up-to-date exploration of his ideas can be found in *The Routledge Handbook of Translation and Ethics*, in which Chesterman wrote an engaging, ground-clearing article on 'Virtue ethics in translation' (Chesterman 2021).

For a fascinating overview of Schleiermacher's thought in relation to translation, **Theo Hermans'** (2019) entry in the *Handbook of Translation and Philosophy* is an excellent starting point. To engage with the ideas from the author himself, **'On the Different Methods of Translating' can be found in translation by Susan Bernofsky** in *The Translation Studies Reader*.

3 Truth

> **Key Questions**
> - How has deontological ethics primarily been applied in TIS?
> - Is there a clearly-definable (and universal) 'right' way to translate, and what is at stake when we translate?
> - Should ethics be universal and, if so, what non-negotiable 'absolutes' exist in translation?

Introduction

Since its emergence as an important area for consideration, much of the work on ethics within TIS has aligned with ethical theories based upon the existence of moral absolutes, with many scholars forwarding their own takes on what it is to be ethical when translating. As Kaisa Koskinen puts it, "[t]hroughout its history, discourse on translation has included strong moralising overtones: many, if not most, contributions either explicitly or implicitly dwell on the issue of how translations ought to be produced" (Koskinen 2000: 13). This mention of both "moral absolutes" and "moralising overtones" is tied to the deontological method, which is based around **universal moral principles that govern what one ought to do**. We will begin this chapter by exploring the theory of deontology in the context of translation, and particularly ethical values relating to traditional notions of textual fidelity. As explored in Chapter 2, the idea of a **textual ethics** and the question of truth (as outlined by Chesterman's ethics of representation) concern the degree to which a target text relates to its source. The discussion here expands this basis in deontology, analysing this idea of a 'right' way to translate, and considers the work of Antoine Berman in detail.

A French scholar and translator, Berman was among the first to construct a translation ethics and offers one of the most persuasive and detailed accounts of specifically text-based ethics. His ideas put forward the most visible case for fidelity to certain features within the text – from a list of

DOI: 10.4324/9781003148265-4

"deforming tendencies" to avoid when translating texts to a specific call for "literalising" translation – and enable us to question the existence of non-negotiable "absolutes" in translation, as well as the **universalisability** of ethics in translation. As will be discussed, these ideas have their shortcomings, but nonetheless represent a foundational contribution to thought on translation ethics and a valuable starting point for a range of subsequent ideas.

Deontology and Translation

Given the difficulties that can arise when tackling a seemingly straightforward guideline such as whether or not it is right to kill somebody, it is understandable that the question of right or wrong within translation presents a serious conundrum (see Chapter 1). Yet overarching deontological rulings continue to provoke scholarly discussion as well as govern the most visible ethical facet of the profession. Indeed, an obvious application of deontology in the translation world is the development of codes of ethics for translators and interpreters. These documents represent one of the most immediate forms of deontological intervention, given their explicit aim of outlining the limits of correct behaviour as well as providing many translators with their only encounter with literature on ethics. Codes of ethics are covered in Chapter 7 and, for now, we instead focus on specific deontological conceptions of textual fidelity and the question of 'how' to go about translating, covering certain methods that are deemed to be right or wrong.

In the absence of divine commands to dictate our methodologies, within translation's deontological musings we are left to call upon scholars, translators, and translation associations putting forward their takes on what is universally wrong or right. As seen in Chapter 2, we find the roots of such deontological imperatives in the many dualistic oppositions that have dominated thought on translation. Pym draws attention to the way ethics has traditionally been perceived as an either/or situation. We either favour "the source language-culture-text-speaker" or the "target language-culture-text-speaker" (Pym 2012: 5), which calls attention back to Schleiermacher's ideas outlined in Chapter 2 and is reflected further within the ideas considered in this chapter.

When translating, we have a range of options at our disposal. Consider the following simple example. When translating a culture-bound term in a text, for instance, "Yorkshire pudding" (a common savoury English side dish), there are multiple choices available (note that this list is not exhaustive but demonstrates a range of possible responses):

- **Paraphrase** – replacing the term with a description, for instance: 'a traditional English side dish';
- **Omission** – simply leaving the reference out;

- **Borrowing** – retaining the foreign element, for example, *Yorkshire pudding* in a Spanish text;
- **Explanation** – for example, retaining the term *Yorkshire pudding* along with an explanation of what it is and its cultural significance;
- Use an **equivalent** (or approximate equivalent) in the target text, for example, choose a similarly common side dish in your target language culture.
    ? What is the 'right' way to translate here?

This dilemma of how to proceed points to the appeal and potential of deontological rulings. They serve to prioritise certain "good" or "right" acts. A deontological theory of translation ethics could prescribe, for instance, that when translating such culture-bound terms, translators should always paraphrase them – provided that it is supported by a source of moral "rightness" – assisting the translator's decision-making process, and enabling them to concretise and justify their course of action. This is precisely what Berman seeks to do, setting out a framework of "correct" ways to approach translation.

Berman's Deontology

As Pym states in his introduction to the 2001 Special Issue of *The Translator* dedicated to ethical issues: "[a] strong tradition in ethical questions is to consider the translator responsible for representing a source text or author. If something is in the source but not in the translation, the translator is at fault and is thus somehow unethical" (Pym 2001: 130). Essentially, translators must be "faithful". As seen in Chapter 2, Chesterman labels this the "ethics of representation", dealing with how we should represent the source text that we are translating, or the author, with issues of fidelity, accuracy, truth, and how to select and transmit a good, or the best, interpretation of a source text. This is at the core of our concern for fidelity and is a pervasive concept.

Exploring this notion of fidelity in a more concrete, ethical manner is the work of French scholar and translator Antoine Berman. As well as providing one of the first explicit accounts of ethical translation and one of the most thorough and influential cases for a specific idea of what is "right" in translation (specifically at a textual level, though it is derived from the wider context), Berman's work has subsequently influenced an array of leading TIS scholars. Berman's evolving work on ethics, which was unfortunately cut short by his death in 1991, enables us to explore the limits of the popular deontological method and represents a seminal contribution to the discipline. Though it is rare for theories of translation to prescribe methodologies for such small-scale decisions rather than offering "bigger picture" general dualistic oppositions, this is precisely what Berman does.

Romantic Roots and Deontological Underpinnings

Berman's most influential work, *L'épreuve de l'étranger: Culture et traduction dans l'Allemagne romantique,* was originally published in 1984 and translated into English in 1992 by Stefan Heyvaert as *The Experience of the Foreign: Culture and Translation in Romantic Germany.* The core ideas from this text have been influential the Anglophone realm, and several other articles and full-length monographs have followed in translation. However, Berman's status is nowhere near as well-established elsewhere as it is in his native France. As Alexis Nouss informs us, "francophone Translation Studies developed through reading Berman" and, the French branch of the discipline took shape "intellectually and institutionally, in parallel with the circulation of Antoine Berman's works" (Nouss 2001: 9, my translation).

The Experience of the Foreign, perhaps Berman's most famous work, was influential not only because of its content but also its methodology, representing a clear precursor to key texts such as Venuti's *The Translator's Invisibility*, which similarly attempted to present a genealogy of translation in a specific socio-cultural context. However, while Venuti's work was anchored in an Anglo-American context, Berman's work provides us with a guide to the conceptions of translation developed and practiced in the German Romantic tradition. He considers the ideas of Schleiermacher, in particular, as well as notable authors such as Friedrich Hölderlin, Goethe, and A.W. Schlegel.

In *The Experience of the Foreign,* Berman painstakingly guides us through the works of several German Romantic authors, placing a heavy focus on the concept of *Bildung*. This concept variously signifies education, experience, or even culture, and represents the continuous process of going beyond oneself to encounter the "Other" and eventually re-find your self. Within German literary culture – and referring to translation in particular – *Bildung* entailed employing a specific translation methodology that enabled the target culture to experience the foreign and subsequently expand their own cultural borders. This sits in stark contrast to the Roman conception of *Bildung*, which Berman presents as a means of developing an empire, proudly appropriating foreign texts as your own to build upon an already-strong culture. This opposition is used by Berman to reflect upon the overwhelmingly binary focus of translation scholarship, with translators seen as either favouring the source or target side. Returning to Schleiermacher's "On the different methods of translating", which (as seen in Chapter 2) influenced a number of key texts on ethics within TIS, "[e]ither the translator leaves the author in peace, as much as possible, and moves the reader toward him. Or he leaves the reader in peace, as much as possible, and moves the author toward him" (Schleiermacher 1813: 42). In Berman's view, the German *Bildung* represents the former method, preserving the foreign author's position and supposedly setting in motion an expansion and growth based upon learning from other cultures. The Roman *Bildung*, meanwhile, aligns with the latter position, domesticating or perhaps appropriating the author's ideas, subsequently aligning with the regularly accepted mode of translation in contemporary professional practice. Throughout *The Experience of the Foreign*, the Roman methodology is labelled as appropriative and likened to the reductionist aim of culture whereby we seek to assimilate everything into our own – supposedly pure – culture, while the German method is lauded for its respect of the foreign and the way in which it enables us to develop the potentialities of language (Berman 1984: 190), thereby moving towards the discovery of the kinship between languages, something that, for Berman, represents one of translation's ultimate goals. In terms of the either/or divisions outlined above, one could argue that Berman's concerns lie primarily on the source side, but the distinction is more subtle than that, with ethics at the very heart of this separation.

Trials of the Foreign

While *The Experience of the Foreign* paints a more large-scale picture, the condensed ideas outlined in his 2000 paper "Translation and the Trials of the Foreign" focus rather at the small-scale, textual level. Primarily, it represents Berman's desire to uncover the "deforming tendencies" inherent in the act of translation. The focus falls upon Berman's critique of translation's tendency to "negate" the foreign through what he calls "naturalization". He instead advocates "alienation" (a distinction that has come to be very closely associated with Venuti's own domestication vs foreignisation divide – see Chapter 5). Berman argues that translation is the "trial of the foreign" (Berman 2000: 284) in the sense that it establishes a relationship "between the Self-Same (*Propre*) and the Foreign by aiming to open up the foreign work to us in its utter foreignness" (ibid.). And it is also a trial *for the* Foreign, because the foreign work is "uprooted from its own *language-ground*" (ibid.).

For Berman, the translating act can reveal the foreign work's "most original kernel", and he limits his discussion to the literary realm, considering that non-literary translation ("technical, scientific, advertising, etc.") only performs a semantic transfer while literary translations "are concerned with *works*" (2000: 285). Based on his experiences as a translator of Latin American literature into French, he decries the way in which literary translation falls into this trap of semantic transfer, with translation becoming – rather than a trial of the Foreign – its "negation, its acclimation, its 'naturalization'". In other words, in translation, we have come to lose this foreignness. The author considers that "[t]he properly ethical aim of the translating act [is] [...] receiving the Foreign as Foreign" (Berman 2000: 285), lamenting the target text's "system of textual deformation" that prevents this foreignness from being made manifest. This is a key point to take forward, as it is this imposition that drives Berman's deontological rulings. Indeed, we could say that this is the metaethical source behind our morality – the right thing to do in translation is representing this foreignness, owing to the nature of translation.

From there he examines a "system of textual deformation" (2000: 286) that prevents this ethical aim from being realised, having been internalised over the course of two millennia within cultures and languages that he deems to be ethnocentric – that is, evaluating other cultures based on standards or preconceptions derived from your own culture. This analysis leads to the development of twelve "deforming tendencies" (see Box 3.1) at work in the literary domain, which the translator must not only be aware of, but must work to be released from. The twelve listed are not exhaustive, but are said to bear on all Western translation. Although Berman does not go so far as explicitly presenting these tendencies as things translators must avoid at all costs, there is a parallel with the Bible's Ten Commandments, replacing the Divine command with Berman's command not to do these things when translating. As he notes: "[a]ll the tendencies noted in the analytic lead to the same result: the production of a text that is more 'clear,' more 'elegant,' more 'fluent,' more 'pure' than the original. They are the destruction of the letter in favor of meaning" (2000: 297). Despite an overall focus on the negative, Berman does offer a brief insight into what "good" translation involves, too. For him, good translation restores the signifying process of works (not just considering their meaning) while also transforming the translating language. However, a clearer image of what ethical translation involves is found in relation to his in-depth analysis of translation and the letter.

Box 3.1 Berman's twelve deforming tendencies

(1) **Rationalization:** This involves the modification of sentence structure and order as well as punctuation, which Berman calls the "most meaningful and changeable element in a prose text" (Berman 2000: 288). For him, these changes alter the work's status, deforming it while seemingly leaving form and meaning intact.

(2) **Clarification:** This works on a similar level to (1) and, though Berman accepts that it is inherent in translation to a certain degree, the way in which translators make certain things explicit can reveal something that is not meant to be apparent in the text.

(3) **Expansion:** Every translation tends to be longer than the original. This is the consequence, in part, of the two previous tendencies. Berman calls it "an unfolding of what, in the original, is "folded"" (ibid. 290) and considers that these additions add nothing.

(4) **Ennoblement:** For Berman, this involves producing elegant renderings that are "readable" and, in so doing, rids the original

of its "clumsiness and complexity". This is part of a tendency for translators to try to 'improve' the text they are working on, and Berman states that the opposite – attempting to "popularize" a translation – is equally harmful.

(5) **Qualitative impoverishment:** Concisely described as the act of "[r]eplacing terms, expressions and figures in the original with terms, expressions and figures that lack their sonorous richness or, correspondingly, their signifying or "iconic" richness" (ibid. 291). When we lose the certain sonorous substance of words throughout a text we lose a great deal of the text's mode of expression or, as Berman puts it, "what makes a work *speak* to us" (ibid.).

(6) **Quantitative impoverishment:** Lexical loss. That is losses of chains of words and meanings ("signifiers and signifying chains") that combine in the ST to give it a certain richness. Berman's neat example comments on Argentinian novelist Roberto Arlt's use of the words *semblante, rostro, cara*. All three mean "face" in Spanish but a translation failing to reflect this variation would considered ethnocentric.

(7) **The destruction of rhythms:** Berman insists that "[t]he novel is not less rhythmic than poetry" and considers that it is "fortunately difficult for translation to destroy this rhythmic movement", though still notes that arbitrary changes to punctuation can cause issues.

(8) **The destruction of underlying networks of signification:** Here, Berman draws attention to a hidden layer of correspondences and links hidden beneath the surface of the text. Again referring to Arlt, he explains how augmentative suffixes are used throughout the text and insists that this level must be something that the translator pays attention to.

(9) **The destruction of linguistic patternings:** Part of the systematic nature of the text is at the level of sentence type and construction and, according to Berman, "Rationalization, clarification, expansion, etc. destroy" these features (ibid. 293), resulting in a text that is standardised and a patchwork of the types of writing used by the translator. Ultimately, this results in a text that is paradoxically more homogenous, but also more inconsistent and incoherent.

(10) **The destruction of vernacular networks or their exoticization:** Here, Berman discusses the serious loss caused by the effacement of vernaculars, or local elements of languages. Examples given include the loss of diminutives when translating from Spanish, Portuguese, German, or Russian, or replacing verbs by nominal

constructions. Berman contends that the typical solution of exoticising (e.g. placing the terms in italics) isolates the terms in a way that is not representative of the source text or artificially includes these foreign elements. Finally, he calls against seeking TL equivalent language varieties or slangs: "An exoticization that turns the foreign from abroad into the foreign at home winds up merely ridiculing the original" (ibid. 294).

(11) **The destruction of expressions and idioms**: This tendency relates to the importance of images and meanings derived from SL expressions, figures, and proverbs. While translators would generally find equivalents for these phrases, Berman argues that finding equivalents is not a substitute for translating and "even if the meaning is identical, replacing an idiom by its 'equivalent' is an ethnocentrism" (ibid. 295).

(12) **The effacement of the superimposition of languages**: Finally, Berman comments on the interaction between dialects and common languages. He argues that translation tends to erase this mix of different forms – for example Latin American versions of Spanish in his work. For him, "[t]his is the central problem posed by translating novels – a problem that demands maximum reflection from the translator" (ibid. 296).

? Which of these tendencies do you feel is the most important when translating a text? Does your answer vary depending on text type? For instance, do they apply if you are translating an instruction manual?

? Do you believe that all twelve of these tendencies are a negative feature? Can they be avoided when translating?

? To what extent do these deforming tendencies apply within the languages you work in and contexts that you are familiar with?

? How would incorporating these examples impact upon your translation methodology of culture-specific terms, for example, the 'Yorkshire pudding' example outlined above?

The "Letter": Producing an Ethical Translation

To recap, in specifically ethical terms Berman states that: "ethical translation is opposed to ethnocentric translation" (Berman 1999: 27, my translation). For the author, the ethical aim of translating is the very opposite of this appropriative and reductive ethnocentric translation outlined above while "the essence of translation is to be an opening, a dialogue, a cross-breeding, a decentering". Translation is "a putting in touch with, or it is *nothing*" (Berman 1992: 4, translation John Milton 2010: 206). Ethics for Berman revolves entirely around representing the Other as Other, as stated above, and articulated concisely, creating a space for the foreign – communicating a communication, manifesting a manifestation. However, when considered in isolation, the notion of receiving the Other as Other remains somewhat abstract. As seen above, Berman goes beyond this abstract call. In *La traduction et la lettre*, he expands our understanding further still, offering concrete guidance designed to inform the translator working on their text. Berman's ethical enquiry presents us with the universal imperative to retain and respect this "letter". As such, it is important for us to pin down what exactly this notion signifies and demands of us.

The methodology of translating the "letter" is something that Berman calls "literalising" translation, which he distinguishes from a traditional understanding of "literal" translation. For Berman, to fully embrace this concept, we must first reformulate the idea of a literal translation, which is widely viewed as a slavish word-for-word rendering. In *La traduction et la lettre*, he states that for professional translators "translating literally is to translate 'word-for-word'" (ibid. 13, my translation). This is a belief that he attributes to a confusion between the letter and the word – two seemingly interchangeable concepts at first glance that he insists are a long way apart – with this conception of literal translation failing to reach the letter. Using the example of the translation of proverbs, he demonstrates how these two terms relate to different visions of translating. As alluded to in his twelve deforming tendencies, he argues that the use of proverbs is "highly symbolic" as it exposes us to the entire problem of "equivalence" in translation. This issue imposes an idealistic sense of invariance across all languages and refuses to expose the target language to the foreignness of the original. Here, he outlines a translation strategy that is not simply a case of producing calques or "problematic" reproductions (which, he argues, respect the "word", as is the case with a traditionally "literal" translation), but rather pays close attention to the play of signifiers at work in the texts. This involves replacing the alliterative structures at work and generally involves respecting the rhythms, sounds, length (or concision), and lexico-grammatical makeup of the original, that is, when he asks that we respect the "letter", this is what he calls for. The chosen example in this case is taken from Berman's own translation into French of Roa Bastos's *Yo, El Supremo*, translated as *Moi, Le Suprême*, and the discussion revolves around the translation of the following Spanish proverb:

ES: A cada día le basta su pena, a cada año su daño.
[Literal translation: To each day is its punishment enough, to each year its hurt]
FR: A chaque jour suffit sa peine, à chaque année sa déveine
[Literal translation: To each day is its punishment enough, to each year its misfortune]

(Berman 1999: 14)[1]

52 *Truth*

Instead of searching for an "equivalent" in French or producing a "servile" word-for-word translation (a traditionally "literal" translation), Berman chooses to replicate the double rhyme in the original (*día/pena, año/daño*) with another rhyme in the French (*peine/déveine*). While this does not necessarily align with a traditional conception of translation equivalence (*déveine* [bad luck, misfortune] certainly would not normally be used to render *daño* [damage, harm]), he feels that it results in a translation that is at once "literal and free" (ibid.). Furthermore, though the rhyme scheme does not match, Berman claims to reassemble the alliterative structure of the original in a new form. Speaking of the difficultly involved in embedding this new view of translation, Berman notes that many of the professional translators who attended the seminar in which he outlined this example were quick to reject such a view of the translating act. He notes: "for them, translating was compulsively about finding equivalents" (Berman 1999: 14, my translation). For Berman, meanwhile, "translating is not about finding equivalents", and "equivalents of a phrase or a proverb do not *replace* them" (ibid. 65). Even though "equivalent" proverbs exist in most languages, using these stock phrases does not suffice for a translation methodology.

Box 3.2 Translating idioms: An example

Imagine you are translating a text from English and you come across the following idiom: 'It's raining cats and dogs'. How would you go about translating it?

In all likelihood, you would perhaps come up with something along the following lines, which all retain the meaning of heavy rain, employing a target-reader friendly idiom:

- French: Il pleut à seaux [It's raining buckets]
- Russian: Дождь льёт как из ведра [Rain is pouring as if from a bucket]
- Mandarin: 下倾盆大雨 [Basin-bending big rain is falling]
- Norwegian: Det regner trollkjerringer [It's raining troll women]

In each of these examples, the translation takes the form of a recognised equivalent in the target language. Yet while this kind of translation would be commonly used in many contexts, this is precisely what Berman is arguing against, as it fails to represent the Other (the foreign language and culture) as Other. In transforming the 'cats and dogs' into the Norwegian 'troll women', we are losing something that he sees as vital to the language – after all, proverbs and idioms tend to be deeply rooted in cultural tradition.

Berman discusses another proverb, commonly translated into English as "the early bird catches the worm" or "early to bed, early to rise, makes a man healthy, wealthy, and wise". Again, most translators would employ a semantic equivalent in their target language. In Spanish, for instance, the translator may opt for "A quien madruga, dios le ayuda", (literally 'God helps those who wake up early'), which is widely considered to be a suitable equivalent for the phrase. The Russian version, meanwhile, could well be 'Кто раньше встал, того и тапки' (roughly 'He who gets up earliest gets the slippers').[2]

For Berman, however, following the "letter" and his version of literal translation, finding equivalents is not a suitable method. In translating the original German proverb "Morgenstund hat Gold im Mund" (literally 'Morning hour has gold in the mouth'), Berman rejects the readily-accepted French "equivalent" ('le monde appartient à ceux qui se lèvent tôt' [literal translation: the world belongs to those who get up early]). Instead he opts for "l'heure du matin a de l'or dans la bouche" [the morning hour has gold in the mouth], claiming that it is precisely the key elements of "gold", "morning", and "mouth" in the German that should be retained or reconstructed in order to enrich the receiving language and to expand awareness of linguistic and cultural difference.

In this way, rather than searching for equivalents in the text, which would thus see us refusing to carry over the foreignness of the original into the translating language, this "*littéralisante*" [literalising] translation engenders a subtle shift that, according to Alain, could subsequently lead to a profound change, with translations that are "more English than the English text, more Greek than the Greek, more Latin than the Latin" (Alain (1934: 56–57) in Berman (1999: 25)).

However, the suggestion that this methodology will see the text become, for example, "more English than the English text" is perhaps misleading. Indeed, the idea of embellishing on meaning supposedly represents a fundamental weakness in translation practice, leading to such ethnocentric renderings and liberal recreations that we confuse for translations. For Berman, when translating the letter, there is a "fundamental agreement" that links a translation to its original and "forbids any exceeding of the texture of the original" (Berman 1999: 40, my translation). This is an explicit call for translation not to exceed the original, with all creativity invested in recreating the foreignness of the original, not producing an over-translation of it. This is supported by Berman's belief that great writing comes from innovation, misuse, and new usages. Traditionally viewed negatively within translational rhetoric (which demands superior, beautiful language), for Berman this provides a text with its "*richesse*" [richness] (ibid. 51). As he puts it: "literality [i.e. translating the letter] is not just about opposing French syntax or neologising: it is also about retaining, in the translated text, the *obscurity* inherent in the original" (Berman 1999: 109, my translation). The further we mimic the tools employed by the other language, the closer we get to the Foreignness that translation is seeking to capture.

Ultimately, Berman leaves us with the notion that this uniqueness inherent in a source language is absolutely vital to ethics and to translation (Berman 1999: 131). Ethically, Berman contends that translation of *la lettre* is our one viable option, respecting the rhythms, sounds, length (or concision), and lexico-grammatical makeup of the original. This deontological call to preserve certain textual features does not entail a slavish attachment to every word and phrase of a text, but rather seeks to carry over the unique features of a language in order to enrich the receiving language and culture. Linguistically, this perhaps calls our mind to the "letter versus the spirit" debate in law and religion. However, for Berman, the "letter" *is* the spirit, in the sense that it is not a slavish fidelity to the shape of every word, but a fidelity to its meaningfulness, its performativity. Though Berman demonstrates that this approach *can* be employed in the specific context of literature and proverbs, doubts remain over its feasibility on a wider level, as we will see below.

Universalisability

Gouanvic's 'Ethos, Ethics and Translation: Toward a Community of Destinies' asserts that "[t]he interest of an ethical theory of translation as we understand it lies in the integration of *all translation* practices" (2001: 204, emphasis in original), thus suggesting that theories should seek to apply to all contexts. In Berman's work too, there is a hint at a certain universality, referring to translation in a general sense despite addressing specific subsections of the activity (i.e. literary translation). Yet whether or not this universality is reflected in practice is a key consideration. Indeed, is there a way to reconcile his ideas with non-literary translation and construct the all-encompassing ethics that Gouanvic suggests? The immediate response from the majority of professional translators would be "no". In contemporary professional practice at least – and this extends to literary translators working in the domain that Berman explores – it would seem that translation of the letter is not a feasible option. Imagine the mystifying looks an interpreter would receive when telling a room of Arabic speakers that "morning hour has gold in the mouth", for instance. Subjecting the target culture to the feel of the foreign language would soon put the translator in question out of work, with client demands invariably necessitating well-written texts that give the illusion of having been originally written in the target language.

More generally, the focus on literary translations found in Berman's work has been criticised by a number of scholars, who have repeatedly remarked upon the elitism present in his ideas. This elitism is clearly reflected in Berman's comments on professional, technical translation, a focus on the translation of poetry and literature, and a rather dismissive attitude to the methodologies followed by professional translators (e.g. his dismissal of the validity of the prevailing translation methodology based on the use of equivalents). However, as Tymoczko suggests, literary translation in particular can serve as an important model for developing overarching translation theories. As she explains, "[i]n developing and testing theory, models are often necessary in order to make sense of a large and complex array of data" and "literary texts and their translations can and do provide foundational models for theorizing various aspects of translation of all types" (Tymoczko 2014: 11–12). As such, although the claims to universalisability may be overly ambitious, these ideas can nevertheless provide invaluable insights to translation theory in general. Indeed, the desire to raise an awareness of cultural tendencies through an encounter with the Other is certainly an interesting and perhaps laudable project.

Finally, in his 2001 paper 'Berman, Unfaithful to Himself?', Charron also questions whether or not Berman's ideas are reflected in his translation work. By analysing numerous passages in the first part of Berman's French translation of the aforementioned *Yo el Supremo*, Charron clearly demonstrates that "'Berman the translator' did not seem to be able to put into practice principles of which 'Berman the translation scholar' was very aware" (Charron 2001: 97). Beyond concerns of compatibility within genres, this paper calls into question Berman's ethical theories and translation methodologies as a whole. Despite providing a fascinating take on his beliefs of what a translation should be and should do, Berman's ideas at this point fail to fully find a way to integrate the theory with practice.

Conclusion

Where does this leave us in relation to deontological accounts of ethics in translation? Notions of accuracy and fidelity undoubtedly have their place in discussions, and deontology's absolute rulings are almost ubiquitous in framing these debates. Although we find doubts over the effectiveness of universal moral rulings in a general ethical sense, translation scholarship has continually called upon this area in its own moral investigations. Generally, however, an unbending approach to moral matters is largely inadequate to deal with the complexities of the translation process. In terms of ethics, it would appear that the general ethical theory criticisms levelled against deontology – primarily that the universal nature of the theory is unable to account for the potentially infinite range of contexts and circumstances that exist in real-world settings – do indeed extend to the context of translation. Gouanvic, for instance, casts doubt upon the idea of a "one-size-fits-all" ethics as follows:

> there are multiple ways of translating the same text, and thus a multiplicity of potentials for various possible texts. If there were just one ethical

way of translating a text, whatever the text, then there should be only one good translation of it.

(Gouanvic 2001: 203)

And, as Juan Ramírez Giraldo puts it, "almost all questions about translation nowadays can be given the same simple answer: 'it depends' " (Ramírez Giraldo 2014: 249).

However, this does not diminish the value of these contributions – we merely need to recognise these limitations. Importantly, the texts considered to this point indicate the kind of questions we need to be asking. The elements that Berman flags up represent something of a checklist of factors to consider when translating – an indicator of the type of minute detail that can affect understanding in translation. His calls for a general respect of Otherness are morally persuasive and his considerable literary knowledge and in-depth critiques uncover tiny nuances in literary work that can also be applied to more general, technical texts. In marketing texts, for instance – a very common specialism among freelance translators, with texts for translation including press releases and advertising copy – elements such as alliteration, rhythm, and syntax can be extremely important. Unfortunately, however, there is no justification for endowing any of these features with particular universal importance when the wide-ranging activity of translation demands unique solutions for unique contexts.

It is certainly not easy to devise universal rulings in translation. Categorical imperatives such as "you should never translate by finding equivalents for idioms" are difficult to uphold in all contexts. But what of the alternative? When learning to translate, we need a way to orient ourselves, to ground our decision-making, and to be cognisant of both the range of potential methods available to us and the potential impact of our decisions. Simply saying "it depends" does not teach a translator how to act. This is a great strength of Berman's deontology and deontological rulings in general. They can provide an insight into dominant modes of translation, and the cases put forward for a specific course of action can demonstrate what is at stake when translating. Whether finding equivalents for proverbs or deleting references that the target reader will not be familiar with, we are not simply making inconsequential lexical choices, but rather shaping the representation of a text/author/language. Translation is not just an arbitrary selection of words or characters, but can impact upon power relations between people, languages, and entire cultures. This is something that Berman was certainly aware of, and his ideas have gone on to shape the thought of a number of other scholars in TIS. Ethics is not just about engagement at a textual level. The next step is to explore the "bigger picture", and to place the translating act into context, a task taken up in Chapter 4.

Discussion, Presentation, and Assignment Topics

1. As a group, read through a text in a shared language and discuss what you feel would be the most important elements to retain if you were to translate that text. Why those specific elements?
2. Find a text that has been translated in your language pair (many online news sites can be a good source for multilingual versions of the same text). Look through the text and its translation, noting any differences. What do you believe is behind these changes? Can you relate these to Berman's deforming tendencies?
3. Try to draw up your own definitive rule(s) for translation. What is something that can apply across a range of contexts? Is it something that only applies to your language pair(s)? It may be interesting to compare and contrast this with guidelines found in codes of ethics (Chapter 7).

Notes

1 The first half of this phrase is an aphorism that appears in the Sermon on the Mount in the gospel of Matthew and is traditionally found in English translation as "sufficient unto the day is the evil thereof". In a less archaic translation, the New American Standard Bible reads, "Each day has enough trouble of its own" while the 'Today's English Version' offers "There is no need to add to the troubles each day brings".
2 It is seen as a bit of a faux pas in Russia to walk around the house in socks or barefoot. You would typically have spare pairs of slippers for guests for them to put on when they arrive (or you bring your own). The reason is that, traditionally, a lot of floors were covered in big fur rugs, which are difficult to clean.

Further Reading

A reasonably accessible starting point for Antoine Berman's thought is Lawrence Venuti's English translation of **'Translation and the Trials of the Foreign' (Berman 2000)**, which offers further detail on the twelve deforming tendencies. Full accounts of his ethical ideals can be found in **Berman (1984) and (1999)**, the latter of which is only available in French. Berman's work developed further in **Berman (1995/2009)**, with a push towards a more hermeneutic understanding of translation, and **Chantelle Wright's (Berman 2018)** translation brings another of Berman's works into English.

For critiques of Berman's ideas, see **Pym (2012)**, which is covered from a different angle in Chapter 4, or **Charron (2001)**. Finally, for another powerful account of a deontological, textual ethics, see **Meschonnic (2007/2011)**. This text, which prioritises the fundamental importance of rhythm in translation, was written by another French thinker who initially influenced Berman, though their thought eventually diverged.

4 Responsibility

> **Key Questions**
> - How has a consequentialist outlook on ethics most clearly been applied in TIS?
> - How have the concepts of loyalty and cooperation been framed in TIS ethics?
> - How does context enter our thinking in relation to translation ethics?

In Chapter 4, we move a step beyond analysing ethical concerns at the textual level and start to consider 'bigger picture' responsibilities. Chapter 3 foregrounded the case for translators' responsibility to lie within the detail of the texts they translate. Chesterman (2016: 167) reminds us that "Berman (1984) […] argued that bad translation negates the strangeness of the foreign and hence makes all texts equally familiar and communicable", and he therefore chose to eschew this tendency and privilege the strangeness of the foreign in his "literalising" translation. For Berman, this desire to represent the Otherness of the source text represents what Chesterman calls a "primary loyalty", and I adopt this word here very deliberately. Indeed, **loyalty** is another crucial concept within translation ethics that has been formulated in a number of key ways and is tied inextricably to the functionalist ideas covered below.

Discussion in this chapter will focus around two central questions, in addition to those posed above: "What are we responsible to or for when translating?" and "How can we balance our range of responsibilities in an ethical manner?" However, as with all of our ethical deliberations, we are unlikely to reach any easy answers. As Kopp puts it, "responsibility" has become something of a buzzword since the 1990s and, despite its wide-ranging meaning, the term is employed throughout many key TIS books "as if its meaning was obvious […] without differentiation, as a synonym of either liability or obligation and duty or accountability" (Kopp 2012: 146). She

DOI: 10.4324/9781003148265-5

offers a nuanced historical exploration of the term and its shifting meanings and draws our attention to an important mix between retrospective and prospective aspects of responsibility – both looking at intentions of your actions and potential consequences thereof, something that is raised below in relation to Pym and recalls consequentialist thought on ethics.

Specifically, we first look at Nord's concept of function plus loyalty (Nord 2001), which discusses the importance of considering the various stakeholders involved in the translation process. After exploring the functionalist roots of this theory, I assess its ethical implications, moving beyond fidelity and function alone to a very specific notion of translatorial responsibility. Subsequently, we consider Pym's influential ideas on ethics (notably from Pym 2012), which embed a translator's responsibility within their profession. In relation to the four types of ethics outlined by Chesterman (see Chapter 2), this chapter focuses primarily on an ethics of service, adding considerations of client needs and expectations and the aims of our translations, while Pym's notions of ethics can be categorised within Chesterman's third model focusing on communication. As a reminder, this model of ethics deals not with respect for the Other in terms of a textual respect (which is covered in Chapter 3), but rather with **the question of communicating with other people** (Chesterman 2001: 141).

? What 'other people' do we have to consider in the context of translation and/or interpreting?
? Is loyalty a concept that you deal with in your daily life? What does it require of you? And what could it require of you in the context of interpreting and translation?

From Function and Fidelity to Loyalty

Functionalism is a school of thought in TIS that emerged in the 1970s and 1980s and saw a move away from previously dominant consideration of individual textual elements (the centre of enquiry in what is known as the 'Linguistic Turn') to prioritise a text's use in more pragmatic terms. This enlarged focus begins to consider the wider context at work and, neatly mirroring our move in relation to ethics, marked a shift from micro-level considerations to a more macro-level approach.

Returning to the ethical theories explored in Chapter 1, we find parallels to both deontological and consequentialist outlooks in functionalist theories of translation. Reiss's text type theory, first of all, is more deontologically focused. It posits three main text types – informative, expressive, and operative – each with distinct characteristics (1977/1989: 108–109) and prescribes different loyalties (or fidelity) depending on the type of text we are translating (Figure 4.1). In an informative text, for instance, our primary loyalty is to the 'reality of the situation', in an expressive text, it is to the sender, in an operative, to the receiver, and these texts can inform our

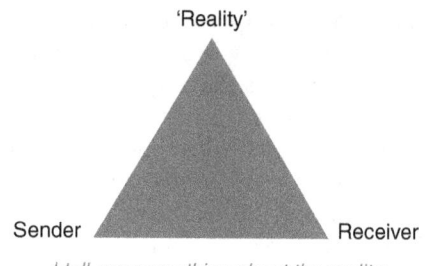

Figure 4.1 Functionalist model of communication.

translation methodology, for example, a translation of an informative text should transmit the full referential or conceptual content of the ST without redundancy (Reiss 1976: 20). The specific content of these maxims is not our core focus here (see Munday 2022, Chapter 5 and pp. 100–105 for a full introduction to Reiss and functionalist ideas) but rather it is important to note that these guidelines suggest an answer to the question of 'how' we should translate that is dependent upon the type of text and – later on in functionalist terms – the purpose. Later in the chapter we will see a shift away from this focus.

Skopos theory, meanwhile, sees us move from ST-centred to TT-centred approaches, from text types to strategies. Nevertheless, we are **still focusing on a mainly linguistic notion of text and of translation within this notion of texts as being 'functionally adequate'**. As opposed to Reiss' text type model, in *Skopos* theory our translation methodology is governed by a predetermined *skopos* (purpose or function) and intrinsic value is bestowed upon this notion of function. The text's final state takes precedence over competing considerations – the TT is determined by its *skopos* (Reiss and Vermeer 1984: 119) and the ends tend to justify the means no matter what course of action is taken.[1] This loosely represents a shift from deontology to consequentialism: we set a certain aim or *skopos* to be achieved (i.e. a consequence), and follow a methodology that will allow us to achieve that aim.

However, this approach has been deemed by some as "unethical sui generis as it accords a disputable power to the translator" (Kopp 2012: 145), allowing misuse (Kadric and Kaindl 1997) via the potential for unscrupulous translators to skew a text to promote their own personal ideological goals, for instance. Though Kopp challenges this "Machiavellian postulate" and the theory's potential link to ideological writing and radicalism with considerable success, this remains a powerful argument and is the point at which ethics has entered the equation explicitly. Indeed, it is important to note that the core functionalist theories were not explicitly conceptualised in ethical terms. Vermeer argued that "ethics must not be mixed up with the general theoretical considerations about other subjects" (Vermeer 1996: 107), conceiving of ethics as culture-specific and thus unsuited to a general theory. However, there is the pervasive argument that all discussions of how we engage with texts can be viewed from an ethical perspective, and the question of responsibility that is central to notions of *skopos* ensures that these ideas are implicitly tackling questions of ethics.

These potential criticisms and the growing importance of ethics led Nord to develop the concept of "Function plus Loyalty". Nord critiques and expands upon existing ideas from this school of thought to form a truly hybrid ethical theory, rethinking basic ideas of functionalism. While she retains the principle of functionality, she argues that this does not allow translators complete licence to make any changes they wish, asking whether or at what point we may be straying too far from the ST. However, this move involves reorienting our roots. **While traditional fidelity is intertextual, Nord argues that translation is actually interpersonal.** It is not just the translator and their text; there are other people involved – our "partners" in the process of translation, towards whom we are also responsible. As an interpersonal relationship, loyalty was meant to replace the traditional intertextual relationship of "faithfulness" or 'fidelity', concepts that usually refer to linguistic or stylistic similarity between the source and the target texts, regardless of the communicative intentions involved. Nord's loyalty seeks to embrace that difference by positing translation as a subjective, personal activity. She is at pains to suggest that this is something different, something new:

> Loyalty is not the old faithfulness or fidelity in new clothes. Faithfulness and fidelity referred to a relationship holding the source and the target texts as linguistic entities [...]. Loyalty, on the other hand, is a category referring to a social relationship between people. It can be defined as the responsibility translators have toward their partners in translational interaction.
>
> (Nord 2001: 195)

In the final chapter of *Translating as a Purposeful Activity*, Nord explains how her concept of loyalty, was developed "to account for the cultural specificity of translation concepts" (Nord 2001: 185) and commit "the translator bilaterally to both the source and the target side" (ibid.: 195). In a bid to move beyond traditional concepts of fidelity, the idea offers an ethical concept governing the translators' responsibility to their partners. Translation is viewed as a cooperative activity and, as noted, the theory sets out with the dual purpose of not only adding an ethical element that was traditionally lacking in functional theories but also addressing several criticisms commonly levelled against the theory. As Nord puts it, the concept of loyalty "was designed to set an ethical limitation on the otherwise unlimited range of possible *skopoi* or purposes of the translation for any particular source text" (ibid. 185), an intriguing addition that undoubtedly provides nuance to the theory.

In ethical terms, **the intrinsic values of loyalty are set to a tripartite distinction: loyalty to source text author, the target audience, and the commissioner of the work.**

> Being loyal means respecting the partners' interests. The commissioner's interest is to obtain a translation that serves the intended purpose (*skopos*), the source text author's interest is not to be interpreted in contradiction to his/her own intentions, and the recipients' interest is to receive a translation that fits their expectations.
>
> (Hebenstreit 2021: 63–64)

This limits the range of available purposes by introducing these other parties and the notion of cooperation, which aligns Nord's thought with contractarian conceptions of ethics.[2] Along with the idea of the social contract, **contractarianism** is all about cooperation (a key tenet that is also present in Pym's ethical thought, discussed in the following section). This revolves around the belief that forgoing some of our liberties (i.e. the freedom to follow any translation methodology we desire in Nord's case) and following the mutually beneficial system of cooperation leaves us much better off than if left in the natural state of everyone competing for supremacy. For contractarians, agreeing not to do something is designed with the understanding that others will agree to the same thing, that is, if we ourselves are drawn to immorality but do not want others to act in the same way, then surely it is within our interests to act morally so that they have no reason to doubt us and will act morally themselves. This is the justification for our being moral. However, doubts remain over whether or not we can overcome rational egoism, where we have good reason to do something only if it serves our self-interest. For example, if we discover that the benefits of acting in a way that is forbidden outweigh the chances or penalties of getting caught, then we run the risk of individuals acting immorally.

Unfortunately, cooperation does not necessarily align with (conceptions of what most people would agree represents) ethical action. For example, if all three parties in Nord's loyalty require a text to be skewed in a particular way, this course of action would presumably be viewed as ethical. This is based solely upon the notion of cooperation and disregards any violation of perhaps well-founded notions of fidelity, for instance. This is where Nord's hybridity and the addition of a deontic maxim aims to bring us closer to a satisfactory solution. With the needs of the various parties often conflicting, Nord suggests that

> [i]f the client asks for a translation that entails being disloyal to either the author or the target readership or both, the translator should argue

this point with the client or perhaps even refuse to produce the translation on ethical grounds.

(2001: 200)

Yet, while this may be feasible in certain situations, the likelihood that a client will be open to these kinds of demands in a professional situation is low. Furthermore, no potential resolutions are offered for occasions where the demands of all parties involved are in conflict.

> **Box 4.1 How to achieve loyalty?**
>
> Nord asks that we are loyal to the source text author, other agents/actors (including clients or editors), and target text users. But can we be loyal to all parties in all situations? What happens when their interests clash? Nord says we should negotiate, tell people what is going on, or even refuse to take on a project. How realistic/practical are these guidelines?
>
> Consider the two following excerpts and the questions that follow:
>
>> The range of the translation purposes allowed for in relation to one particular source text is limited by translators' responsibility to their partners in the cooperative activity of translation (loyalty principle). If the client asks for a translation that entails being disloyal to either the author or the target readership or both, the translator should argue this point with the client or perhaps even refuse to produce the translation on ethical grounds (cf. the example in Nord 1997a:126f.)
>>
>> (Nord 2001: 200)
>
>> [L]oyalty can be achieved by making the translation strategies explicit in a preface, by adopting clear choices at points of source text ambiguity, and by using the most advanced theological and philological scholarship to ensure loyalty to the source-text author's intentions.
>>
>> (Nord 2001: 185)
>
> ? What is a 'clear choice' when it comes to ambiguity?
> ? How do we intuit what the author wanted/meant?
> ? How do we access our target users?
> ? Do you have full, detached control over your translation strategy? Could you always reflect this in a preface?
> ? How useful is the most advanced theological and philological scholarship beyond the context of Bible translation?

Moving forward, Nord suggests that we do not simply do "what the others expect you to do (because this would lead into an insoluble dilemma if the interactants expect divergent forms of behaviour)" (ibid. 196) and says that we, as translators, must "consider the subjective theories of [our] partners and explain their translation purposes and methods if [we] behave in a way that may be contradictory to these theories" (ibid.). This notion of appreciating the viewpoints of others and of initiating a dialogue to explain and defend translational decisions is illuminating and will resurface in subsequent chapters, albeit within a different ethical framework. Indeed, though the idea holds a great amount of appeal, Nord does not go into significant depth regarding the inner workings of such a system. Instead, her analysis returns to an ethics of explicitness, which accords ultimate responsibility to the translator and enables any course of action based on transparency and accountability (see Box 4.1). Here, the translator is very much allowed to do as they wish as in the consequentialist *skopos* theory idea of "function", just as long as they are open about doing it. In this way, Nord's theory demonstrates an acknowledgement of the translator's partially subjective role in text creation and attempts to negotiate this issue via the explicit reporting of any alterations.

Prefacing a translated text (also suggested by Chesterman) seemingly represents a beneficial course of action when feasible but the assumption of an ability on the part of the translator to intuitively know where this subjectivity arrives and in what form seemingly underestimates the complexity of such a task. The idea of "adopting clear choices at points of source-text ambiguity" (ibid. 185) equally relies on intuition and equates a clear choice with the right choice (ethically), which is not necessarily the case nor a simple matter. Furthermore, "ensur[ing] loyalty to the source-text author's intentions" both contradicts her tripartite loyalty outlined above and makes light of what is itself surely another subjective category (if the preface is to discuss all points at which a subjective decision has been made, arguably the text should be covered in its entirety) and one that again returns us to problematic discussions of fidelity.

Ultimately, though problems remain when we are to decide what course of action is to be taken when the interests of individual parties conflict, Nord's framework has multiple strengths. It demonstrates a keen awareness of the importance of considering the needs and interests of a range of agents involved in the translation process, incorporates conceptions of subjectivity, and counters some of the criticisms previously levelled against *skopos* theory by attempting to bind the translator's decisions to these various agents. Nord's hybridity is also an interesting feature. Deontology again emerges at various points, traditional notions of function are consequentialist, and contractarianism is contained within the notion of cooperation and an insistence upon loyalty to various parties. Yet through all of these theories, various issues of compatibility see responsibility return to the translator a problematic call for transparency.

Translator Ethics: Anthony Pym on Cooperation, Risk, and Trust

A particularly telling contribution to ethics in TIS, which builds upon the consequentialist basis at the heart of this chapter, comes from eminent scholar Anthony Pym. Pym's core ethics is outlined in his 1997 work, *Pour une éthique du traducteur,* which was subsequently translated from French into English in 2012 as *On Translator Ethics*. This seemingly commonplace choice of title is important in the context of this chapter as a whole. While previous discussions could be more neatly termed under a *translation* ethics – which Chesterman concisely notes as "principles governing what makes an ethically good translation, as a text" – Pym's conscious choice of *translator* ethics considers the human beings at the heart of the process as explicitly "bringing to the fore issues such as the translator's responsibility and agency" (Chesterman 2021: 15). Pym's ideas in this text revolve largely around the notions of cooperation and interculturality, and he reflects upon and critiques the ideas of Berman and Schleiermacher as he seeks to move away from translation theory's obsession with binarisms. In subsequent work, Pym has explored the notions of risk and trust as further, essential components of ethics, as we will see later in this chapter.

On a general level, Pym views the ethics of translation as twofold – it contains "collective, professional aspects as well as the translator's individual morality" (Pym 2012: 15) – and argues that "[i]f any decision includes moral aspects, it follows that any act of translation, and any theoretical treatise on it, can be read from the point of view of ethics" (ibid. 16). With these statements, Pym equates the act of translation with an ethics of translation. Yet, rather than seeking to address the question of ethics within the act of translation, as Corinne Wecksteen puts it, "Pym proposes to replace the fundamental question, 'How should one translate?' (the answer to which is usually based on the binary opposition between source- and target-oriented theories) by the question, 'Should one translate?'" (Wecksteen 2000: 125), considering that "if we know why we translate, then we can deduce how we should translate and perhaps even what we should translate in each situation" (Pym 2012: 12). This move can be equated to shifting from a deontological ethics to a consequentialist one, with the question of "how" relating to what we ought to do and the question of "why" insisting that our end goals drive our course of action.

From there, Pym views translation as a cooperative act and creates a social ethics that seeks to promote the process of translators' professionalisation. This acts as a guiding principle to contribute to intercultural cooperation, a central concept in Pym's ideas that he describes as "abstract but situational, since the nature of cooperation depends on numerous factors specific to each case" (2012, 9), a signal of the importance of contextual factors within ethics. Pym goes on to produce a number of overarching principles: the translator's first loyalty is to their profession, and then they

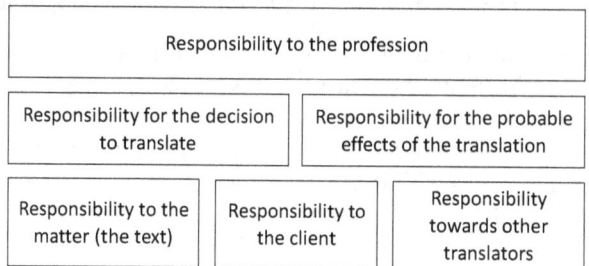

Figure 4.2 Areas of responsibility in Pym's ethics of cooperation.

are responsible for the decision to translate, to the probable effects of their translations, and subsequently to the matter (the text), the client, and other translators (illustrated in Figure 4.2). These domains overlap to a degree with Chesterman's ethics of representation and ethics of service and Nord's loyalty, but they paint a more clearcut picture in terms of the hierarchy that is drawn and the range and extent of responsibilities.

Importantly, in more recent years Pym has also been at pains to point out what cooperation is not. He states that it is not about faithfulness or equivalence, as all texts must be interpreted – inevitably, change is going to happen, as explored in Chapter 2. It is not about fulfilling a purpose, like *skopos* theory, as purposes must be construed and mercenaries who simply set out to get the job done regardless of the context or demands placed upon them cannot be seen as being ethical. And finally, it is not a simple deontological code: he forcefully states that we need more than limits and, just because a certain model has become traditional (e.g. accuracy or fidelity), that is not enough of a reason to retain it (Pym 2021b: 10).

For Pym, "the benefits of cooperation are the final measure to evaluate the necessity of translation", and "[t]here is also a more profound ethical aim behind his ethics of cooperation: cooperation, or even social solidarity, is seen as the general goal of social relations" (Koskinen 2000: 73). **The goal of any translation project should be long-term cooperation between cultures.** This reinforces the consequentialist outlook, setting cooperation that leads to intercultural relations as the ultimate goal to be achieved. In an article published in 1995, Pym even went as far as to formulate the ultimate goal of translation in general within a wider social ethics as "the attainment of happiness" (Pym 1995: 602). This means that, for Koskinen at least, his work represents "an extended effort to think through the ways in which translators as a collective could fulfil this goal of 'happiness'" (Koskinen 2000: 110), and offers not only consequentialist strands but, more specifically, utilitarian ones.

Box 4.2 Cooperation in action

In outlining what cooperation means in the context of translation and interpreting and how it differentiates itself from other ideas of ethics, Pym provides the following example of a meeting between Donald Trump and Vladimir Putin in Helsinki in 2018, during which State Department interpreter Marina Gross took notes (Pym 2021: 18–19). After the meeting, a US congressional committee asked Gross to reveal what was in her notes, and Pym asks us whether or not she should have agreed.

Referring to codes of ethics, the answer would be no, as confidentiality is one of the key principles in these documents. Indeed, Pym reports that "[t]he International Association of Conference Interpreters (Field 2018) swiftly issued a statement saying that the interpreter should not testify, and the American Translators Association was reported as taking the same position (Segal 2018)". In terms of cooperation, meanwhile, we have to consider whether revealing the notes from the private meeting would result in a benefit to cross-cultural communication. For Pym, "a good argument can be made for the practice of private meetings as trust-building exercises between heads of state" (Pym 2021: 18), which leads him to agree with the principle of confidentiality, but not because it is enshrined within codes of ethics. This logic of decision-making introduces a subtle yet important difference.

? What do you make of these ideas? Is the shift to cooperation clear in this case?
? Can you think of any cases in which cooperation would not be the ideal (or your chosen) solution?

Aside from notions of cooperation, one of Pym's principal postulates is that translators are primarily intercultural agents located in the intersections of cultures and not within one single culture. His opening chapter of *Pour une éthique du traducteur* is dedicated to a critical re-reading of Schleiermacher's 'On the different methods of translating'. He concludes that Schleiermacher's binary opposition presumes that translators take only one side in their interventions, excluding the middle ground within which Pym believes that the future of translation could lie. In this middle ground, translators are "dominated by the ethics of cooperation", "primarily responsible not to the source text writer, the client or their readers but to their fellow translators" (Koskinen 2000: 80). Though Pym accepts that translators may have to choose between two sides at certain points, the fundamental core of his ethics is "strictly intercultural" (2012: 167). As Chesterman puts it:

> For Pym, a translator's primary loyalty is neither to the source culture nor the target culture, but to others inhabiting this space, i.e. to other intercultural mediators, to the translating profession as a whole: in short, the primary loyalty is to something intercultural [...] Pym stresses the translator's responsibility for the translation, as soon as he/she has agreed to translate it, and the utilitarian importance of translations in contributing to stable and mutually beneficial intercultural relations.
>
> (Chesterman 2016: 168)

Some commentators at the time remarked that translators were being portrayed as somehow detached from national interests, as benevolent but impartial helpers. It creates an "aura of innocence and moral disinterestedness" (Koskinen 2000: 74) in a tactical move aimed to raise the profile of translation – an innovative rethinking of the traditional binary dichotomies dominating the field, yet a claim that left some fundamental concerns. Indeed, though there is undoubted promise in implicating translators within their profession, this idea of translators as neutral characters in between cultures has been criticised.

Tack, for instance, states that "Pym's cooperation model [...] takes little notice of the more covert aspects that prevent human communication from ever becoming a mechanically transparent exchange of immediately accessible goods: hidden agendas, unconscious biases, diffuse connections to power relations." Importantly,

> [i]nformation does not flow freely, not even in intercultures; it is inevitably anchored, situated, appropriated and inscribed in complex ideological contexts. The mutual benefit, as the guiding principle for the question whether or not to translate, is not always clearly in sight.
>
> (Tack 2001: 301)

Once again, this raises the problem of competing issues between various stakeholders, which proved to be a significant shortcoming in the ethical thought of Nord. Furthermore, in 'Ideology and the position of the translator', Tymoczko outlines the translator's inevitably non-neutral position and emphatically concludes that the translator's position is "not a space in between" (Tymoczko 2003: 201). Translators are always rooted, and their clients are always rooted. Interculturality is certainly a feature of the translator's existence, but a translator lives somewhere, is from somewhere, and those things are not homogeneous wholes in themselves. The translator is not value-free or universal, a theme that is explored in greater depth in subsequent chapters.

From an ethical perspective, it is important to recognise identity as complex and organic: it is not possible to be free of ideology and still be human. This objection is vital, as it not only potentially problematises some of Pym's ethical underpinnings but also articulates a much wider point in terms of professional translator ethics. Though it features in both professional documentation and scholarly thought, it is widely accepted that total neutrality or impartiality on the part of the professional translator is an illusion. For Koskinen, further questions such as "How does one position oneself in the intercultural space", "How does one evaluate the benefits of cooperation?", and, again, "How does one choose between conflicting interests in cases where an obvious middle ground ensuring long-term cooperation simply does not exist?" represent "[d]ifficulties of application indicat[ing] a fundamental weakness in Pym's ethics of interculturality" (Koskinen 2000: 73).

However, the fact that Pym's text was re-published in 2012 and his continued use of the ideas in more recent articles (see, for instance, Pym 2021a and 2021b) demonstrates their ongoing relevance to the discipline. In his introduction to the 2012 version, Pym accepts that while technological developments and the translation community's attitudes towards scholarship in the profession engendered certain changes in focus – and this is an element that continues to transform our understanding of ethics, as we will see in Chapter 8 – the crucial ethical thrust behind the work required no alteration before its republication in translation. Even more importantly, perhaps, Pym himself has subsequently sought to clarify his stance and claims that many of these critiques misunderstood his intentions. He states that cooperation does not assume equal parties, neutrality (the translator as "honest broker"), hard work, or high-effort translations (cheap translations can be socially beneficial), or access to truth (rational egoists can be trusted to lie […] a little). Rather,

> all parties act in their own interests but do so in such a way that they all acquire more value than what they started with. Non-cooperation is a zero-sum game where if I win, you lose. In cooperation, I win something and you win something, and that possibility gives us a very good reason to communicate.
> (Pym 2021b: 10)

Importantly, he states that

> [t]he approach does not assume any symmetry or equality of the communication participants; it does not require any pre-established community of purpose: as long as both sides benefit, no matter how unequally, then the interaction is considered cooperative and thus ethically good.
> (Pym 2021a: 151)

Whatever the case, the preceding discussions are enough to draw ample attention to the importance of questions of neutrality in relation to ethics and emphatically overturning this possibility represents a key point of focus in Chapter 5.

More recently, Pym has also commented on risk as an important concern within what he terms as translation as a cost/benefit analysis, requiring that we weigh up the potential positive and negative outcomes of a project. For Chesterman, Pym's ethical translator "invests a translation effort that is proportionate to the value of the resulting translation", where the value is calculated based on the amount of mutual benefit and cooperation "leading to an increase in social wellbeing" (Chesterman 2016: 168). These risks and costs can be financial, but also refer to other less-tangible assets such as credibility and covering for uncertainty. This is in part done to clarify potential weaknesses that were flagged in terms of his focus on interculturality.

Overturning the accusation of implied neutrality, Pym states that the translator is not just another communication participant but also one who could be a traitor and, therefore, part of the cost involved is spent on 'buying' trustworthiness. Though the basic transaction cost does rather controversially suggest that cheap translations can be a laudable (and ethical) option for many communicative purposes, "since the savings thus made allow more scope for cooperation between the main communication partners, and thereby more future work for the translator" (Pym 2021a: 152), in some contexts translation requires considerable attention and investment. Pym continues:

> [a]s a rule of thumb, the greater the risks involved in the communication act, the higher the permissible transaction costs and the more resources should be invested in establishing the trustworthiness of the translator. **Translator ethics thus becomes a question of trust.**
>
> (ibid. bold added)

Indeed, trust now underpins our ethical decision-making and Pym states that the "greatest risk the translator faces might be loss of trust (by clients or receivers), so translation decisions can be seen as ways of gaining or maintaining that trust, rather than just representing a foreign text" (Pym 2017: 364).

And this consideration of risk and trust works on both a wider scale – for instance in terms of the rates that we can charge – and on a small-scale level in terms of concrete translational decisions. Pym allies translation solutions such as omission, which are "not usually condoned by approaches based on equivalence" (ibid.), with low-risk situations where the potential impact on trust is low. And much of this focus on trust hinges around the information asymmetry that is inherent in much of translation (Pym, Grin, Sfreddo, Chan, 2012; Chan, 2008). It is assumed that the translator's clients do not know the languages that the translator knows and that translators know more about quality in translation than their client. As a result of their client's lack of oversight, they can therefore "bend the truth" in terms of the value of their work if they so desire, thus meaning that clients do not know whom to trust. As noted above, translators may be acting in the interests of the other side.

This consideration of the risk and trust inherent in translation reinforces the need for Pym's cooperative framework, bringing us full circle. With the aim of this cooperative framework being (not necessarily equal) benefits for *all parties* involved, including the translator, "the translator is primarily trusted to seek those benefits" (Pym 2017: 364) rather than clients hoping that they are simply a good person who will look out for their interests and not a mercenary. Ultimately, through these clarifications via risk and trust, cooperation remains a central component of Pym's thought, and he states that this attainment of mutual benefits as our aim of cross-cultural exchanges, with all parties benefiting, remains a "sublime ethical aim, no matter how naïve one might consider it to be in practice" (2017: 365) that is "a more powerful, socialized aim than the static alternatives available in equivalence theory and the like" (2017: 33).

Pym's ideas can be summed up as followed:

1. Translators […] are responsible for the capacity of their work to contribute to long-term stable, cross-cultural cooperation (2012: 167).
2. In order for mutual benefits to be achieved, they must be greater than the transaction costs put into organizing and carrying out the exchange (2017: 363).
3. "[T]he greatest risk the translator faces might be loss of trust (by clients or receivers), so translation decisions can be seen as ways of gaining or maintaining that trust, rather than just representing a foreign text" (2017: 364), a notion that Pym sees as anathematic to institutions and understandings of translation based on linguistic equivalence.

Box 4.3 A case study on loyalty and cooperation

Consider the following example drawn from Chesterman (2018) – the full example is also included in Chesterman (2009):

A literary translator, Stefan Moster, translates a Finnish novel by Arto Paasilinna into German. In this story, set in Finland's pagan past, a semi-divine hero is born who will save Finland from the threat of the new Christian religion. The hero is born on 20 April. But the German version says he is born on 19 April. Why is this the case?

The answer is that 20 April was Hitler's birthday. Many German readers will know this, so there is a risk that the novel will be taken as neo-Nazi propaganda, and this is a risk the translator refuses to take. On his own responsibility, he changes the date. He informs the German publisher, but not the author. Asking the author's permission would have run the risk of being refused, and this was a risk he was not willing to take. Later (Moster 2003), he makes the reasons for his decision public. Recognising the date and the significance with regard to Hitler, he feared that readers would "interpret the ending of the novel as referring to a Nazi saviour who will improve the gene-pool of the nation" (ibid.). Moster argues as follows:

> Quite possibly, the book had what it took to become a cult novel in right-wing circles, and I did not want to let that happen to it – or, most of all, to me – for which reason I replaced 20 April with another date. And I did not actually ask the author, as I am wont to do in similar cases, for I wanted to avoid him disallowing the (to me) essential modification [sic].
>
> In doing so I valued my stake as originator of the text more highly than that of the author. Is that allowed? Yes, when you think you have to do it. Is it a problem? Not really, when you know what you're doing.
>
> (Moster 2003: 60)

? In what ways can we say the translator was/was not 'loyal' and to whom?
? In this case, what would you do? Or what *should* we do as a translator? And why? Again, is it the principle of 'loyalty' that guides us? How would the notion of trust impact upon our decision-making?
? Can the translator realistically flag issues to the client every time something problematic comes up? This is an extreme example, but where do we draw the line?

For Chesterman, though he questions the solution ("Why not just 'in the spring'?"), he respects the decision and considers the ethical justification to be utilitarian: he weighs up the importance of textual fidelity and the need to consult the author against possible undesirable consequences and decides that those consequences weigh more heavily.

In terms of loyalty, the translator was loyal to the publisher (an agent?), and arguably the author in terms of avoiding this potential reading. The translator's subsequent article also showcases the potential of paratextual (or extratextual) visibility, as mentioned by Nord, though how feasible is this in all circumstances?

In terms of cooperation, we could also argue that this does fall in line with Pym's notion of all parties benefiting: the author is saved from being presented as a Nazi sympathiser (presumably something he would be happy about), the translator benefits financially and in terms of his career (as a culturally sensitive translator), and the publisher avoids a potential scandal. But is it this clearcut?

Perhaps the date's significance would not have caused any negative readings. Perhaps the translator no longer holds the trust of a range of potential clients because they worry that he will make similar changes without consulting them in the future. Importantly, this example demonstrates how the translator is an active, interventionary being with their own needs, desires, and beliefs entering the equation. Moster did not act in a neutral way. Clearly, there is more at stake than textual fidelity, as demonstrated in this chapter and yet how and where do we draw the line with what is considered to be professional? We will explore this personal dimension to ethics further in subsequent chapters and will get to the professional dimension in Chapters 7 and 8.

Conclusion

Beyond exploring various potential partners to whom we are responsible when translating, the ideas covered in this chapter begin to allude to both the context-based and the personal, ideological dimensions of ethics. Ethics is inescapably subjective and situated, and no detached balancing act can respond to all situations. However, like Berman's ethics, loyalty and cooperation provide us with a further set of vital considerations to bear in mind when we translate or interpret. We must always remember that we are involved in an interpersonal interaction – though that may be easier to grasp when interpreting, with (potentially) the client, target user, and ST author all present in real time, the Moster example above shows that these divergent needs and desires are very real in cases of translation, too.

Repeating Chesterman's distinction between macro- and micro-ethical considerations is helpful to reorient ourselves at this point. While micro-ethical matters pertain to the "relation between the translator and the words on the page", macro-ethical issues encompass broad social questions "such as the role and rights of translators in society, conditions of work, financial rewards and the client's profit motive, the general aims of translation as intercultural action, power relations between translators and clients, the relation between translation and state politics" (Chesterman 2016: 168). In this chapter we have moved away from the micro-ethical level and added new levels of responsibility to consider. While responsibility to the text and ST author is a challenging, pertinent area of consideration, here we have seen that other answers include responsibility to our client, our audience, to other translators, and our profession. That is not to say that these previous answers lose all importance. Indeed, while moving away from the micro-ethical side of things is an important step to make, the two levels of course feed one another and the way we engage with the Otherness within a text is crucial. This mutual interaction between the two levels is central to the coverage of Venuti's ideas in Chapter 5, expanding our enquiry further still and taking into account a commitment to representing other languages and cultures within a highly personal, non-neutral framework. This personal, moral dimension is further accentuated in Inghilleri's ideas, which consider interpreters' responsibilities to society at large, while also seeking to overturn the image of the neutral, conduit translator and interpreter. This focus on our own inevitable, personal, human input brings the agent involved in this process even more clearly to the forefront.

Discussion, Presentation, and Assignment Topics

1. Discuss the notions of 'fidelity' and 'loyalty' in relation to functionalist approaches to translation.
2. To what extent does the principle of cooperation enable us to sidestep "either/or" models of translation ethics?
3. Group discussion: Using the Moster case study in Box 4.3, work in small groups and share your take on the example.

Notes

1 This is reflected in Cristiane Nord's succinct functionality principle: "[t]he translation purpose determines the choice of translation method and strategy" (Nord 2001: 200).
2 "The range of the translation purposes allowed for in relation to one particular source text is limited by translators' responsibility to their partners in the cooperative activity of translation" (ibid. 200).

Further Reading

Kopp (2012) offers an illuminating exploration of the link between *skopos* theory and ethics. She covers the development of the notion of responsibility, including a fascinating dive into its etymological roots and emergence as a key ethical concept, grounds the idea within *skopos* theory, and considers potential future directions. For a comprehensive yet accessible account of ethics in a functionalist context, meanwhile, **Nord's (2018)** *Translating as a Purposeful Activity* is an excellent resource. In terms of Pym's ethics, his 2021 paper **(Pym 2021b)** offers a concise and typically engaging overview of his wide-ranging ideas, while his entry in *The Routledge Handbook of Translation and Ethics* on **'Translator Ethics'** **(Pym 2021a)** is another accessible point of entry. Finally, for coverage of Chinese ethics and responsibility, see **Guangqin (2021: 30–31)**.

5 Justice

> **Key Questions**
> - How has TIS tackled problematic perceptions of translators and interpreters as neutral conduits?
> - What is visibility and agency in translation and interpreting?
> - When we look beyond neutrality, how does this impact our role as translators and interpreters?

In Chapter 4 we began examining the translator's role in more detail, introducing differing directions of responsibility; in this chapter we take this enquiry one step further. Chapter 5 consolidates the non-neutral, subjective nature of translation and ethics and considers the role of the translator and interpreter as a key agent in shaping knowledge transfer, laying the foundation for the exploration of activist roles in Chapter 6. It begins with an exploration of Lawrence Venuti's pre-2000 contribution to ethical thought, which places critical scrutiny on the ethical underpinnings outlined in Chapter 3, seeks to raise the translator's global profile via discussions of **visibility**, and tackles questions of what could be termed as linguistic injustice – with power imbalances feeding global hegemonies in terms of language and culture. Though often misunderstood as a general call to 'foreignise' texts – and thus representing a deontological call, which returns to the more narrow, textual level explored in Chapter 3 – we will see how Venuti's work is in fact rather consequentialist in nature, seeking to promote cultural innovation and challenge dominant norms above all else.

These appeals to responsibility on a wider level and a link to notions of justice are echoed by a number of prominent scholars. Here, we also consider Inghilleri's (2012) illuminating ideas, which place the translator within a network of power relations and offer a powerful critique of universal theories of ethics, paving the way for more relativistic views. Within these calls for wider moral consideration, the role of the translator changes further still. In Chapter 4, we saw how Pym's work initiated a reconceptualisation

DOI: 10.4324/9781003148265-6

of the translator as an active mediator, and this role is examined further here, particularly in the context of interpreting, where we see the emergence of the role of a **cultural mediator**. Ultimately, the translator remains firmly at the centre of enquiry – and is pushed even further into the spotlight by both Venuti and Inghilleri, in different ways – as we consider this wider commitment to society at large.

- ? How visible would you say that translators or interpreters are?
- ? In what way do translators and interpreters play an important role in global events?
- ? In your daily life, do you feel that you are able maintain neutrality? Are there any specific situations in which you might struggle to maintain that neutrality?

Overturning Neutrality and Looking to Emancipatory Translation

In Chapter 4, concerns were raised over the potential for translators and interpreters to be seen as merely neutral conduits, and we saw how Pym has been critiqued (mistakenly, in his view) for a supposed neutrality at the centre of his early ideas of interculturality. As Chesterman puts it, "[d]oubts have been raised about the validity of the conduit metaphor for translation and interpreting, according to which the mediator is no more than a neutral channel for the exchange of information" (Chesterman 2021: 17). For him, there is more at stake than "ensuring that packets of information reach their destination" (ibid.). Interculturality and exchanging information are certainly features of the translator's existence, but **the translator is not value-free.** Abdallah eloquently encapsulates a generalised view of non-neutrality by stating that "in the end it is the moral agent herself who decides which course of action to take in resolving an ethical dilemma, based on her own moral values" (2011: 148). This quotation points to the inherently subjective and non-neutral nature of both translation and ethics. At the heart of enquiry in both areas, we are dealing with human beings who have their own personal interest, beliefs, and needs to consider, and this problematises images of translation as simply a linguistic transfer activity. Though Pym and Chesterman have both sought to separate professional and personal ethics, others have argued that there is no way to fully extricate ourselves from the contexts we work in, and all decisions must include personal considerations (this tension will come up again in more detail in Chapters 6 and 7). From an ethical perspective, we must question the personal and examine what it is that these active agents are interested in and concerned about.

As we will see below, Inghilleri contends that interpreters in particular should be afforded more room for maneuver in their decision-making, being allowed to take their own belief systems into account, even when these may clash with professional codes' guidelines (these codes are covered at length in Chapter 7, but it is worth noting here that these documents regularly state that translators and interpreters should be neutral in their professional activities and not take sides). As such, overturning neutrality and fidelity (which we problematised in Chapter 2) is an important step in moving towards empowering activist translators and interpreters, who "may be more motivated by ideals such as social equality and justice than by the neutrality or fidelity principles" (Chesterman 2021: 21). In terms of the translator's overall role, we see something of a sliding scale from neutral conduit to an emancipated and active participant in communicative situations – "from humble slave to independent expert or equal partner" (Chesterman 2016: 187) – who "assumes the right to break norms" (ibid.) in a manner that is justified by an appeal to higher-level personal values, norms, and ideals.

Box 5.1 Ethics and subjectivity

Bearing in mind the consequentialist principles covered in Chapter 4 (and Chapter 1, of course!), which ask us to prioritise the consequences of our actions, and the personal dimension of ethics that is central to this chapter, consider the following example (adapted from Robinson 2012: 101):

> There are two people drowning in a river. One is your translator friend and the other is a world-famous brain surgeon, who is a stranger to you. You are standing on the shore with the one available lifejacket.
> ? In this situation, what would you do?

Deontological calls to save lives or minimise death are useless here, as there is no way to save both people. Utilitarian principles, meanwhile, being superficially impartial, would recommend that we save the surgeon, as this would result in the greatest amount of happiness – after all, he would undoubtedly save hundreds of lives, unlike your translator friend. However, this is not overly satisfying, and in reality we would all probably want to save our friend. As Robinson puts it "[f]riendship makes us subjective and partial, and we don't think much about 'ends' when we see our friends in trouble" (ibid.). This example points to the inevitably subjective and partial nature of ethics, and this is something that we will continue to address in greater detail in this chapter and chapters to come.

Venuti, Visibility, and Cultural Innovation

In some ways, Venuti's ideas on ethics take us back to the discussions of fidelity and respect for the Other covered in Chapters 2 and 3, and certainly he was hugely influenced by the ideas of Berman. Indeed, Venuti states that

"I follow Berman [...]. Good translation is demystifying: it manifests in its own language the foreignness of the foreign text" (Venuti: 1998, 11), but his own ideas also mark a clear break from more 'pure' considerations of textual ethics, focusing on questions of visibility and invisibility of translators and translation as a whole, as well as broader aims of cultural innovation and breaking norms. These ideas sit comfortably within expanded notions of ethics that are not simply considering the words on the page, translators as neutral channels of communication, or professionals seeking to balance loyalties, but rather wider social concerns and personal notions of justice. While we viewed Berman in a more static, textual context, his choice of primary loyalty is undeniably ideological and this has led to far-reaching impacts within translation ethics. Chesterman gets to the crux of this matter, noting how scholars such as Venuti and Eric Cheyfitz (1991) place our linguistic choices within a broader cultural context, analysing "these choices in terms of theories of imperialism, colonization, nationalism, economic issues, power struggles between cultures, and the global domination of European or Anglo-American cultural value" (2016: 167)." **For Venuti, translation is always a political act.**

Venuti's key terms, developed in his pre-2000 writings on ethics, have been readily adopted by translation scholars worldwide and are among the most influential contributions in the discipline to date, Laaksonen and Koskinen rightly note that he has the rare status of having been "a household name in Translation Studies since the 1990s" (2021: 131). His two most influential texts – *The Scandals of Translation* and *The Translator's Invisibility* – are widely cited across and beyond the discipline, emerging as vital sources for both TIS students and translation professionals looking to gain a grasp of the discipline. It is *The Scandals of Translation* – published in 1998 – with its subtitle of 'Towards an ethics of difference' that is perhaps of greatest interest to us here, although the 1995 *Translator's Invisibility* can be seen as sharing many of the same themes, albeit presented from a different perspective. Both works outline Venuti's core theory of translation, formulated around the basis of hermeneutics. He initially builds upon largely philosophical ideas from Schleiermacher and Berman to distinguish between **"foreignising" and "domesticating" types of translation** and forwards his ideas of deviation from dominant linguistic forms.[1] Venuti begins by placing translation within a wider sociocultural framework, considering the impact of social institutions (publishers, editors, people who market books, reviewers) as well as political ones, and explores the way in which Britain and America export/import texts, revealing a trade imbalance that, he argues, indicates English-speaking countries are not as open to foreign cultures.

Venuti describes the Anglo-American translation market as characterized by a domestication of foreign texts. Publishers and readers consider acceptable only translations that 'read like original texts' and 'conceal their foreignness' behind a veneer of naturalness, that is, we like translations that are smooth and natural. He laments this dominant domesticating strategy that prevails throughout Western literary translation and renders texts as fluent, readable target language pieces. He argues that this approach has ideological foundations (appropriation of foreign culture for American consumption) and has been detrimental to the recognition of translation in society and to the status of translators, making them invisible. As he provocatively puts it, "[t]he purpose of transparency/invisibility is to inscribe foreign texts with English-language values and provide readers with the narcissistic experience of recognizing their own culture in a cultural other" (Venuti 1995: 15). Insofar as **the effect of transparency effaces the work of translation, it contributes to the cultural marginality and the economic exploitation that translators have long struggled with.** Ultimately, translation is seen as a low-status activity; translators are invisible, poorly paid, and disadvantaged by copyright laws, and publishers exploit this situation (see Lambert and Walker 2022 for a conceptual exploration of status and rates of pay). With Anglo-American cultural values imposed on vast foreign audiences, the United Kingdom and the United States have become "aggressively monolingual", "unreceptive to the foreign", and "accustomed to fluent translations" (Venuti 1995: 15). Thus, "the translator's invisibility is symptomatic of a complacency that can be described – without too much exaggeration – as imperialistic abroad and xenophobic at home" (ibid. 16-17).

Instead, Venuti calls for us to foreground the foreignness of the translated text. While domestication smooths over the uniqueness of the foreign, he seeks to prioritise this element in order to release the "remainder", defined as "[t]he collective force of linguistic forms that outstrips any individual's control and complicates intended meanings" (Venuti 1998: 108), and which allows the disturbing and stimulating effects of translation to be shown in the domestic setting. Put simply, foreignisation happens whenever we eschew conventional modes and forms of translation, and the key factor is the translator's ambivalence toward domestic norms and the institutional practices in which they are implemented. All of this is carried out in accordance with Berman's idea that a bad/unethical translation negates the foreignness of the text and sets out to counter institutions' predilection for a translation ethics of sameness. While Venuti stands as another advocate of the idea that translators should include prefaces and notes with their work where possible, his ethics of difference departs from Nord's loyalty, as it can require the translator to be disloyal to domestic cultural norms – something that the commissioner of a translation is generally very unlikely to agree to. Indeed, Venuti's ethics requires the translator to call attention to what these norms enable and limit and admit and exclude in the encounter with foreign texts, although he insists that a translation can deviate from norms without being so estranging as to be self-defeating. Foreignising makes readers aware that what they are reading is not an original, but a mediated and manipulated text and makes the translator more visible. It puts "an ethnodeviant pressure on [TL cultural] values to register the linguistic and cultural difference of the foreign text, sending the reader abroad" (Venuti 2008: 20). The aim is "to force translators and their readers to reflect on the ethnocentric violence of translation and hence to write and read translated texts in ways that recognize the linguistic and cultural differences of foreign texts" (Venuti 2008: 34).

Venuti's ethics represents a reflection upon and reaction against trends in translation scholarship at the time and was made in order to forward his ideas of deviation from dominant linguistic forms. However, while his easily dichotomised distinctions seemingly represent a deontological imperative to always deviate from domestic norms, we sense a softening in his stand in *Scandals of Translation* that resituates his ethical underpinnings. As his terminology moves from "foreignising" to "minoritising", Koskinen sees Venuti as moving beyond basic ideas of fidelity and foreignisation. This move places him alongside other approaches aimed at giving greater prominence to marginalised groups in society, such as feminist and post-colonial translation in aiming "never to acquire the majority, never to erect a new standard or to establish a new canon, but rather to promote cultural innovation as well as the understanding of cultural difference" (Venuti 1998: 11). As Koskinen explains:

> Unlike most (post)modern translation theories, Venuti seems to have overcome the obstacle of fidelity. Even though he has not renounced the origin of the translation, his ethics of difference, as the name implies, is not based on any reformulation of the notion of fidelity. For him, the important issues and ethical aims are located elsewhere than in fidelity or loyalty towards the source text or clients and target readers. The most important considerations are, instead, to be found in the wider framework of cultural exchange.
>
> (Koskinen 2000: 58)

While critics such as Folkart contends that "the foreign" for Venuti seems to be simply the opposite of the mainstream, this offers a rather reductive understanding of the concept of foreignisation.[2] Venuti applies Berman within his own political views. Berman retains the deontological sense of translating the foreignness, while Venuti contextualises the methodology and aligns it with a cause – translate the foreignness to decentre established practices and to foster innovation and politico-cultural communication. Indeed, Venuti's method is not a simple binary opposition between good and bad, as has often been considered to be the case. Rather, adopting a domesticating method can be a good thing, and translations almost universally contain elements of both methods. This being the case, along with his postmodern streak, Venuti's thought actually resides in the rule consequentialist category of ethics. **Subversion or deviation from cultural norms that promotes innovation is set as his ultimate value, even when this – seemingly paradoxically – entails the use of a domesticating method.** For him, if we achieve the end result of subverting or destabilising established norms (subsequently increasing cultural communication) then we have acted ethically. To be ethical, our aim is "to force translators and their readers to reflect on the ethnocentric violence of translation and hence to write and read translated texts in ways that recognize the linguistic and cultural differences of foreign texts" (Venuti 2008: 34). Indeed, through his wide-ranging discussions, drawing attention to imbalances in global flows of literary translation and invisibility, Venuti "has urged his Anglo-American and international readers to cultivate attitudes hospitable towards foreign literary influences, with the overall calling to contribute to more democratic cultural relations (1995: 20; 1998: 25; see also Koskinen 2000: 109)" (Laaksonen and Koskinen 2021: 132), and it is through foreignising methods – involving bold, heterogeneous translation choices with clashes of register and archaisms drawing attention to the translator's active role – that we can achieve these aims.

However, this assertion poses a troubling question that he leaves unanswered. In deviating from the established norms, are we really representing the culture of the source text (presumably this "traditionally" ethical representation of the source culture, which once again wraps us up in issues of fidelity, is a necessary component in promoting innovation and cultural communication?). Or, are we merely opposing our own culture in order to give a suggestion of the foreign or in mere fulfilment of a personal, ideological need? As Pym suggests in his review of *The Translator's Invisibility:* "[a]s long as the translations are kept distant from the masses' cheap understanding, the professors will be employed to read and talk about those translations", thus stressing the importance of Venuti's own continued visibility in academia (Pym, 1996: 175). This once again highlights the importance and inevitability of our personal, subjective input in matters of ethics, and also points to the genre-dependent nature of certain considerations or manners of decision-making in ethics. Indeed, Venuti's intellectualism and exclusion of non-literary translation dictates that the technical translator cannot realistically follow his ideas in their present form. This is due to the economic concerns and client demands foregrounded in the professional setting. This is not necessarily a fault on the part of Venuti; his focus on literary translation is entirely deliberate and he makes no claims to apply his ideas beyond this field. However, he is perhaps in the fortunate position of being able to translate with a degree of cultural experimentation rather than bending to commercial constraints and publisher demands as would likely be the case with most professional translators, literary or otherwise. While he does suggest a new limited copyright enabling translators and publishers to gain rights more easily and to encourage increased publication of translations as earlier ones become dated (and, subsequently, more freedom for publishers to take on translation projects, more translation and more creative, less domesticated translation), the professional situation is unlikely to change dramatically in the foreseeable future.

Venuti's focus on the literary field is criticised by Gouanvic who contends that such compartmentalisation of the translation process is unsuitable when developing an ethics of translation. Gouanvic attempts to expand traditional borders of discussions on ethics within translation to include both low- and high-brow material, critiquing Berman's and Venuti's ethics for their elitism and their desire to destroy dominant theories and practices of translation. This foregrounds the important link that exists between an ethics of translation, the sociology of translation, and contemporary philosophy, before leading him to conclude that "[t]he interest of an ethical theory of translation as we understand it lies in the integration of *all translation* practices" (Gouanvic: 2001, 204, emphasis in original). This is an interesting, if daunting, notion, and in today's increasingly fractured translation landscape, where rapid industrialisation has moved attention to areas such as translation technology, the possibility of addressing all areas at once seems utopian.

Ultimately, the contribution that Venuti's key works in the late 1990s have made to the field – and indeed to the understanding of translation beyond the confines of our own discipline – cannot be overstated. Furthermore, despite being criticised for his primary focus on high-brow literature and intellectualism, this narrowed focus in some ways allows for a more comprehensive discussion of the specific requirements of a particular situation and less of the generalisation found in other ideas. It is clear that Venuti does not always provide all the answers, but his ideas remain unerringly relevant as translation continues to produce and reveal "imbalances, asymmetries and inequalities" (Laaksonen and Koskinen: 2021, 144). He demonstrates with numerous examples that this process of domestication is taking place in the literary domain and, just as culture changes, historical conceptions of right and wrong and ethics change over time, and the way in which translations are produced now is not a fixed method – it can be changed. Venuti's work is designed with this potential for change in mind.

Box 5.2 Foreignisation in practice

As Laaksonen and Koskinen note, "Venuti offers his readers little in terms of hands-on translation solutions that would fall into categories such as fluent or domesticating, let alone visible or foreignizing translation" (2021: 137). The reason for this is that the effects of certain small-scale choices are not generalisable and therefore "a particular choice may contribute to a domesticating effect in one context while promoting foreignization in another" (ibid.). Indeed, as Venuti puts it, the terms do not "describe specific verbal choices or discursive strategies [...] but rather the ethical effects of translated texts that depend for their force and recognition on the receiving culture" (Venuti: 2018, xiii), emphasising the primordial nature of context. That said, there are still a number of perhaps typical strategies outlined in *The Scandals of Translation* that offer some insight into the kind of methods he sees as leading to cultural innovation and a destabilisation of dominant norms.

In terms of wider, macro-level choices, Venuti contends that **the very choice of text to translate is invaluable,** favouring non-canonical, marginal, experimental, or innovative texts, possibly with subversive themes, rather than more mainstream texts and authors. In his own practice, for instance, Venuti has translated works by Iginio Ugo Targhetti, a minor writer who produced challenging, experimental novels in the nineteenth century, a choice of subject and author that is minoritising in its very nature.

In terms of translation methods, meanwhile, **he recommends mirroring elements of source language structures and syntax, mixing up different registers and different varieties of language (such as combining slang and archaisms, resulting in a heterogeneous style), and keeping the original cultural references** (borrowing or calquing foreign terms as opposed to replacing them with general terms or domestic references).

It is important to remember, that while foreignising often involves retaining culture-specific elements from the source text and using calque renderings, it is not the same as literal translation nor is it just about fidelity. Rather, it is about drawing attention to translation, making the translator visible and disrupting dominant norms.

Ultimately, all of these methods are used with the aim of making sure that the translation is not fluent. The example below is provided by Venuti to exemplify these methods:

> *Italian ST*: Egli non è altro che un barattiere, un cavaliere d'industria, una cattivo soggetto
> *Literal translation*: He is nothing more than a swindler, an adventurer, a bad person
> *English TT*: He is nothing but an embezzler, a con artist, a scapegrace
>
> (Venuti: 1998, 17)

Of particular note in the example is the mismatch in register between 'con artist' and 'scapegrace', juxtaposing more modern American slang and archaic British usages. For Venuti, this technique "immerses the reader in a world that is noticeably distant in time, but nonetheless affecting in contemporary terms" (ibid.), and he builds up these effects by using this and other techniques throughout his translation. As the

> back translation suggests, the Italian 'una cattivo soggetto' is a far less marked usage [a bad person], and is certainly not an archaic British usage. From a reader's perspective, consider the following:
>
> ? How would you respond to coming across a sentence such as this in a text?
> ? What would the odd, juxtaposed usages signal to you, if anything?
> ? Do you feel that this example is successful in making the translator visible?

Inghilleri: From Textual Justice to Wider Justice

Within Venuti's ideas, there is a clear ideological belief in where we should stand. This aim of making the translator visible and promoting cultural innovation is, at its core, a personal take on what is ethical and what is right and just, not just in terms of the words on the page, but in terms of our position in the world more generally. Moira Inghilleri is another scholar who offers a detailed personal take on matters of justice, problematising notions of neutrality in the context of interpreting, raising "important ethical issues concerning the clash or overlap between professional and personal ethics" and provocatively defending the importance of an interpreter's personal ethical issues (Chesterman 2016: 193). This leap from translation to interpreting explicitly is worth noting here. While, as mentioned in the introduction, interpreting is subsumed within many of the discussions of translation, this is a clear break, and it is important to consider the points of overlap and difference between these practices, and the symmetry in some of the developments across the domains. As Boéri and Delgado Luchner put it, "the physical proximity of the interpreter with third parties imposes a tangible limit on invisibility and impartiality (Angelelli 2004; Tipton 2008; Wadensjö 1998)" (2021: 249). Indeed, Venuti's invisible translator often works alone and will never meet clients, authors, or intended audiences, while an interpreter is inescapably 'right there', which has a clear impact on the nature of their interventions (responses are uttered in real-time, often with little opportunity for clarification, let alone extended reflection), the nature of their relationships with the people around them (it is much more difficult to be an impassive, neutral conduit when working in highly charged situations such as warzones, or court proceedings, for instance), and the toll of the work on the interpreter personally (see Chapter 8 for considerations of the psychological impact of interpreting work in particular, where ethical stress is seen and felt more acutely than in many cases of translation). They continue by stating that impartiality is no longer viewed as an accurate description of "the translator's actual positionality" but acknowledge that these research ideas have not had a huge impact on the professional context and education settings, "which still largely subscribe to impartiality and neutrality as inherently good". This final remark is particularly important as we get into Inghilleri's work.

Pollabauer and Topolovec (2021: 211), meanwhile, describe how Public Service Interpreting often involves high-stakes encounters that may possibly entail life-changing decisions for public service users' futures – think, for instance of interpreters working in medical or legal contexts: does translation carry a comparable level of jeopardy? They state that the interactants are driven by different motives, with interpreters being granted access to confidential and private information, though I would argue that translators too are privy to such information (and we will discuss this area in more detail in relation to professional codes and standards in Chapter 7). In terms of asymmetries, it is worth noting that interpreting similarly suffers with problems of information asymmetry (see Pym in Chapter 4), a relative lack of regulation, and often poor understandings of what the role entails, meaning that considerations such as trust and risk do apply in this context. Finally, for Inghilleri, interpreting represents translation in action, offering:

> a first-hand unmediated glimpse into what all translation is, in whatever form: an instrument to reveal and represent the 'living dialogue' that contributes to the formation of worldviews, opinions, values, and beliefs that are formed and transformed by human interaction and the intervention of different environments.
>
> (2012: 130)

Dismantling Neutrality and Impartiality in Interpreting

In the aptly-titled *Interpreting Justice* (2012), Inghilleri opens with an account of the philosophy of language and critiques both objectivism and relativism. The former is the belief that values, knowledge, truth, and morality are absolute and objective, and that they can be found in reality, while the latter argues that they are relative to particular people, places, times, or cultures, that is, that they depend on the individuals involved and cannot be grounded. She considers the pragmatic importance of language functioning and the inter-subjective nature of meaning – that is, meaning happens in context between people who have their own beliefs, thoughts, and opinions – which sets the foundation for a critique of neutrality within codes of ethics (critiquing codes of ethics is a common theme in scholarly discourse on ethics in TIS, an important point to bear in mind when we reach Chapter 7), while also critiquing the potential of lapsing into a moral free-for-all (see Chapter 6). She states that though codes offer some protection, they make the mistake of assuming that the "principle demand on interpreters is a linguistic or sociolinguistic one" (2012: 16), viewing "the interpreter's job as one of resolving questions of semantic uncertainty" and frequently appealing "sometimes simultaneously, to relativist arguments about language and culture and to objectivist accounts of meaning" (2012: 13). The interpreter is both a cultural mediator "whose role it is to identify and explain difference in order to overcome it", while also being expected to recover some meaning that is "out there". This implies that the interpreter works on a linguistic level to ensure that nothing changes – "[t]he consequence of either of these perspectives is to perceive the interpreter's role as one of seeking to establish the sameness of a world beyond language" (ibid.). For example, the ITI (Institute of Translation and Interpreting, a prominent UK-based translation association) requires that members

> shall **interpret impartially** between the various parties in the languages for which they are registered with the Institute and, with due regard to the circumstances prevailing at the time, **take all reasonable steps to ensure complete and effective communication between the parties, including intervention to prevent misunderstandings and incorrect cultural references.**
>
> (2016: 9, bold added)

This implies that complete semantic accuracy is expected of interpreters, who are also expected to step in to resolve points of confusion. As we will see below, this is not an easily resolved tension and, while interpreters will sometimes justify their methods based on these ethical principles, at other times they are compelled to deviate from them.

Rather, Inghilleri argues that the decisions interpreters make extend far beyond their linguistic abilities, confronting "the boundaries of their knowledge, their beliefs, their prior experiences, and their ethical practice both professionally and personally" (2012: 17), particularly in situations of conflict – asylum hearings or war zones, for instance. For her, this is where loyalty and impartiality "confront questions of justice and individual conscience" (ibid.), and she goes on to provide example cases from interviews with interpreters and written accounts from military interpreters. These examples illustrate instances in which interpreters use their cultural and experiential knowledge to clarify points or redirect arguments in asylum cases to assist or uphold speakers' "communicative objectives", perhaps to gain asylum, or to undermine a case for asylum in (2012: 16). In her chapter on warzone interpreting, meanwhile, she shows how impartiality and neutrality are less central in taking up their roles – many interpreters choose to work for one side or another for ideological or financial reasons, but this is still occasionally seen as a virtue. She concludes the discussion of objectivity and subjectivity as follows in a key passage:

> Acknowledging semantic uncertainty as an aspect of all communication and all interpreted interactions does not imply that confrontations of beliefs and attitudes in communicative encounters must lead to

misunderstanding or reinforce divisions. All confrontation is productive communication in that it defines over and over again, from one communicative context to another, how we understand perceive and experience the world. There is, however, no way to stand outside of our beliefs to check their validity, or to check whether our beliefs coincide with the beliefs of others.

(Inghilleri: 2012, 24)

This sees us arc away from suppositions of truth and veracity, with this inevitable, personal, active mediation on the part of the interpreter/translator calling for us to reconsider images of neutrality and impartiality. Inghilleri goes on to comment how this widespread image of interpreters as neutral participants limits their ability to make "independent and specialist contributions toward the achievement of communicative objectives" (2012: 31) and, crucially, breaking with neutrality is an important tool in achieving justice. In their professional roles, interpreters act depending partially on the range of groups and communities that they belong to, each often having contradictory roles. This move is made through Habermas's discourse ethics – an intersubjective approach to ethics, which is tailored to the social and communicative practice of interpreting. It recognises the inherent inter-subjectivity of ethics, "links the ethical beyond the question of duty, and demonstrates how communicative reason and reciprocal recognition can work together to achieve expanded worldviews or consensus amongst many different individuals and groups" (2012: 38). But this is undermined by the assumption that all conversation partners "share a common communicative framework" (ibid. 39) and just like interpreter ethics, "views impartiality and rationality as the means to guarantee equality" (ibid.). Ethics is indeed inherently intersubjective – an interaction taking place between people – but not all conversation partners share a common communicative framework. Rather, the framework in which this dialogue takes place is full of unequal power relations and incompatible interests, "where equal participatory rights are not a given[,] and distorted communication remains the norm." Importantly, "even in institutions explicitly committed to giving a voice to the less powerful, the norm of interpreter impartiality can serve a prohibitive function in the fulfilment of this agenda" (2012: 40), and "when domination-free communication is not only not guaranteed but is positively constrained by legal and political institutions or between nations at war, the idea that impartiality guarantees the equal rights of interlocutors has a hollow ring" (ibid. 50).

Cultural Mediators

The alternative proposed by Inghilleri, placing language in context "shifts the focus of attention to language as a tool which along with other tools helps interlocutors to achieve their communicative objectives in a given context" (ibid. 13). Instead of just absent mindedly carrying across information, interpreters are to become mediators who actively select and make choices in relation to the various (self)interests involved, a move that often goes "under the radar" (ibid. 30) because of the prevailing codes and professional norms. Inghilleri forcefully states the case for this shift to a model of mediation by asserting that "[i]nterpreters must be permitted to exercise their agency to voice their concerns, to make what they deem to be the right ethical choice in the moment, even if their professional duty suggests otherwise" (ibid. 48). Inghilleri then turns to communitarian approaches, which "detach ethical subjectivity from notions of impartiality and universal concepts of justice", instead attaching it to notions of culture, community, and solidarity (ibid. 42). Within this school of thought, "as moral discourse is always situated within individual, social, and historical contexts, the issue of the right thing to do is always about the right thing for us to do, according to whatever substantive conceptions of the good presently inform a community" (ibid. 42–43). This cannot address global issues, nor can it reconcile a plurality of views within the same community, but she argues that this and discourse ethics both "recognize the significance of communication and political community to broaden our thinking with a view to increase understanding and reduce misunderstanding between ourselves and different others" (ibid. 45). Factors to consider in interpreting include (ibid. 14) the following:

- What is at stake for individual participants in an interpreted event?
- What are the professional, ethical, political, social, or personal risks involved in the interaction?
- Is there a potential for conflicting views over what may be reasonably meant or understood by an utterance in the particular situation?
- And, what ethical, political, or social factors may lie behind a claim that one participant's understanding of an utterance is reasonable or that another's should be challenged?

Finally, to return to the aforementioned similarities and differences between translation and interpreting, when discussing progress in Interpreting Studies in relation to Translation Studies specifically (and literary translation ethics in particular, e.g. Venuti), Inghilleri posits that both translation and interpreting ethics can invest their practitioners with more agency to increase the general status of languages in cultures in an array of contexts. However, she notes that developments cannot consider the meaning of utterances in isolation from the producers of those utterances (2012: 128–129). Authors, or rather speakers, are right there in interpreting.

Box 5.3 A critique of cultural mediators

Angelelli (2004: 129–133) similarly argues that an 'invisible' interpreter model is inadequate to capture what happens in the role but, an example also cited by Hale (2008: 111) and Skaaden (2019: 706–709), demonstrates potential difficulties within the cultural mediator model too. The following example, an interpreted exchange in a US medical setting, illustrates the 'visible' interpreter and their effect on the communication between interlocutors – here, the doctor and patient. The interpreter, Joaquín, enacts his full potential of agency by deciding what to render and what to omit. The dialogue is included in full below. For the sake of clarity and concision, I have simply included literal English translations rather than the Spanish (in square brackets). The doctor's input is in bold italics, the interpreter in plain text, and the patient's input in bold. Bear in mind considerations of maximising communication, advocacy, and information asymmetry when reading the dialogue and consider to what extent the interpreter's active intervention is helpful.

(1) Doctor: In a scale from one to ten, how would she rate her pain?

(2) Interpreter: [Let's see Mrs. Rita, on a scale from one to ten, what number would you assign to your pain? For example, if one is a pain that would allow you to go dancing, and you almost don't feel anything and ten is so painful that you are dying, where would that pain be?]

(3) **Patient: [What did you say?]**

(4) Interpreter: [What […] what number would you give to your pain?]

(5) **Patient: [Well, it hurts a lot.]**

(6) Interpreter: [How much is a lot, Ma'am? Does a lot mean you are dying from the pain?]

(7) **Patient: [Well […] no […] not dying, but –]**

(8) Interpreter: [Which things can you do when you are in pain?]

(9) **Patient: [Well, I don't know […] When it is very bad I sit down.]**

(10) Interpreter: [But, can you cook when you are in pain?]

(11) **Patient: [Sometimes it is very bad, and I can't.]**

(12) Interpreter: [And at those times, does it feel like you are going to die, or is it not that bad?]

(13) **Patient: [No, not like I'm going to die, it just hits me hard.]**

(14) Interpreter: [Do we give it an eight or a nine?]

(15) **Patient: [Well, I don't know, well yes …]**

(16) Interpreter: When it is most painful it would be close to an eight, Doctor.

(17) Doctor: Okay.

? What do you make of the interpreter's role in this case?
? The interpreter clearly did more than simply carry across a message in a neutral, invisible manner, but was their input of use?

Skaaden (2019: 708) comments on the way in which the interpreter "singlehandedly interviews the patient in Spanish", depriving the doctor of "insight into the patient's pain experience" as they are left oblivious to the patient's lack of understanding of the numeric scale. Ultimately, she never answers the doctor's question. In this way, interpreters displaying their agency may hinder the interlocutors from clarifying misunderstandings and expanding their common knowledge, which are two central aspects of human communication. Rather, as Angelelli (2004: 138) observes, the consequence is often the opposite of the parties achieving their communicative goals. It is also worth noting that the practitioner observed in this case lacked interpreter training, which could perhaps instil a greater understanding of the mediatory role.

On a wider level, Skaaden comments that the fluid, dynamic role that many suggest interpreters should play would allow them to act as 'negotiators' and even 'co-diagnosticians' (Skaaden 2019: 709). This role sees interpreters adapt their actions as an interaction develops in order to pursue their intended outcome, with a consequentialist outlook replacing prescriptive, norm-based guidance rooted in fidelity. However, Skaaden asserts that questions remain as to the consequences of this role fluidity and that it does not necessarily fully alleviate issues of prescription. Indeed, "[w]hether the mandate is to be an advocate or to be a faithful renderer of the utterances, it is equally prescriptive" (Hale: 2008, 101) and ill-defined or confusing roles or an absence of a clear, prescribed role are all damaging.

Conclusion

Ultimately, these calls for greater respect for difference and justice are exceptionally compelling and have been echoed by other scholars. Tymoczcko, for instance, calls for "a more just world where difference is welcome" (Tymoczko: 2007, 232). Returning to our overarching ethical divide – as we have done at several points – we are firmly in the macro-ethical realm at this point. While Venuti's foreignising strategies can be on a small-scale textual level, their purpose is to enact change on a wider social (and political) scale, demonstrating the interaction between the different levels of ethics illustrated in the Introduction. There is a parallel between ideas from Schleiermacher here too – both he and Venuti are striving for change, but their ideological aims are very different. While Venuti is promoting recognition of the foreign – his transgressive methods seek to do "justice to the ethos of the foreign culture" (Chesterman 2016: 170) – Schleiermacher's project was to ultimately promote the target language. All of this ties to questions of status, power, and the translator's role in society.

Koskinen (2000: 99) helpfully breaks visibility down into three different types: **textual visibility, paratextual visibility, and extratextual visibility**. Textual visibility allows the translator to mark their presence within a text, for instance by using foreignising techniques. Paratextual visibility is seen in translator's introductions, prefaces, and footnotes, for example. Extratextual visibility, meanwhile, looks beyond the translation task to the translator's social role and wider status – marketing, public appearances, interviews, and so forth, can all be considered part of this domain. Venuti's work seeks to tackle each of these areas, and it is vital that we engage on all three levels. Again, Chesterman captures it nicely: "[i]nvisible translators, who seek to efface themselves textually, also tend to get effaced socially" (2016: 167). Beyond the text, issues including copyright, conditions of work and pay, acknowledgements and understandings of the translator's role and input, and the promotion of translation and TIS all feed into ongoing wider attempts to change the status quo. We will return to many of these questions in a professional context in Chapter 8.

For Inghilleri, meanwhile, there is a similarly social undercurrent to her thought. "Translators are pivotal players in global events, operating at the grinding edge of their associated conflicts and controversial politics" and, particularly in situations of conflict, the question of translation goes beyond linguistic or cultural judgement to take on ethical and political dimensions, which require an **ethics of translation that "takes as its starting point the actual social conditions in which translators operate"** (Inghilleri 2008: 212). Inghilleri's provocative thought points out the impossibility of standing "outside of our beliefs to check their validity, or to check whether our beliefs coincide with the beliefs of others" (Inghilleri (2012: 24), with translators and interpreters becoming active, key players in communication, "facilitating open negotiations over meaning" (2012: 51). This shatters thought grounded in neutrality and impartiality and calls for personal and social responsibility to be included within our ethical calculations, particularly where questions of justice and fairness are concerned. Inghilleri productively brings the personal dimension of ethics into focus and this is where our attention lies in Chapter 6. Building upon this active, non-neutral basis to translation, we pick up some threads in relation to personal and professional ethics and push the idea of agency even further from the neutral conduit model critiqued here.

Discussion, Presentation, and Assignment Topics

1. Presentation task: To what extent do the same ethical challenges apply to both translation and interpreting? What are the key differences between the two practices?

2. As Boéri and Delgado Luchner put it, "the physical proximity of the interpreter with third parties imposes a tangible limit on invisibility and impartiality" (2021: 249). Does this mean that impartiality is less possible in the context of interpreting/more possible in the context of translation?
3. Venuti argues that translation is fundamentally domesticating, but the translator can choose an 'ethics of difference'. Should translators adopt this 'ethics of difference' and make themselves visible in the text? And is this visibility empowering or problematic for the translator?

Notes

1 Though we only cover these two key texts by Venuti here, his work on ethics has extended into the twenty-first century. Indeed, his 2012 collection of papers, *Translation Changes Everything*, tracks the development of his thought on ethics, in some ways departing from the works considered in this chapter, though Venuti retains his ethical commitments explored here. We consider some of these later ideas in Chapter 9.
2 In what is a particularly scathing account of Venuti's take on translation compared to Berman's, Folkart goes even further in suggesting that "[w]here Berman's reasoning is complex, audacious, and profound, Venuti's account of it is simplistic and impoverishing. Of the crucial terms "original," "pure nouveauté," « pur surgissement" and "manifester dans sa langue cette pure nouveauté en préservant son visage de nouveauté" he has understood nothing" (Folkart 2006: 295).

Further Reading

Inghilleri's wonderful (2012) *Interpreting Justice* is worth reading in full for its wide-ranging and illuminating thought on neutrality, conflict, politics, and language. While it deals with the context of interpreting specifically, the way in which it reshapes theoretical and professional perspectives on language make it an invaluable source for anyone involved in the language industry. Similarly, **Venuti's** *The Translator's Visibility* **(and perhaps to a slightly lesser extent** *The Scandals of Translation*) are must-reads for anyone interested in the world of translation. However, for a more accessible entry point to Venuti's ideas, **Laaksonen and Koskinen's chapter in** *The Routledge Handbook of Translation and Ethics* **(Chapter 10: Venuti and the ethics of difference)** is a wonderful source. Finally, for applications of politics and difference in the Chinese context, see **Guangqin (2021: 31–33)**.

6 Commitment

> **Key questions**
> - As translators and interpreters, how embedded are we with the content we translate?
> - How can (or should) we engage with the world in a meaningful manner?
> - How has translation ethics been theorised in relation to activism? And how can we combat the relativism that ensues from a more activist approach?

Consolidating our transition from actions to people, this chapter considers viewpoints that could fall under the ethical school of thought known as moral particularism – emphasising context, responsibility, and accountability. While some limit personal accountability, others place a more central emphasis on the importance of this side of ethics. Indeed, in contrast to detached views of professional ethics, scholars such as Inghilleri and Baker – whose ideas we explore further below – make the case for the translator's active engagement in society, enacting a 'higher' social and ethical aim of contributing to the improvement of society (this theme also returns in Chapter 8 in the professional context). In addition, Gouanvic insists that the translator "retains **a responsibility to the future of target societies**" (Gouanvic 2001: 209). From focusing purely on texts, to thinking about the various agents in the translation encounter, we are now building upon the ideas in Chapter 5 to consider how we can or should handle the potential current and future societal impacts of our work.

With the translator's role increasingly viewed as that of an active mediator, and even the potential for activist roles, in ethical terms we must be able to assume responsibility for our work. While traditional accounts of neutrality shield translators from this level of scrutiny, a closer look exposes a trade-off between power and responsibility. This chapter continues by exploring the continuum of agency and the limitations of pure relativism in

DOI: 10.4324/9781003148265-7

94   *Commitment*

TIS. Finally, we consider Andrew Chesterman's (2017) emerging notion of a translational *telos* (as opposed to *skopos*) as a conception embedding this personal agency and accountability.

?   What do the terms 'advocate', 'activist', and 'accountability' mean to you? Are there any points of overlap or key differences?

Personal versus Professional Ethics and Commitment

To begin with, let us return to a topic that has been at the heart of many of the discussions so far: responsibility. Now, however, we must add a commitment to the content we are working with to our range of considerations. While Phelan (2001: 56) reports that codes of ethics (see Chapter 7) enshrine the belief that "[i]nterpreters/transliterators […] are not at all responsible for what is said, only for conveying it accurately", this image has sparked debate in TIS, where responsibility "for the broader socio-cultural effects of translation is precisely where schools of thought in TS seem to diverge" (Phelan et al. 2020: 64). Consider the following somewhat opposing viewpoints as a starting point to illustrate this personal-professional split:

- Pym (2012: 67): "there is no need for translators to claim (or to be attributed with) any commitment to the content of what they are translating."[1]
- Kruger and Crots (2014: 149): "there is a responsibility to resist situations of injustice or unfairness founded on responsibility towards society at large."

Pym's early work on ethics puts forward a case for detachment from any commitment to the content of the work we take on. He states that non-translational ideologies, such as a refusal to translate certain content, must lie beyond "the space in which a professional ethics can be developed" (Pym 1992: 151). In other words, while accepting that "professional subjectivity never suppresses individual subjectivity in the intimate space of doubt" and that personal beliefs do not go away, these personal desires are viewed as incompatible with or at least exterior to professional needs (Pym 2012: 80). This is a powerful argument – particularly in the context of professional formulations of ethics, perhaps unsurprisingly, as we will see more clearly in Chapter 7. However, as we have seen in exploring Inghilleri's work in Chapter 5, the personal dimension to ethics can be very hard to avoid and simply deciding not to translate is not always feasible.

A fascinating counterargument comes from Kruger and Crots, whose 2014 paper 'Professional and personal ethics in translation: a survey of South African translators' translation strategies and motivations', not only offers a concise history of the development of thought on ethics in TIS, but also provides empirical data exploring key ethical questions. In their study, the authors distributed 9 texts containing elements that could be seen as ethically problematic (racist or sexist language, for instance) to 31 South African translators. The translators were then asked what their translation methodology would be if they were presented with the texts as professional translators. The authors found that respondents selected strategies based on personal and professional reasoning at almost the same rate (professional ethics 51% of the time, personal 49%). This led them to conclude that

> [i]t therefore seems as if personal ethics does play a substantial role in the decisions made when translating a text, and professional status does not suppress the tendency to articulate ethical motivations from a personal, rather than a professional, subject position and frame of reference.
>
> (Kruger and Crots 2014: 165)

This conclusion leads them to accord a greater level of importance to personal ethics than is the case in others' thought and to give increased prominence to the translators' wider socio-cultural responsibility, situating "the professional activity of translation as an intrinsic part of a larger social practice with a clear ethical mandate (of social justice)" (Phelan et al. 2020: 64). Placing this in the context of what has come before, professional translator ethics should not only consider professional responsibility to the client, the text, and the profession, but also a personal ethics "founded on loyalty towards the translator's own system of beliefs" (Kruger and Crots 2014, 149). Phelan et al. (2020: 64) label this as a "[l]oyalty to a higher level".

There is a complex interplay between these systems in the translator's decision-making processes and, while there remains a distinction between personal and professional ethics, Kruger and Crots afford it a more central role in ethics overall, acknowledging that "[t]ranslators are humans, and like all humans, they have a system of beliefs that inform how they choose to live their lives" (2014, 149). By contrast, Pym's move to the question of "why translate?" which is answered with the call to promote cooperation, limits a translator's responsibilities and sidesteps the issue of personal engagement. For him, the ethical translator may sometimes decide that it is better not to translate at all. Unfortunately, this is not fully representative of the way that professional translators work, in part due to the asymmetrical power relations that Pym notes elsewhere (see Chapter 4, 5, and 8). Cooperation is not the professional translator's only consideration, and the decision to translate is often taken based upon their own sense of what is or is not acceptable, or necessary (or, indeed, how much they are getting paid!), not simply whether their input will benefit the profession as a whole. For instance, using the example of morally questionable content in a text, in a 2020 survey of 1,264 freelance translators, UK-based professional translation agency Inbox Translation asked translators whether they had ever refused, or would refuse, to work on texts relating to a wide range of traditionally taboo subjects. Only 17 per cent of respondents said that they would not refuse work in any subject area, reaffirming the inescapably personal nature of decisions on what is and is not acceptable (personal correspondence with managing director of Inbox Translation, April 2020). Considering the human agent involved and their personal beliefs and moral viewpoints represents another step forward in the development of the field.

Finally, returning to Inghilleri, this exclusion of personal ethics – the assumption that translators and interpreters' roles can be detached from personal responses – denies them the ability to give expression "to what Zygmunt Bauman has described as the inescapable burden of individual conscience and our moral proximity to others" (Inghilleri 2012: 40). Bauman eloquently captures this personal demand in a quote that is well-worth repeating here (Bauman 1993: 53, original italics):

> Pointing my finger away from myself – 'this is what people do, this is how things are' – does not save me from sleepless nights and days full of self-deprecation. 'I have done my duty' may perhaps get the judges off my back but won't disband the jury of what I, for not being able to point my finger at anybody, call 'conscience'. *'The duty of us all'* which I *know*, does not seem to be the same thing as *my responsibility* which I *feel*.

If we view the translator's role as that of an active mediator, in ethical terms they must be able to assume responsibility for their work. While domains such as literary and religious translation often engage with questions of taste and morality in more depth, Baker (2013, n.p.) argues that the "prototype" of professional translators or interpreters presented to students is an apolitical servant to their fee-paying client, a viewpoint supported by the influential status of *skopos* theory, accused of creating "mercenary experts" (Pym 1996: 338) (see Chapter 4 for more on *skopos* and its link to ethics). The case studies in Box 6.1 will help to place these competing concerns in context. After reading the cases, consider the following questions:

? What is your take on the "I'm just a translator" defence as a justification for taking on ethically problematic projects? Is there any content that you would refuse to translate?
? Do you believe that it is possible to separate our personal and professional selves in some contexts?
? Should we always commit to specific causes when we translate/interpret? (We'll return to this question below)

Box 6.1 "I'm just the translator"

In the late 1940s and 1950s, many Nazi leaders on trial for war crimes claimed that they were simply following orders and thus doing their duty, which they viewed as a moral law of the highest order. Ultimately, however, the tribunals passing sentences concluded that everyone is morally and legally responsible for their own actions, and being commanded to act in an illegal or immoral way does not override personal responsibility for that action (Phelan et al. 2020: 17).

In recent years, a number of nonagenarians of lesser status have stood trial for Nazi war crimes, and the nature of their roles forces us to question whether we can ever simply argue that we are just "doing our job". The case of John Demjanjuk is particularly fitting here (see Pidd 2011). In 2011, then aged 91, Demjanjuk, was found guilty of accessory to murder on the basis of having been a guard at a concentration camp. Dutch Nazi war crimes expert, Professor Christiaan F Rüter, described Demjanjuk as "the littlest of the little fishes" (*Guardian* 2011) when he became the lowest ranking person ever tried in Germany for Nazi war crimes, lowering the standard of proof needed for a conviction for playing a part in the Holocaust. Though Demjanjuk died in March 2012 before a final judgement could be made on his appeal, therefore technically remaining innocent, the initial conviction set a legal precedent in Germany and sparked a number of further prosecutions.

In the context of translation specifically, cases this shocking are harder to come by, but the appalling murder of Hitoshi Igarashi, the Japanese translator of Salman Rushdie's *The Satanic Verses*, again blurs the lines. Rushdie's novel caused considerable controversy within Muslim communities, and the author was forced into hiding in February 1989, when Iranian spiritual leader Ayatollah Ruhollah Khomeini issued a death sentence or *fatwa* against him, charging that *The Satanic Verses* blasphemed the Islamic faith. Following the issuing of a further *fatwa* in 1991, Igarashi was stabbed repeatedly by an unknown assailant, nine days after the Italian translator of the controversial book was attacked and wounded in Milan in an event that was suspected to be linked to the murder (these cases resurfaced once again in August 2022 when Rushdie himself was stabbed repeatedly ahead of a lecture in Chautauqua).

Interestingly, and somewhat in contradiction with the arguments stated at the start of this chapter, Pym (2012: 56–57) considers this particular case and writes that each translator is deeply responsible for what they do with the material they work on: "[i]n terms of strictly intercultural ethics there is no reason to believe that the translators of *Satanic Verses* are somehow less responsible than the author who wrote the book or the editor who chose to publish it. [...] In this, translators are not simple messengers. [...] They have choices, and thus responsibility."

Though rather extreme examples, these cases force us to question the extent to which we are complicit in the events that we are privy to or content that we translate. Though it may seem far less likely that we are likely to court controversy when translating in more banal contexts, a sensitivity to the wider contexts in which we are working and how that fits in with our own beliefs and convictions (and indeed what our beliefs and convictions are to begin with) is vitally important. Even a seemingly innocent translation of a short press release could raise questions. For instance, who are the company we are translating for? Do they hire/treat/pay their employees in an ethical manner? What is their impact on the environment (see Chapter 8 for more on sustainability)?

From Mediators to Advocates

If we follow the argument that there is an inescapable personal dimension to our ethical decision-making, a new scale emerges. While the section above separates personal and professional, these are not simple, one-dimensional constructs. We will explore various takes on what makes a "professional" in the next two chapters, and here we turn to examining the sliding scale of "personal" involvement. Indeed, there are degrees of agency, as the discussions in the previous chapter hopefully began to make clear. Below we examine the sliding scale from mediation to activism, via advocates.

Figure 6.1 provides an adapted continuum of agency that allows us to glimpse where these enquiries fit in relation to what has come before more clearly. Pollabauer and Topolovec consider something of a continuum in the field of PSI, mainly exploring the two poles in the figure, while I adapt this model to represent more of a sliding scale and to add a little more detail, suggesting varying degrees of agency and involvement from the translator or interpreter.

At the far left-hand side of the continuum, we find the least active role that is "distinctly distant and non-activist", calling upon notions of invisibility and neutrality that we critiqued in Chapter 5. In the middle, we find our cultural mediators or communication facilitators, who are more involved in the meaning transfer process. Pollabauer and Topolovec's comments on the context of healthcare interpreting provide a fitting example for this mid-point on the scale. As they explain: "[s]ome healthcare providers and patients alike 'expect interpreters to adopt **a more engaged role**, including, for instance, the articulation of personal opinions, providing practical

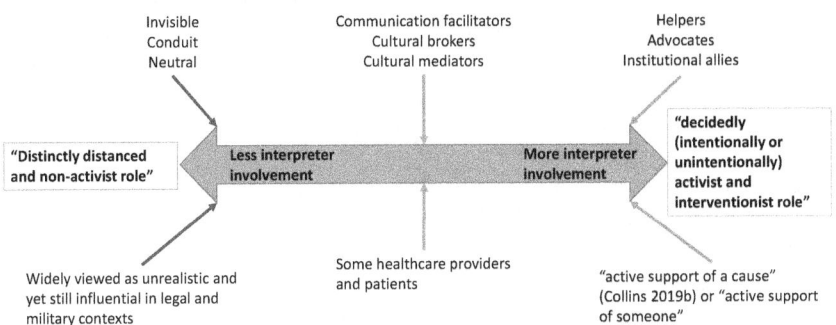

Figure 6.1 The continuum of agency, adapted from Pollabauer and Topolovec 2021: 215–219.

support and emotional comfort, and keeping interactants' secrets (e.g. Hsieh 2006, 726-727; Zendedel et al. 2016, 983)'" (2021: 216). At the right-hand edge, meanwhile, we get into activist territory, with interpreters described as helpers, advocates, or institutional allies. Here, their role is decidedly interventionist and actively supports a cause or an individual. While Inghilleri champions mediation (a concept that is not straightforward or unproblematic, as illustrated in Box 5.3), the thought of Mona Baker, discussed in the next section, takes us into the realm of activism proper.

In a professional context, meanwhile, **advocacy** has also begun to come more to the forefront in recent times and was the subject of a February 2021 guide from the NCIHC (National Council on Interpreting in Health Care) in relation to healthcare. Though, as we will see, there is a stark difference in the way advocacy is conceptualised and employed between theoretical and professional contexts. The association astutely comment on an important distinction to make between general message conversion and advocacy. As they note,

> [m]ost commonly, interventions such as asking for clarification, cultural brokering, or managing the flow of communication have, at times, been mistakenly called advocacy. These interventions, as we will explain later, are not acts of advocacy because they support the healthcare interpreter's primary function of facilitating accurate and complete communication and understanding within the encounter.

Rather, they define advocacy as

> 'the act or process of supporting a cause or a proposal' (Definition of ADVOCACY, 2019). It is 'the act of speaking on behalf of or in support of another person, place, or thing' (Your Dictionary, 2020). Advocacy,

therefore, is the act of coming to the aid of another by supporting their cause or issue to arrive at a desired resolution.

(NCIHC 2021: 12)

They add that advocates are defined by two conditions:

> Speaking for, acting on behalf of, or representing an individual, group, issue, or cause. A person who advocates supports the interests of the person, group, or issue (ibid. 12).
>
> Seeking to persuade or influence those with the authority to come to a resolution in line with the (best) interests of the person(s), issue, or cause they represent. Such persuasion goes beyond simply informing those in authority that a problem exists (ibid. 13).

They conclude by attempting to overturn the image of the advocate as an adversarial stance "in which a third party enters a conflict or disagreement to support, promote, or defend the interests of one party against the interests of another" to instead consider it as a collaborative approach – still speaking on behalf, but doing so by engaging in "collaborative problem solving" (ibid.). Importantly, the NCIHC also argue that

> [h]ealthcare interpreters should only consider the need for advocacy after they have tried all other interventions to alert the parties to the potential for serious imminent harm to the patient, whether physical or emotional, and the attempts have failed to address the concern.
>
> (2021: 32)

Far from being a default position when interpreting, advocacy is an extremely rare occurrence and, in some ways, a last resort. It is also tempered by several questions to ask yourself, which raise some rather troubling points. For instance, they ask you to ensure that your assessment is "unbiased by your own feelings and opinions" and that "no one else will recognise and correct the potential for serious harm before harm occurs" (ibid. 36) and "[h]ave you exhausted all the interventions you have at your disposal to transparently alert the parties to the potential for imminent harm without having to advocate" (ibid. 38). While obviously an important step in surpassing traditional notions of neutrality, the neutral, accurate translator is still hierarchically superior in this framework, and intervention is kept to a bare minimum.

Overall, these are challenging, slippery terms, with different bodies and thinkers using different definitions. And, though the continuum above groups activism and advocacy together – and there is crossover between the two terms as activism can be viewed as a form of advocacy – the means are often different. Advocacy involves working to make needs heard while activism involves taking direct action to achieve a political or social goal.

Indeed, the NCIHC seek to view advocacy as a non-adversarial relationship, while activist stances tend to lean towards a more militant context.

Narrative Theory: From Advocates to Activists

Though Venuti is not included under the umbrella of activist translation, his work can arguably be seen as feeding into this important and challenging area of translation practice. Boéri and Delgado Luchner (2021: 246) agree with Venuti in claiming that every act of translation can be seen as being ideologically motivated, at both a macro and micro level. At the macro level, choosing what gets translated is an ideologically motivated decision, while on the micro level the linguistic choices we make (such as those contributing to domesticating or foreignising effects) are at stake. Boéri and Delgado Luchner define activist translation and interpreting as practices that set out to "connect across the globe and to bring about social and political change" (Boéri 2019: 1) and **to disrupt dominant discourses and institutions**. Activist movements have "agendas that explicitly challenge the dominant narratives of the time" (Baker 2006: 462) – that is, "practices that are *intentionally and explicitly* geared towards social change and a *disruption* of existing power structures" – and within the context of this definition there is clear overlap between Venuti's ideas and activist, feminist, humanitarian, and developmental translation.

However, it is only in the twenty-first century that this has been used as an explicit label to describe these endeavours in TIS. Baker's work on ethics is a hugely influential and thought-provoking contribution to this field. While we will explore some of her general thoughts, which lead us to accountability later in this section, it is first useful to look into the theoretical backdrop she uses to foreground the activist role of the translator: narrative theory. This framework is based upon a sociological understanding of narrative as an active, reality-constructing tool. It has been adopted by several translation and interpreting theorists as a powerful tool for exploring practitioners' choices, as well as for examining the ethical implications of those choices. When thinking about what a narrative is, a traditional answer might be: 'It's a story, with a beginning, a middle and an end. It's something people tell. It's a way of communicating or expressing experiences.' This literary description depicts narrative as primarily representational; we have experiences – or we invent imaginative experiences – and use language to relate these back to an audience. Yet this concept raises many questions: How do we decide what to include in our narrative, for example? Why do different people tell different narrative versions of the same events? 'Narrative' in this context means much more than a straight-forward representation of reality. It is a problematisation of storytelling.

As Somers and Gibson (1994: 59) state, "[i]t is through narrativity that we come to know, understand and make sense of the social world, and it is through narratives and narrativity that we constitute our social identities." Baker uses this concept of narrative to explain both the ideologies underlying translation choices and our understanding of what translation is. Translators, she argues, occupy a privileged position as mediators of these stories because of the nature of their work. One of her fundamental assumptions is that translators can never be entirely neutral. For her, the idea of translators as neutral mediators is not only unrealistic, but it should not be held as an ideal either, precisely because we are always inevitably embedded in complex political, institutional, social contexts. Translators do not inhabit a borderland in between different cultures, a hybrid 'third space', they are embedded in situations which are often unavoidably political.

Narratives in this view are public and personal 'stories' that we subscribe to and that guide our behaviour. They are the stories we tell ourselves, not just those we explicitly tell other people, about the world(s) we live in. Narrativity does not only help us to understand reality, it makes up that reality, which shifts and changes over time. Every person subscribes to a selection of narratives about various aspects of reality, and our belief in these narratives guides our actions and therefore helps to construct reality. Its value lies in the fact that is it considered to solve a number of issues perceived in TIS including: moving beyond a traditional preoccupation with equivalence, binarisms, and linguistic analysis; overturning the assumption of neutrality (like Inghilleri does); embedding translators in the wider context of their work; and turning our attention squarely towards ethics.

Somers and Gibson divide narratives into four broad, overlapping categories, which interact with one another, and there is a porous, evolving, and mutually enriching level of interaction between them:

- **Personal/ontological narratives** – As Baker (2009: 226) puts it, "[p]ersonal narratives are narratives of the self, typically stories which locate the narrating subject at the centre of events."
- **Public narratives** – According to Somers and Gibson, public narratives (also known as 'shared narratives') are the stories which circulate amongst groups larger than the individual, such as in the family, workplace, church, government, or nation. Examples could include narratives about Islamic fundamentalism or gay rights (Baker 2006: 33). Baker (2009: 226) describes public narratives as "the bread and butter of the translation and interpreting business."
- **Conceptual narratives** – These are specialist/expert accounts of some phenomenon in the world. Baker (2006: 39) defines them as "the stories and explanations that scholars in any field elaborate for themselves and others about their object of enquiry." Despite their scale and often a supposedly detached, scientific status, they are no more authoritative than other types. Baker gives the example of discourse around slavery, which was used as a "scientific" approach in the nineteenth century to define a hierarchy between black and white people.

- **Meta (or master) narratives** – These are shared stories with extensive temporal and spatial reach, and are often conceptual narratives that have acquired an almost inescapable breadth. "Metanarratives are the 'master-narratives' in which we are embedded as contemporary actors ... the epic dramas of our times" (Somers and Gibson 1994: 63).

Baker points out that translators and interpreters are often involved in translating personal narratives (the autobiography of a Holocaust survivor, for example). But, we can never fully step out of our own narrative position, we are always governed by our own beliefs and positions. There is no magically neutral vantage point and, at the level of public narratives in particular, translators and interpreters assist their proliferation across linguistic and cultural borders. Indeed, due to the international nature of metanarratives, Baker (2006: 46) argues that it is impossible for public narratives to rise to the status of metanarratives without the involvement of translators and interpreters. Importantly, however, translators and interpreters can also challenge and subvert those narratives – the idea of **renarration** – and this is where the idea of activism comes into play.

Translators can use their personal narratives to resist dominant public narratives and promote alternative versions, and activist translation is precisely the act of subverting these dominant narratives and/or promoting the narrative(s) that they subscribe to. In her work, Baker explores numerous cases of translators taking 'direct action' to subvert narratives. Ultimately, "[w]hether the motivation is commercial or ideological, translators and interpreters play a decisive role in both articulating and contesting the full range of public narratives circulating within and around any society at any moment in time" (Baker 2006: 38). Importantly:

> [R]omanticizing our role and elaborating disciplinary narratives in which we feature as morally superior, peace-giving professionals is neither convincing nor productive. Instead, we need to recognize and acknowledge our own embeddedness in a variety of narratives. Whether professional translators or scholars, we do not build bridges nor bridge gaps. We participate in very decisive ways in promoting and circulating narratives and discourses of various types. Some promote peace, others fuel conflicts, subjugate entire populations, kill millions.
>
> (Baker 2005: 12)

Below we consider the impact that agency has on our role. It is of crucial importance at this stage to consider how this fits in with your translation and/or interpreting practice:

? Are there any particular voices or beliefs that are marginalised/amplified in your work?
? Do you support a more active, advocate role for translators/interpreters?
? Or do you feel that this falls beyond the role that we are taking on?

From Activists to Accountability

All of this narrative positioning ties the translator to an undercurrent of moral responsibility. Translators and interpreters face a basic ethical choice with every assignment:

> to reproduce existing ideologies as encoded in the narrative elaborated in the text or utterance, or to dissociate themselves from those ideologies, if necessary by refusing to translate the text or interpret in a particular context at all.
>
> (Baker 2006: 105)

Translators must make choices, selecting aspects or parts of a text to transpose or emphasize. These choices create necessarily partial representations of their source texts. This "partiality is not merely a defect, a lack, or an absence in a translation – it is also an aspect that makes the act of translation partisan: engaged and committed, either implicitly or explicitly" (Tymoczko 2000: 24). Clearly, translators are not neutral or invisible, but rather must be committed to the causes they speak up for and accountable for their choices. According to these viewpoints, translators and interpreters need to be aware of the impact they have on society and take responsibility for that impact. Translators and interpreters must be able to justify a decision (morally) to themselves as well as those who might question it (see Baker 2011, Baker and Maier 2011).

In a separate contribution to ethics that consolidates this turn to accountability, Baker devotes an entire chapter to the subject in the 2011 second edition of her translation handbook *In Other Words*. This addition is included to reflect the discipline's (and her own) evolving interests since the book's initial publication in 1992. In this chapter, Baker claims to move beyond codes of ethics in order to prepare translators to think critically about ethical choices of which they are often unaware. She takes the time to outline the most commonly encountered forms of ethics, something that is entirely praiseworthy and a significant step to establishing a more solid foundation for future progress.

Despite not explicitly setting out a theory for herself, Baker's introduction hints at her own position in the framework, advising as she does against the uncritical use of "abstract codes". For her, these codes are often used as an institutional device to constrain behaviour and are unable to "predict the full range of concrete ethical issues that may arise in the course of professional practice" (Baker 2011: 274). Instead, she pushes translators to develop critical skills that can help them to make ethical decisions for themselves and to follow their own moral leanings despite contradictory forces. These comments signal a definitive shift from such prescriptive ideas. Indeed, Baker moves away from any ethical framework setting out *a priori* laws or codes, initially affording her contribution with a much closer fit in virtue ethics. Despite this close link to virtue ethics, however, there is another area of ethical theory that neatly aligns with certain elements of Baker's thought. The notion of moral particularism, a lesser-known theory favouring an appreciation of the context of each situation, is also present. As with virtue ethics, this theory rejects the idea that there are any universal moral principles while also asserting that moral judgement can be found only as one decides particular cases, either real or imagined. It is founded on the claim that there are no uniformly morally relevant features of the world and, as such, no decisions can be taken before an event. Rather, a sensitive appreciation of the entire context is always required, and particulars are normatively prior to universals. This places particularism at the far end of ethical theory to monisms – such as act utilitarianism and ethical egoism, where one overriding value governs the entire theory, in this case happiness or self-interest respectively – in that it allows for no all-powerful rules. British philosopher Jonathan Dancy is one of the most prominent defenders of particularism, and he demonstrates how there are a number of moral reasons but no moral principles because of this dependency on context. For him, "[t]he question is always, 'what is the nature of the case before us?', not 'in what way is my decision here determined by previous decisions, or general principles?'" (Dancy 2013: 773). While this move away from the continuous development of ethical knowledge forwarded by Baker distinguishes her ideas from Dancy's, a shared focus on contextual importance is emphasised in her assertion that ethical issues have no ready-made solutions.[2]

This particularist strand of thought is one that is shared by Inghilleri who, in 'The ethical task of the translator in the geo-political arena', clearly sets out an ethics based around a similar appreciation of context. Exploring military linguists' accounts of their own work in the midst of the "war on terror", she suggests an ethics that is not guided by professional codes of ethics based on the notion of impartiality, but that is instead informed by the nature of the ethical encounter itself. Within this conception, social conditions disturb and disrupt our view of the ethical, leading to a misrepresentation of the other, and therefore necessitate a close consideration of the factors at play. We are offered "a translation ethics that resists the wish to transcend the violation of the other through codes based in transcendent ideals", which could include accuracy or fidelity, as the right thing to do cannot be calculated or predetermined "and is instead guided by the nature of the ethical encounter itself" (Inghilleri 2008: 222).

So, for both authors, we are responsible for the choices we make and must be able to back them up when required to do so. No one, translators included, can stand outside or between narratives. Translators and interpreters should "develop critical skills that can enable [them] to make ethical decisions for themselves […] rather than fall back uncritically on abstract codes drawn up by their employers or the associations that represent them" (Baker 2011: 274) and we must critically consider the range of options available to us, "because however difficult the decisions we have to make we are still accountable for them, to ourselves as well as others" (Baker 2011: 283).

? Which role (mediator, advocate, activist) do you find most realistic and/or appealing, and why?
? Do you feel that the labels apply equally well to both translation and interpreting (or other contexts)?
? How can we be accountable for the choices we make as a translator or interpreter?

Box 6.2 Activism, accountability, and conflicts of interest

While not quite tackling the same contexts addressed by Mona Baker, the example below provides a concise illustration of narrative positioning and commitment in a professional context, foreshadowing discussions to come in the following chapters. Read the case study and then consider the questions below it before looking at the responses.

The Case

A New York-based translator describes an ethical dilemma (in Cohen 2010): "I was hired to do the voice-over for a French version of the annual video report of a high-profile religious organization. The video opposes gay marriage, a view untenable to me. During the recording session, I noticed various language errors. Nobody there but I spoke French, and I considered letting these errors go: my guilt-free sabotage."

? What should the translator do in this situation? What would you do?
? How does the idea of activism come in here?
? After reading Chapter 7, consider what they should do according to the professional code of ethics.

The Translator's Course of Action

"Ultimately I made the corrections. As a married gay man, I felt ethically compromised even taking this job."

? Did the translator follow their personal ethics, advocate for a particular narrative?
? What do you think of his decision?

Cohen's Response

In his article, Cohen argues that the translator was right to complete the work to their usual standards, contending that "if you accept a job, you must do it professionally" before questioning whether the translator should have accepted the job in the first place. He goes on to call working on the video a form of advocacy for and promotion of the "policies you revile", and an act of betrayal to the communities he is part of. He finishes with an update, explaining that the translator was subsequently asked to be the voice and face of additional videos for the organisation and refused.

? Do you agree with Cohen's response?
? Do Cohen's views change your opinion at all?

As we have seen, the decision of whether or not to translate/interpret in the first place is a common theme. In the context of interpreting specifically, Prunč (1997, 2008, and 2012) argues first that interpreters may decline assignments on moral and ethical grounds, in cases such as interpreting that would contribute directly to suffering or endangering life and "goes further by justifying withdrawal or termination of service when clients seek to deny the interpreter's autonomy to make ethical judgments" (Setton and Prunč 2015: 145 in Pöchhacker). When it comes to interpreting objectionable content, however, opinions are mixed – some legal systems would protect interpreters who refuse to speak on behalf of Holocaust deniers, for instance, as these remarks would be deemed to incite racial hatred, while "Prunč even justifies subversion of the message in extreme cases" (ibid. 147). It is also worth keeping this case in mind when reading chapters 7 and 8.

The Translator's *Telos*

We draw discussions to a close in this chapter by returning to the crucial and complex personal-professional divide and examining a final viewpoint that considers centralising personal concerns in a perhaps more flexible manner. While we have discussed Chesterman's thought on ethics at various points in this book, his multifaceted work contains a number of strands that we can call upon at different points. One idea that has emerged within his ethical thought is that of a translatorial *telos*, which further explores the idea of accountability to ourselves, simultaneously returning us to questions of consequentialism while also introducing ideas of **individual responsibility**, which are explored in more detail in Chapter 8.

This idea highlights the crucial importance of incorporating the human side inherent in the translating act into an ethical framework and first emerged in a question Chesterman posed to Baker in a published 2008 interview. Taking inspiration from use of the term *skopos*, which introduces a consequentialist ethics focusing on ends rather than means (as outlined in Chapter 4), Chesterman makes the innovative move of transferring this aim from the text to the translator. His idea of a *telos* hints towards the translator's own personal desires. Below is part of the interview with Baker in which we find this initial hint towards the development of the translator's *telos*, which was later elaborated in 2009 in the paper 'An ethical decision', as well as a brief explanation of what such a notion would entail.

> Chesterman: [...] What interests me in this context is the way the skopos is tied to a text: it is the function of a text, not the goal of a person. It occurs to me that translation theory might need a new concept to describe the ultimate motivation of the translator (or interpreter, of course). Translators work to stay alive, yes. But they also have a number of other motivations: a love of languages no doubt, an interest in other cultures, perhaps a desire to improve communication, and so on. [...] There is a traditional Stoic distinction between skopos and telos that has been much commented on by classical scholars and theologians. Skopos is usually taken to refer to more immediate intentions, the visible target literally aimed at by an archer for instance (originally, skopos means a watcher, an observer), whereas telos refers to a more distant or ultimate state, such as the more abstract goal of life as a whole, ideally perhaps a final harmonious state. The telos is a result rather than an intention. Suppose, alongside skopos, we adopt the term 'telos' to describe the personal goal of a translator, firstly in the context of a given task. Some tasks are done just for the money, but others might have different teloi.
> (Baker 2008: 31)

Potential benefits of this concept of a *telos* are immediately clear. Rather than being tied to textual fidelity or being governed by neutrality, there are a number of personal factors involved in our decision-making. For instance, I may want to translate to forward my own career, to get paid and to satisfy the commissioners of the work in order to ensure that I continue to get paid. This is, presumably, all part of my *telos*. Or, I could choose to follow a personal cause. For her part, Baker states that a "telos is a more productive concept than skopos because it connects with the wider context of a whole society, and potentially of humanity at large" (Baker 2008: 32).

In a later article, Chesterman exemplifies the notion of *telos* by using the Moster example covered in Box 4.4. After reflecting on Moster's (traditionally "not ethically justified") decision, Chesterman argues that there is an inevitable need to consider the person behind the translation. For him, Moster's decision has serious implications for the way we view the translator's role in general. Whereas traditionally "we have become accustomed to seeing the translator as a mediator, a bridge-builder between cultures" (Chesterman 2009: n.p.), Chesterman argues that this simplistic view inevitably ensures that we see translation "through rose-coloured spectacles, as if translators never acted as bridge-destroyers, as if translation could never be used for destructive ends." He argues that examples of historic instances in which translators and translations have misled, distorted facts, and caused misunderstanding, whether intentionally or not, are easy to come by and concludes with a variation on the theme of interpretation, with the firm but fair judgement that "[a] translator is never totally neutral. All translation is also an intervention." Furthermore, the translator's decision to take a stand "against the potential risk of encouraging neo-Nazi fanaticism", and his defence of this decision are, for Chesterman, "evidence of what we might call his translator's telos (Greek 'end, goal')", "conceptualizing the ultimate goal of a translator, the source of personal motivation, values and priorities." He adds that this *telos* can influence not only a translator's means of handling a specific text and the ethical issues that it entails, but also their decision to translate a certain text in the first place.

Box 6.3 *Telos* and accountability in action

Maitland (2016) outlines an example from her own translation practice that reflects these notions of *telos* and accountability. She recounts how in 2011 she was invited to translate *Dentro de la tierra*, Paco Bezerra's multi-award-winning play for performance in London. As she puts it, "[s]et in a family-run tomato farm in rural Andalusia, the play is a macabre tale of a father's ambition and his violent verbal and physical abuse of the North African workers he employs" (Maitland 2016: 27). The translation dilemma in this instance stems from the problematic language used by the father and his son who repeatedly refer to these workers as *moros* [Moors] or *negros* [blacks].

Maitland concluded that the use of such loaded terms (as opposed to more neutral terms such as *trabajadores* [workers]) and the responses from various interlocutors in the play signalled a "clash of multicultural values" (ibid.). At this point, she explained that her "challenge was to find a translation that would communicate the family's racism while resisting the potential for harm when performed for English-speaking audiences" (ibid.). While the author himself suggested "Moors" and "niggers" as a translation, Maitland rejected these terms as problematic in the context of a play staged in England. The challenging nature of the terminology stems from the ambiguity inherent in the Spanish term *negros*. For the translator, a number of competing interests become clear. As Maitland explained:

> As a "reader" of the text my task was to assess the context of its usage both from the perspective of the author and the characters in the play. But given my commission, to translate for a UK performance, my readerly concern had to take into account the Spanish text and its English-speaking audience.
>
> (ibid. 2016: 28)

She suggests that the author's suggestions of "niggers" ran the risk of moving beyond signalling this racist insult built into the Spanish play, and instead placing the audience in a "place of real discomfort" (ibid.). Instead, Maitland considers the various choices available. "Could 'blacks' convey the Father's racism without alienating spectators? What about the references to moros? 'Moors', 'North Africans' or 'Maghrebis'?" (ibid.).

Subsequently, after proposing the various options to a stage director (who "initially balked at the family's use of language" (ibid.)), Maitland opted for "Arabs", playing on a familiar, pejorative usage with a choice that she felt would reflect the shocking language used and "ensuring it did not take the audience beyond my belief in the dramatic clash of multicultural values the play was offering, towards a place of offence, confusion, or hostility" (ibid.). This process of questioning what the terms are used for in the source text, the connotations of various possible renderings, their potential impact upon the final audience, and the best means of negotiating the various interests at stake in the final analysis reflects a personal engagement with the text and a series of individual, idiosyncratic responses that will vary between translators.

Just like Moster in the example from Chesterman, Maitland outlines the complex considerations that occur within seemingly small choices and highlights the amount of cultural sensitivity and concrete input required on the part of the translator. Here, for instance, Maitland had to engage in research into the history and context of the terminology and communicate with various agents involved in the translation before making a personal decision that drew upon all of this information without bowing to the interests of one particular party, a choice she later advocated for in her article.

In both of these examples, what is most interesting perhaps is this foregrounding of the translator's personal and studied intentions and objectives. By linking *skopos* theory and the notion of a *telos*, Chesterman attests to the consequentialist link between the two theories. In describing the *telos* as "the personal goal of the translator", his ideas move towards a non-judgmental, flexible conception of ethics. For instance, his acceptance that translators do indeed translate to stay alive and that translating just for the money is an acceptable *telos* both call our attention to the egoistic notion of doing what is "right for you" as opposed to following a supposedly universal "right". This extended range of responsibility specific to the translation profession is explored in more detail in Chapter 8 and potential applications of egoism are briefly considered in Chapter 9.

Moral Relativism

While a primary focus on the specific context of an ethical encounter and individual agency is an invaluable step to consider in refining our considerations of the ethical, the total rejection of guiding principles is far from an unproblematic solution. Indeed, the void created by the addition of contextual factors provides us with the ability to let ourselves off the hook, so to speak: even though we know the context, we still do not necessarily know how to act. Indeed, an overriding reliance on context can turn the answer to every question into an emphatic 'it depends'. For all of the freedom, agency, and power that ideas of advocacy, accountability, and *telos* can impart, how, where, or when do we draw the line when it comes to the leeway afforded to translators and interpreters in their actions? This is a complex and, as always, very personal question, which is encapsulated within the ideas of moral relativism.

Moral relativism asserts that judgements are only true or false relative to a certain standpoint. It primarily stems from the questionable status of moral objectivism – the argument that there is an objective, universally valid moral truth. As the name suggests, it relativises the truth of moral claims, casting doubt upon the existence of a single true morality and enabling us to account for divergent viewpoints, supposedly increasing tolerance as we are ready to accept others' ideas, views, and beliefs. Hopefully the link to translation is clear here. We have scholars such as Inghilleri and Baker who question the universalisable nature (or even the possibility) of ideas such as neutrality and impartiality and we instead have to decide based on individual cases, with a hope that individuals will be self-critical.

Despite claims to tolerance and an acceptance of diversity, however, criticisms of moral relativism abound. Firstly, many claim that there are indeed some common core values that are shared across all cultures – perhaps trustworthiness or the wrongness of killing (is this universal?) – and that there is a factual basis to some values, with differences merely arising from a lack of understanding or access to these facts. The key objection, however, is that this approach risks an 'anything goes' view of ethics if taken to its limits. **If we maintain that right and wrong is relative to an individual standpoint, then how can we say that *any* standpoint is wrong?** For instance, if in the present day an individual contends that slave ownership is right, how can we refute that if we are guided by the principle of relative rightness?

Baker's stance outlined above addresses ethics on a case-by-case basis and asks us to be critical and to reflect on our choices, but never asserts a 'right' way of doing things. Similarly, Chesterman's notion of *telos* allows for non-traditional ethical courses of action and to cover personal needs and desires, but at what point do omissions, changes, and interventions in a text, or work taken for purely financial reasons regardless of the questionable nature of the content or the source of the financing, for instance, become a problem? Is it enough to say that, as long as we are willing to accept responsibility for our actions, then we can act however we see fit? What makes a good, laudable, or ethical cause? Discouraging neo-Nazi fanaticism (as in the case of Moster's translation) may be a principle that many of us can agree upon, but who is the arbiter of the 'worthiness' of these causes? Does a certain number or nature of omissions/changes make a rendering as a whole ethically problematic? Does changing one term, like the *negro* example in Box 6.3, throw into question the translator's 'ethical' role?

> **Box 6.4 Unbridled relativism: The fake sign language interpreter**
>
> An example that neatly illustrates the limits of pure relativism in the context of TIS is the famous "fake sign language interpreter." In 2013, Thamsanqa Jantjie stood alongside world leaders at Nelson Mandela's memorial service in South Africa and produced a series of meaningless, "childish hand gestures") in the place of legitimate signs when interpreting for speakers, including US president Barack Obama. Surely no amount of posturing and rule-bending can realistically claim that his actions were ethical? Unsurprisingly, Jantjie was heavily criticised for his work and yet, following the line of argument that translators must stand by their choices, we struggle to disarm the practice. Speaking to *Talk Radio 702* in South Africa following the event, Jantjie claimed that he felt that he had been a "champion of sign language" (On Demand News 2013), confirmed that he held a formal qualification in interpreting and explained that a schizophrenic episode caused his inability to sign properly. He clearly stood by his practice and showed no remorse for any potential problems.
>
> ? What can we do when faced with this kind of situation where somebody contradicts what may seem like a clear view, arguably increasingly common in our post-truth world?
> ? While a vital cog in our ethical machine, personal accountability alone is not enough to resolve disputes in all contexts, does this change your view of the theory at all?
>
> However, there are several interesting perspectives that could be added here. From a professional point of view – and particularly in light of mental health concerns (see Chapter 8) – should Jantjie have

been provided a greater level of support? Not only was his employer presumably aware of his diagnosis and potential complications but, when conducting his role, best practice suggests that interpreters should be able to take a break roughly every twenty to thirty minutes and that, for meetings longer than two hours, two interpreters should be present to enable them to take turns.

Hendrietta Bogopane-Zulu, the deputy minister for women, children, and people with disabilities argued that best practice was not followed and that, though mistakes were made, Jantjie was unfairly criticised. She contended that having to translate from English to his first language Xhosa to sign language caused him to get tired and lose concentration. Could these be considered as mitigating factors? Following the event, the company providing the translation services reportedly "vanished into thin air" and had been paying under half of the standard fee for an interpreter, alluding to issues of regulation and pay, which we will explore in Chapter 8 (Smith 2013).

? Where would you personally draw the line in terms of how an interpreter or translator can act? What are the guiding principles that would help you?
? Do you feel that strict rules or greater freedom are more practical/ethical in the context of translation and interpreting?

Conclusion

This chapter has seen us explore the full range of agency at work when we translate or interpret. From a commitment to the content that we translate, to the place of personal beliefs in our work and accountability for the choices that we make. We have moved from a more detached professional take on projects to the activist notion that we should select projects that are oriented toward (our notions of) social justice. For Baker, accountability is a central concern for all modern professionals, requiring "every professional and every citizen to demonstrate that he or she is cognizant of the impact of their behaviour on others, aware of its legal implications, and prepared to take responsibility for its consequences" (Baker 2014 n.p.). This would subsequently require that translators and interpreters think more critically about their stances, overturn perhaps over-simplistic models of neutrality and impartiality, and open space for activist, subversive methods.

However, doubts remain about how feasible it is for working translators and interpreters to adopt the kind of militant, politically driven activist positions described here. Pym disagrees with Baker's contention that one should translate only those texts to which one is committed ideologically

(Pym 2012: 59–60; Baker 2008). Indeed, in the economically driven context of professional translation, with a number of asymmetrical power relations at work means that, as Pym memorably puts it (2012: 87–88), "[a]sking a translator to save the world is sometimes like asking an infant to read."

Does this mean that we can stand back and deny responsibility, using the defence of "I'm just the translator"? The examples covered in Box 6.1 would seem to suggest otherwise. Phelan et al (2020: 65) offer a pertinent note in this regard, acknowledging that it is vital that we recognise the complexity of the process of translation and interpreting and the negative effect translations or interpretations can have on the community, while also contending that combining activist and professional concerns "may lead to confusion", as the two are qualitatively different categories. They contend that **"[t]aking a stand in favour of a just cause does not make someone a good translator or interpreter, although it may make them a good person."** Yet what exactly is *just* is undoubtedly a personal, subjective, and dynamic issue. We cannot easily conflate or separate personal and professional concerns, and these two areas merit further exploration.

In Chapter 7, we look at perhaps the most purely 'professional' invocation of ethics in the translation profession – codes of ethics – considering a range of professional standards that have become well established across numerous geographical areas, contexts, and practices. This exploration of codes responds directly to questions above, as these documents represent a very clear attempt to set out principles for good practice (or, arguably, the *just*) in translation and interpreting. As we will see, these codes sit a long way from moral relativism and allowing practitioners to follow their personal needs and desires.

Discussion, Presentation and Assignment Topics

1. To what extent do you feel that the translator/interpreter is responsible for the content that they translate?
2. Translators should always follow their personal convictions when translating, even if that means making changes to the text / speaker's utterances. Discuss.
3. Group presentation: Find a case of a translator/interpreter who has made the news for making changes to a text or utterance (or, use one from this book or the Routledge Translation Studies Portal) and prepare both arguments for and against their course of action.

Notes

1 In Pym's account, we are also not fully responsible for the consequences of our translations, though once we have made the decision to translate, he does soften this stance (see Box 6.1).

2 Dancy is not referenced in Baker's chapter on ethics, a further example of the lack of engagement between translation studies and ethical theory.

Further Reading

For a more comprehensive exploration of activist translation, see **Boéri and Delgado Luchner (2021)**. **Kruger and Crots (2014)** offers a fascinating reflection on the divide between personal and professional ethics. For an accessible breakdown of narrative theory and a range of insights into its applications in translation studies, see **Baker (2005)**, while *Translating Conflict* (**Baker 2006**) offers a rich, challenging exploration of the domain. Finally, **Chesterman (2009)** is a useful site for exploring notions of *telos* and also reflects on the Moster case study in relation to a range of theories of ethics (this paper is also included in **Chesterman 2017**).

7 Standards

> **Key Questions**
> - What are codes of ethics and how are they used in the context of translation and interpreting?
> - What are the key ethical principles that translators and interpreters are required to follow?
> - What are the potential shortcomings of these guidelines, and how realistic or helpful are the principles used?

In Chapters 3–6, we explored a range of key ethical issues for translators and interpreters to consider in their work. Though often quite practical in nature, these insights largely came from a theoretical backdrop. This chapter marks a shift in focus, considering how ethics has been grounded in the professional context. We will begin with an exploration of codes of ethics for translators and interpreters in this chapter, before exploring other perspectives on "ethical professionals" in Chapter 8.

I begin by setting out what exactly these codes of ethics are and what they aim to do. I then cover the key principles contained within these codes, considering concrete examples from representative codes from some of the most well-established translation and interpreting associations worldwide. Given their key role in codifying ethical behaviour it is necessary to not simply acknowledge the codes' existence in their current form, but also to engage with a wide range of ongoing critiques of these documents. As noted by Baker in Chapter 6, we are responsible for the choices that we make ethically and cannot simply fall back uncritically on these codes, and both scholars and professionals readily acknowledge that codes offer contradictory and sometimes confusing guidelines. I consider criticisms of codes from both translation and interpreting backgrounds, with considerable shared ground between the two. Indeed, despite the considerable differences between the two practices, it is noteworthy that translation and interpreting both share many of the same values (and even the same code in many instances!). Finally, I briefly address some thoughts on how to move beyond these limitations.

? Based on the discussions in previous chapters, what principles would you expect to see in translation and interpreting codes of ethics?
? In your work or study, is there a code of ethics that you have to follow? How prominent/wide-ranging is it?

What are Codes of Ethics?

A codes of ethics is a set of rules or principles put in place by an institution (or sometimes an individual) to govern behaviour or decision-making processes, and in some ways to help employees or practitioners to distinguish from good or bad or right and wrong in their particular domain. As Hale puts it (2007: 103), **codes offer guidance on how practitioners should "conduct themselves ethically for the benefit of the clients they serve, the profession they represent and themselves as practitioners."** This definition is important in the way that it echoes the questions of responsibility that we have considered in previous chapters, and it is interesting to compare and contrast theoretical and practical conceptions of ethics.

It is also important to note that while there are strong practical strands within the ideas explored in previous chapters, working translators largely do not engage with these academic sources – either due to a lack of access (academic texts can be expensive and often require institutional or journal-based subscriptions) or a lack of time, interest, or awareness of their existence (understandably, professionals' primary focus is placed on the *doing* rather than the *theorising*). As such, codes of ethics undoubtedly represent most working translators' primary point of contact (if not their only point of contact) with thought on ethics in the field and are a key tool in defining ethical translation and informing ethical decision-making.

The codes act as a shared set of guiding principles and are a key element in the professionalisation of a practice, providing certain standards to uphold. Indeed, using Wilensky's model of professionalisation (1964), Pym et al. (2012: 80) describe the development of formal codes of ethics as one of five steps towards professionalisation found in many "newer and marginal professions". In this view, the codes set "rules to eliminate the unqualified and unscrupulous, rules to reduce internal competition and rules to protect clients and emphasise the service ideal." In terms of ethical theory, meanwhile, codes return us to a focus on deontology. Leong Ko notes that they are almost universally deontological in nature, setting out "principles of ethics and a series of rules which then flowed from these principles" (Ko 2015: 349).

Zooming out to the wider professional world for a moment, codes emerged as a key tool in the 1990s and soon started to be adopted in the context of translation and interpreting. Though translation codes emerged as early as 1963 with the Fédération Internationale des Traducteurs (FIT) *Translator's Charter*, it is really in the twenty-first century that they became a must-have document for translation associations and, to a lesser extent, Language Service Providers (LSPs). Most professional associations now have a code that members are expected to follow. The Institute of Translation and Interpreting (ITI) code, for instance, is intended to "ensure that the highest standards are consistently maintained amongst its members" (ITI 2016: 3).

Codes are attractive to associations and agencies for a number of reasons. Aside from the surface-level value of providing shared values and principles of practice that professionals (should) adhere to, they also act as a symbolic badge of honour by sharing a marketable, ethical image. Indeed, it is appealing to clients to see that the translators and interpreters they hire will supposedly behave in an appropriate, professional, predictable, and "ethical" manner. Codes also confer elevated status to and trust in the profession and its institutions (Baixauli-Olmos 2021: 311). Baixauli-Olmos – a key voice on codes of ethics in translation – describes them as "textual embodiments of professional power struggles" (2017: 262), concretising a link to efforts to improve our position as a profession. In many professions, they will sit hand-in-hand with professional training, though in the unregulated world of translation and interpreting (see Chapter 8), where qualifications, accreditations, and ethical training are by no means a prerequisite for entering the profession, this is unfortunately not an option (indeed, training in ethics has only recently begun to take on a more central position: see Drugan and Megone (2011), for a fascinating exploration of the ways in which ethics has been and can be further brought into the translation classroom).

At this point it is also important to note that the terms "code of conduct", "code of practice", and "code of ethics" are used almost interchangeably in some academic literature, and even in professional documentation, despite the differences that exist (see, for instance, Drugan and Megone, 2011b: 186). Phelan argues that the key difference is that codes of ethics focus on ethical standards or principles, while codes of conduct or practice focus on behaviour. Some associations do adhere to these different characteristics, publishing distinct documents addressing ethical standards and behaviour, but others use generic titles or even titles that "are not always thought through" (Phelan 2020: 90). This flexibility of terminology reinforces a more general trend for using the terms interchangeably and, here, for the sake of clarity and simplicity, I will use "code of ethics" throughout except when referring to a document that has the title "code of conduct".

Box 7.1 The ATA Code of Ethics and professional practice

Below is the code of ethics in force for the American Translator's Association (ATA) reproduced in full (note that the ATA does have a commentary available on their website alongside the code to expand upon and clarify some of the concepts below but, owing to space restrictions, I have limited myself to the core document here). This code has been chosen as a concise and representative example of a code of ethics. Read the code and reflect on any strengths or weaknesses that you see:

? Are there any gaps, issues, or contradictions?
? Do any of the guidelines surprise you?
? Do you feel that the code will be useful in your work as a translator or interpreter?

We the members of the American Translators Association accept as our ethical and professional duty:

1. *to convey meaning between people and cultures faithfully, accurately, and impartially;*
2. *to hold in confidence any privileged and/or confidential information entrusted to us in the course of our work;*
3. *to represent our qualifications, capabilities, and responsibilities honestly and to work always within them;*
4. *to enhance those capabilities at every opportunity through continuing education in language, subject field, and professional practice;*
5. *to act collegially by sharing knowledge and experience;*
6. *to define in advance by mutual agreement, and to abide by, the terms of all business transactions among ourselves and with others;*
7. *to ask for and offer due recognition of our work, and compensation commensurate with our abilities; and*
8. *to endeavor in good faith to resolve among ourselves any dispute that arises from our professional interactions, mindful that failure to abide by these principles may harm ourselves, our fellow members, the Association, or those we serve.*

As approved by the ATA Board of Directors October 2010

Guidelines within Codes

There is no one definitive code across or within the translation or interpreting professions. Codes vary in length and detail, from just a few sentences on general ethical behaviour to detailed explanations of key terms and principles. However, there are common features to be found. Codes will generally introduce the organisation publishing the document and provide some context on what ethics requires and why it is important, before offering a list of normative guidelines, which tend to follow very similar patterns, as explored below.

Though academic engagement with codes is still relatively sparse in the context of translation specifically – the standout contribution remains McDonough Dolmaya's (2011a) study of 17 translation codes of ethics – there have been a number of surveys of codes in interpreting that can serve as a basis for exploring the guidance offered in these documents. As noted above, despite the differences between these practices, the core code values are consistent across practice types, and this increased attention in Interpreting Studies makes it a more fertile ground to orient our discussions here. Schweda-Nicholson (1994), Bancroft (2005), Hale (2007), Mikkelson (2000/1), and Phelan et al. (2020) have all provided useful surveys of ethical codes in interpreting studies. This includes multiple types of interpreting (conference interpreting, public service interpreting, court interpreting, etc.), with interpreting studies scholars often commenting on ethics within their specific branch of interest, for example, Donovan (2011) or Martin Ruano (2015).

In her influential early study of codes of ethics for interpreters, Bancroft (2005) found five (near-)universal ethical principles – **competence, integrity, confidentiality, neutrality, and fidelity** – while Schweda-Nicholson (1994: 82) listed seven key points covered in codes (integrity was removed, neutrality became **impartiality**, fidelity became **completeness and accuracy**, and **continuing professional development, role boundaries, and conflicts of interest** were added). Skaaden (2013) later highlighted neutrality and fidelity in particular as guidelines that specifically differentiate interpreting from other activities. Indeed, all professions aim to guard against conflicts of interest and seek to protect confidentiality, though these areas do of course apply to translation and interpreting in specific ways. General or not, it can certainly be argued that some of the principles are more straightforward than others – questions of impartiality and accuracy, as we have seen in the preceding chapters, are incredibly complex and contested areas of consideration. This can cause guidance on different topics to vary wildly, from one sentence to entire pages.

Phelan (2020: 93–98), meanwhile, studied twenty codes of ethics from international, regional, and national associations available in English, with Schweda-Nicholson's seven principles in mind and, while her findings echoed prior studies in the area to a degree, her data also quantifies the amount of variation in coverage of each key topic. Confidentiality is the only ever-present principle, arguably marking it out as one of the most necessary and/or perhaps least controversial guidelines in the codes. The other areas were ranked as follows: impartiality (17/20), competence (14/20), completeness/accuracy (14/20), continuing professional development, or CPD (13/20), conflicts of interest (11/20), and questions relating to roles (7/20). Phelan also goes on to consider other prominent areas in the codes beyond these "traditional" values and finds that advertising (8/20), credentials (7/20) and remuneration (9/20) are among the most common inclusions in this regard. Finally, she draws our attention to a range of principles that have emerged to a lesser extent, often in response to instances of bad practice. These include "issues such as payment of taxes, illegal activities, bribery and corruption, and criminal records" (Phelan et al. 2020: 122) and point to some willingness on the part of associations to update their codes as the need arises. However, this is far from being a concerted effort to modernise codes in line with professional struggles, as explored further below. As a demonstration of the similarities between translation and interpreting, McDonough Dolmaya (2011a: 30) stated that the seventeen translation-specific codes she analysed agree on very few ethical and professional practices and that

> only two principles are stipulated by all seventeen codes: confidentiality and competence. Other principles for impartiality, accuracy, conflict resolution, professional development, advertising, translator rights and working conditions are addressed by only some of the codes and their guidelines are occasionally in conflict.

This variation in the topics included points to a lack of common understanding of what exactly ethics requires in a professional sense and undermines the overall hope of setting consistent standards of behaviour for professionals across geographical borders and practice types. On this note, McDonough Dolmaya concludes by asking "[s]o what, then, makes a translator ethical?" If we assume that each translation network considers their principles to be the cornerstones of ethical practice, then "this means that whether a translator is acting ethically when practicing the profession depends on what network he or she belongs to, as no general consensus about ethical translation behaviour seems to exist" (2011a: 49).

Lambert (2023), meanwhile, attempts to shed light on the development of translation codes of ethics since the publication of McDonough Dolmaya's study and uses an adapted version of the principles outlined by Schweda-Nicholson. He found once again that competence and confidentiality were ever-present, while accuracy (14/20), conflicts of interest (13/20), CPD (13/20), and impartiality (13/20) all featured to a relatively significant extent. Combining this array of studies leaves us with a list of eight common ethical principles in translation and interpreting, as follows (in alphabetical order):

1. Accuracy (fidelity and completeness)
2. Competence (and skills required)
3. Confidentiality
4. Conflicts of interest
5. Continuing Professional Development (CPD)
6. Impartiality/neutrality
7. Integrity and professionalism
8. Role boundaries

It is worth noting that these principles have remained largely static across time and space. Many prominent association codes have remained in force unchanged for years and even decades, while this persistence extends to different countries, languages, and practices. Below, we explore each of these core areas of focus in detail, before considering critiques of these documents in the next section. Beneath the heading for each principle, I have included the relevant Australian Institute of Interpreters and Translators (AUSIT) code of ethics definition (2012) to present a real-life example of guidance. This code was selected as it covers every one of the areas outlined above and is a prominent and representative code.

Accuracy (fidelity and completeness)

"*Interpreters and translators use their best professional judgement in remaining faithful at all times to the meaning of texts and messages.*"

This broad guideline enshrines a commitment to translating meaning in an accurate or faithful manner. As we have seen in previous chapters, this is not only a core issue in terms of ethics but. in TIS more widely, with a plethora of sources examining questions of fidelity and equivalence. As we have seen, this is a complex area, and guidelines such as these that demand fidelity to meaning and intent of the original message, are one of the more problematic guidelines. The apparent simplicity of the request fails to acknowledge the complexity contained within the statement. Indeed, the question of how we go about transferring a message from one language to another in the most faithful, accurate, and impartial way possible is far from self-explanatory.

Competence (and skills required)

"*Interpreters and translators only undertake work they are competent to perform in the languages for which they are professionally qualified through training and credentials.*"

Competence means a commitment to reflecting expertise and qualifications honestly, and/or working to "appropriate" (usually high, or the highest!) standards. Associations will sometimes underscore this principle with reference to training and qualifications and, when applicable, these are often courses and accreditations offered by the association themselves, offering something of a "seal of approval" in relation to the standard of work that the translator or interpreter can offer.

Confidentiality

"Interpreters and translators maintain confidentiality and do not disclose information acquired in the course of their work."

This commitment is recognised as one of the central principles, not just in translation and interpreting, but in the professional world more widely, representing an oath to not divulge sensitive information. Despite its key status, however, it is also a principle that can be broken when legal constraints or "a higher moral imperative" (Setton and Prunč 2015: 146 in Pöchhacker) require it, for instance, an obligation to report criminal activity, or a duty to save lives. Setton and Prunč (ibid.) contend that the "emphasis placed on confidentiality in many codes reflects its vulnerability to pressure – for example, from the media, but also potentially from the interpreter's employers."

Conflicts of interest

"Interpreters and translators frankly disclose all conflicts of interest, e.g. in assignments for relatives or friends and those affecting their employers."

This guideline represents a commitment to disclose any occasions when your judgement or actions at work could be affected by a factor unconnected to your role. We have seen examples of this kind of case in previous chapters, for instance Box 6.2, which reflects on a conflict between the translator's personal beliefs and those shared in a text. However, conflicts of interest extend further than ideological disagreements, and can include personal relationships, financial interests, or past, present, or future affiliations with interested parties.

Continuing Professional Development (CPD)

"Interpreters and translators continue to develop their professional knowledge and skills."

Principles related to CPD are generally quite simple and self-explanatory, as well as perhaps being the least controversial of the guidelines. These require a commitment from interpreters and translators to continue to work on enhancing relevant skills, for instance language skills, domain-specific expertise, business and marketing skills. Given the fast pace-of-change in the professional world and the very real prospect of skill (and language) attrition, this commitment to development is entirely logical. Training often takes place through professional memberships, with associations offering a range of CPD activities and formal certifications (as with the training mentioned under 'Competence' above, this ironically brings to light something of a conflict of interest on the part of the associations, requiring members to sign up and often pay for the courses that they themselves run (Lambert and Walker 2022: 14).

Impartiality/neutrality

"*Interpreters and translators observe impartiality in all professional contacts. Interpreters remain unbiased throughout the communication exchanged between the participants in any interpreted encounter. Translators do not show bias towards either the author of the source text or the intended readers of their translation.*"

There is a close link between impartiality and accuracy, with impartiality acting as "a means to the end of ensuring accurate renditions" (Baixauli-Olmos 2020: 306). As the guideline above implies, a biased (partial) translator would lean towards either the source side or the target audience. However, as we have seen in previous chapters, the issue of partiality is complex and contested, with many scholars questioning the very possibility of impartiality. Nevertheless, impartiality is nearly universally present, and most codes will present it in a relatively straightforward manner, often – as is the case in the above guideline – simply requiring a commitment from the translator and interpreter to be impartial or neutral.

Integrity and professionalism

"*Interpreters and translators respect and support their fellow professionals, and they uphold the reputation and trustworthiness of the profession of interpreting and translating.*"

This is something of a nebulous construct that can cover a huge swathe of different areas. It undoubtedly covers values (virtues perhaps?) such as honesty, keeping your promises, cooperation with colleagues, and a commitment to maintaining the dignity of the profession. It could also relate to generally maintaining high standards in your work – for instance, by making sure that you have enough time to complete any work to the required standard – or even cover elements such as appearance and dress codes, something that is much more common in the context of interpreting than freelance translation! Yet integrity itself can also be understood as having strong moral undertones, making our understanding somewhat circular. The AUSIT code actually places integrity under the heading of "professional solidarity", and this powerful idea of respecting and supporting fellow professionals echoes Pym's ethics in concretising our responsibility, not to texts or authors and so forth, but rather to our fellow professionals and our profession as a whole.

? How might we show solidarity with our fellow professionals?
? What would be likely to undermine the reputation of the profession?

Role boundaries

"Interpreters and translators maintain clear boundaries between their task as facilitators of communication through message transfer and any tasks that may be undertaken by other parties involved in the assignment."

An important element within the move to personal ethics and advocacy in Chapter 6 was the question of role boundaries for translators and interpreters and these debates again emerge in the professional context. Role boundaries require us to confine ourselves to the specific tasks of a translator or interpreter, and this is often articulated by asking that we refrain from personal involvement in cases (echoing the personal-professional divide covered elsewhere, and guidelines relating to conflicts of interest) or providing counsel, advice, or personal opinions.

The benefits in many cases are clear, as this guideline allows an interpreter or translator a framework to remove themselves from potentially problematic situations. If asked 'what would you do/say?', for instance, an interpreter can cite the code of ethics' role guidance to sidestep a need to respond. Another example here could be in legal translation where good practice dictates that legal translators do not attempt to disambiguate (potentially purposefully) ambiguous language. It may have been written that way for a reason by the lawyer, so the ambiguity needs to be retained. Similarly, it is not their job to explain specialist terminology or to explain specific meaning from case law or similar. In short: legal translators are not lawyers.

These guidelines offer an image of the detached, focused professional, something that has been problematised in previous chapters. Indeed, problems emerge in relation to questions of advocacy, which blurs the lines of our role. Where exactly does our involvement start and finish? As covered in Chapter 6, associations such as the National Council on Interpreting in Health Care (NCIHC) have introduced advocacy as part of the role in certain limited situations, and Phelan (2020: 111) considers it to be one of the most controversial issues in interpreting codes, offering a detailed examination of its emergence as an important principle.

Hopefully, it is clear from this range of ethical principles that there is significant crossover between the topics addressed in the profession and the academic debates that we have explored in previous chapters. However, it should also be clear that codes approach many of these principles from a different perspective to that of TIS scholars, and that there is nowhere near the same level of depth available in this professional context. The far-reaching, categorical nature of many of the rulings result in rather imperfect documents and in the next section I explore several criticisms commonly faced by codes of ethics.

The Effectiveness of Codes

Despite codes being well established across different languages, countries, and practices, nowhere can we find a deep sense of satisfaction in their composition. Surveying practising interpreters for their views on codes of ethics, Hale (2007: 101–102) reported viewpoints ranging from blind adherence to the codes ("I set it as the bible of my daily life practice"), to entirely negative viewpoints ("The code of ethics is a mess and quite ridiculous") and noted widespread indifference to codes, which are seen as overly general or simplistic, despite support in principle for the documents. Translation associations, meanwhile, are often reticent to take on the (rather daunting) task of updating and modifying the codes, while scholars have regularly drawn attention to an array of limitations. In this scholarly context, a number of now-familiar voices re-emerge. Chesterman, for instance, reiterates that "many national (and international) codes of ethics are in need of revision" (2019: 672) and points towards a range of "loose ends" that still exist in the area, including when a translator can or should intervene, their divided loyalties, and the expanding range of stakeholders involved in the translation process. As such, in this section, we explore some potential shortcomings in these documents - including **problems with coverage, enforcement, internal conflicts, specificity, and the nature and content of the guidelines** – from the perspective of both translation and interpreting (as with the codes and guidelines themselves, there is a lot of shared ground in the critiques).

Internal conflicts

In her influential critique of translation codes, McDonough Dolmaya points to conflicts between a range of guidelines as a key shortcoming. For instance, the National Association of Judiciary Interpreters and Translators (NAJIT) code simultaneously requires that "[s]ource-language speech should be faithfully rendered into the target language by conserving all the elements of the original message while accommodating the syntactic and semantic patterns of the target language", that "[t]he rendition should sound natural in the target language", that "[a]ll hedges, false starts and repetitions should be conveyed", and that "[t]he register, style and tone of the source language should be conserved." This is a daunting if not impossible task and, as alluded to above, it is the guidelines relating to accuracy that often conflict the most. As we saw in Chapters 2 and 3, the nature of equivalence and fidelity makes this a topic that is rather unsuitable to simple, universal deontological guidelines. The AUSIT code, meanwhile (which generally offers an excellent example of good practice in the area), asks that "[i]nterpreters and translators do not alter, add to, or omit anything from the content and intent of the source message." The irreducible differences between languages surely ensure that it is impossible to simply replicate the form of the original, and anyone who has worked on a translation or interpreting project will know that alterations, additions, and omissions are commonplace in many domains of professional practice. How can we reconcile this guideline with subtitling practice, for instance, where space and time constraints necessitate the widespread use of omissions and ultra-concise paraphrasing?

Elsewhere, Donovan (2011: 112) draws further attention to how calls for accuracy and impartiality are embedded in confused and contradictory rulings. As she notes, "the Australian Association, AUSIT, states in its code under Article 5(iii) that 'interpreters shall convey the whole message'", while also entitling interpreters to take "reasonable steps to ensure effective communication" where necessary and demanding "complete fidelity while allowing interpreter intervention to guarantee understanding." This ultimately leaves us with a rather paradoxical relationship between guidelines, with codes juxtaposing "the strictest rules on impartiality and objectivity together with demands for an interpreter-improved communication" (Diriker 2004: 34).[1]

Enforcement

This incompatibility with actual professional practice in relation to accuracy and impartiality (and more generally) also alerts us to the issue of enforcement. Though, as noted above, associations explicitly require members to adhere to codes, instances of enforcement of these guidelines are rare and, in the case of accuracy, these documents would become entirely untenable if they were (Returning to the example above, do we automatically label all subtitlers as unethical because they are unable to conserve all elements of meaning?). If nothing else, these problems remind us how the stringency of ethics can lead to its rejection; as Blackburn explains, "[t]he centre of ethics must be occupied by things we can reasonably demand of each other" (2003: 43).

While many of these codes are drawn up by translation associations – bodies that are designed to assist and organise groups of professionals, often in specific geographical locations or fields – association membership is not obligatory for practising professionals, clouding the effective implementation of the codes. Furthermore, though the codes are presented as binding (often with a line to the effect of "members agree to ..."; see Box 7.1 for an example), there are considerable doubts as to how realistic it is that translators and interpreters can follow all of the prescribed guidelines and even whether they should follow them. As Phelan puts it, codes are all too often an "attempt at self-regulation in an unregulated environment" (2020: 88). Finally, associations do not necessarily have the power to uphold the principles stated.

Beyond undermining the credibility of the codes, from a more cynical point of view it also points to a different purpose. As Lambert (2018) argues, this image of accurate and impartial meaning transfer is not designed to accurately represent the way that translators and interpreters work, but rather offers a marketable image to clients, which indirectly help LSPs and associations to sell translations and memberships by fostering a "sense of trust and confidence around a skewed image of the translation process and a fictional construction of the translator as a neutral conduit" (Lambert 2018: 269). It is much more appealing to tell a client that their text/message will be replicated in another language without additions, omissions, or distortions, than to explain that translation is a fundamentally personal and subjective activity. Of course, this image can benefit translators, too. For Donovan, translators and interpreters themselves are willing to emphasise professional neutrality and confidentiality as pillars of their professional practice, as this stance "protects them from awkward and even threatening criticism and deflects potential pressure from powerful clients", while also enabling them to retain authority over their output (Donovan 2011: 112–113).

Coverage

While, as seen above, there is a core set of generally accepted principles, gaps undoubtedly remain, and this is complicated further by the dynamic nature of ethics and the fast pace of development in the profession. In this regard, McDonough Dolmaya noted that "codes often do not address many of the issues translators are encountering as part of their practice" (2011a: 45), and this is a criticism that has somewhat divided scholars. Drugan and Megone (2011: 187–188) rightly note that the heavily context-dependent nature of translation and interpreting means that codes are unable to refer to the infinite range of potential situations facing practitioners. Indeed, "a code of ethics is not designed to provide an answer to every specific problem" (Mikkelson 2016: 84, in Baixauli-Olmos 2021: 309). However, there are a number of areas that are deemed to be of crucial importance to practising translators and interpreters that are not covered in codes, including rates of pay and technology (both are covered in more detail in Chapter 8). These areas in particular have been flagged as pressing ethical concerns by translators in industry and professional surveys. For instance, in the ITI's Spring 2020 Pulse Survey (ITI 2020), 42 percent of respondents selected "rates/conditions asked to accept" when asked which ethical issues they had faced in the previous three years. However, as Lambert (2023) shows, half of codes include no mention of rates, and when they do it is generally with loose reference to the principle of fairness (in various guises). For instance, guideline seven in Box 7.1 above provides a good example of this phenomenon. McDonough Dolmaya similarly notes that "slightly more than half the codes include a clause about the rates professional translators should accept for their work" while three "stipulate that members must not agree to work for rates significantly below those set by the association" (McDonough Dolmaya 2011a 31–32). In terms of technology, meanwhile, no codes currently approach the area in an engaged manner (if at all!), and further technological advances "will undoubtedly give rise to additional gaps in these codes of ethics" (Bowker 2021: 269). Ultimately, though codes cannot cover everything, there is a balance to achieve, and covering topics that are of interest to practitioners is a powerful means of bridging the theory-practice gap (Asiri 2016; Baixauli-Olmos 2021: 309; Ozolins 2014).

Problems of interpretation and application

A further issue is that, even when codes do include a guideline highlighting a specific issue, it is not always straightforward to interpret the principle and work out exactly how to act. As Drugan and Megone (2011: 187) put it, "difficulties in understanding arise because ... codes do not interpret themselves, they require intelligent deployment." Ko echoes this conclusion in noting that while the codes are "useful", they "can only serve as guidelines for translators and interpreters" as "[t]here are situations in the real world which may be contrary to, unrelated to, or not included in these general guidelines" (Ko 2015: 349). In attempting to pinpoint the cause of such flaws, Abdallah suggests that translators are caught between two different ethical systems: the "utilitarian business ethics" that requires the translator to forge a trusting relationship with the client and to work quickly in order to get paid and make a profit, and the "translators' deontological ethics as outlined in the various codes of conduct provided by professional associations" (Abdallah 2014: 131). Abdallah summarily concludes that "translators' professional ethics cannot be guided by theoretical, universal statements that are presented haphazardly across the curriculum and focused only on deontological issues. Instead, ethical issues need to be situated, and their complex and collective nature must be revealed" (ibid. 132). Ultimately, with a number of codes relying upon vague guidelines that are left without adequate explanation, practitioners are forced to draw their own interpretations of what the code requires of them and act accordingly. This leads to translators taking divergent courses of action despite following the same codes. As Martin Ruano puts it, "seemingly sacrosanct notions such as fidelity, when invoked as guidelines in difficult situations, do not provide specific solutions" (Martin Ruano 2015: 142). Even in the case of a universally acknowledged principle such as confidentiality, legal obligations conspire to undermine any simple application. If, for instance, a translator is given access to information that could negatively affect the lives of many unaware, innocent parties, is it intrinsically good for them to continue to withhold this information?

> **Box 7.2 A case study: Confidentiality**
>
> Imagine that you have been hired as an interpreter by a defendant in a criminal case. The defendant has been accused of murder and, when speaking in a private consultation with their lawyer, the defendant says that they committed the crime.
>
> ? What is the recommended course of action for the interpreter in this situation?
> ? Should you reveal this information to the lawyer?
> ? Should you tell the police? Why?
> ? Would your course of action differ if you were hired by the legal firm itself or by a local authority?
>
> Of course, the principle at stake here is confidentiality. Returning to Box 7.1, the ATA code requires that we to "hold in confidence any privileged and/or confidential information entrusted to us in the course of our work", would you abide by the code of ethics, or would a personal/legal drive supersede it? Whose interests are you representing? Confidentiality in this case can conflict with public interest.
>
> There is of course a risk of harm if you do not share that information, as somebody else may be convicted of the murder. As mentioned above, there are very limited exceptions that can enable you to breach confidentiality, for example, to protect a life by disclosing information about homicidal or suicidal intent, but does that apply here? If your partiality is compromised, should you withdraw from the assignment? In this case, it is doubtful that your evidence would be valid in the eyes of the law and there is no guarantee the person really did it. Somebody may have paid them to confess, for instance.
>
> Though perhaps a rather extreme example, hopefully this shows that even seemingly straightforward guidelines (e.g. maintain confidentiality) are not always easy to interpret in a real-life context.

Content

For many authors, a key area of discussion when assessing the codes' content more closely is the focus on accuracy, fidelity, and neutrality. In ethical terms, these calls for accuracy and neutrality at best fail to account for all of translation, and at worst misrepresent the translation task and call for something that is impossible for translators to achieve. As Chesterman puts it (2021: 16), principles relating to fidelity "are highly relevant to much of professional translation, but less relevant to situations where a translator sets out to break norms, to intervene in the text, to edit or even censor the text or radically change its meaning."

Just like accuracy, neutrality "embodies a seemingly 'monolithic, non-negotiable' concept" (Rycroft 2011: 220), which hints at the importance of ensuring that these codes receive treatment that suitably encapsulates the complexity and gravity of these topics. As Martin Ruano notes "[c]laims for strict compliance with neutrality are often put forward as a guarantee for the professionalisation of translation and interpreting in the legal field." However, the propagation of this conflictual notion risks blinding translators to the consequences of their actions, and she argues that, if neutrality is internalised by an inexperienced translator, they could well end up undermining the professional image that they strive to present. As she explains: "[t]ranslators accurately reproducing the substandard wording of many texts, which have to be translated daily in international organisations or court interpreters mimicking the incoherent and disjointed discourse of uneducated speakers could well appear as incompetent rather than neutral" (Martin Ruano 2015: 149).

Returning to ideas from a key figure discussed in Chapter 5, Inghilleri carried out a sustained and powerful critique of the documents in *Interpreting Justice*. As you would imagine from her wider arguments explored in Chapter 5, she fundamentally disagrees with the image of the interpreter the codes put forward. She contends that the central position of principles of neutrality and impartiality abdicate interpreters from the personal and social responsibility in their role, which she conceives of as being "active, key players in interpreted communication, facilitating open negotiations over meaning and maximizing the possibility that the communicative objectives of all participants are met" (2012: 51). Elsewhere, she challenges the separation between role-specific morality and legal morality, contending that role occupants should have space to "reflect upon or challenge the rules and principles of their professional code and to enter into open and transparent dialogue in situations where gaps are perceived between the norms and interests of the profession and those attached to specific individuals, communities, or the wider society" (2012: 56) and permitting this space allows occupants to extend and redefine the morality of the role itself, particularly in relation to questions of justice.

Ultimately, these codes all reiterate the image of the neutral, conduit translator or interpreter and simultaneously conceal the fact that interpreting and translation involve a reworking of texts (or indirectly enable interpreters to rework the texts). While some scholarly thought has called for codes to move beyond this image (see, for instance, Lambert 2018, who calls for overturning the regularly-used image of translation as an unproblematic transfer of meaning), there has been very little progress made, particularly in translation. In interpreting, however, there are some signs of a move towards embedding advocacy more widely. Phelan, for instance, devotes considerable attention to the development of the notion of advocacy in interpreting codes, noting the conflict between guidelines requiring strict impartiality and calls for interpreters to advocate on the part of a certain party. However, she notes that advocacy remains a restricted and relatively uncommon principle, with most codes still calling upon impartiality. While some outliers do now allow for advocacy in restricted circumstances, others still prohibit it entirely (Phelan et al. 2020: 122). She astutely notes that there is no great call from interpreters for increased agency in codes as they already know that they have this agency in this role regardless of the codes' stipulations – again reinforcing the unenforceable, unrealistic nature of the guidelines.

> **Box 7.3 A case study: Neutrality**
>
> In what is a revealing example of how an interpreter's supposedly neutral positioning can easily slip, Matthew Maltby analysed Asylum Aid's (AA) code of ethics and uncovered inconsistency and contradiction in how neutrality is presented.
>
> Within this code, interpreters are simultaneously expected to give the impression of favouring neither interlocutor, while also making decisions on the clients' behalf when linguistic problems arise, for example, deciding when the client requires interpreting if they have some competence in English. AA advisors can also take an additional interpreter along with them to official hearings to assess (or even question) the performance of the official court interpreter.
>
> In this instance, the interpreter's role is certainly not neutral, for they are clearly working for one side. This is something that Maltby alludes to in stating that the interpreter is not only a quality-control element, ensuring that a message is transferred in a suitable manner, but rather interprets "for us", that is, for AA. As Maltby puts it, interpreters are permitted to have an "active, advocacy role as an additional advisor in client consultations", challenging or clarifying any information. However, this role is kept to being off-the-record, maintaining the illusion of neutrality – introducing "a double-faced conceptualization of the interpreter" (Maltby 2010: 229). In this instance, institutions present the interpreter to clients as a transparent conduit while simultaneously calling upon the interpreter's partiality when it is convenient for them, and the organisations also enlist interpreters who are ideologically predisposed to helping their cause, explicitly endorsing active intervention that can be of benefit to them.
>
> ? What is your take on these guidelines and on this practice?

Conclusion and Moving Forwards

Codes of ethics remain a cornerstone of consolidating professional activity and are "a means of progressing towards the professionalisation of a low-status activity" (Martin Ruano 2015: 142). Clearly, however, despite Inghilleri and Maier's belief that "there is no current consensus on the nature and status of professional codes of ethics" (Baker 2011: 102), the limitations explored above suggest that more work is required to provide codes that are fully relevant to the day-to-day work of interpreting and translation. Problems of inconsistency alone are enough to provide serious obstacles to potential progress and, in the context of deontology, the variable assignment of value and the stringency of the rulings represent significant shortcomings. In terms of realistic enforcement, Phelan aptly notes that these documents are "toothless" in many contexts – members *can* be suspended or expelled but associations generally cannot impose wider sanctions (Phelan et al. 2020: 122).

Ultimately, as a result of these limitations, translators and interpreters unfortunately do not or cannot always adhere to codes in their practice. Though a possibility, this is not necessarily due to a lack of willingness from the practitioner. Several authors have assessed codes and labelled them as inadequate or contradictory, but suggestions for changes have not been made in terms of the codes themselves. Instead, what ensues from many of these discussions of codes is a turn to pedagogy within translation and interpreting. Indeed, several authors suggest that students must be made aware of the contradictions and shortcomings within codes of ethics before outlining methods of putting this into practice. For Donovan, this turn to pedagogy is rooted in the belief that "[i]f codes are to be internalized and integrated into practice, they need to be anchored in training" (Donovan 2011: 123). Ko (2006: 48), meanwhile, suggests that translators need to be taught to assess each situation in order to act ethically, a line of thinking that is unsurprisingly echoed by Baker, who comments on the risk of codes turning "translators into unthinking cogs in the wheel of an established social system rather than reflective and ethically responsible citizens" (Baker 2011: 284). One way that is suggested in this regard is the implementation of teaching practices that employ real-life examples, case studies, and role plays (see Introduction) – a suggestion echoed by several authors, including Drugan and Megone, whose 2011 paper is specifically geared towards outlining why and *how* we should teach ethics in translation studies courses.

Education is undoubtedly a key concern and training emerging translators and interpreters to develop a critical awareness of their role and the current state of the industry will benefit the long-term health of the professions. However, in an area that has historically struggled for professional status due to a largely unregulated nature (see Chapter 8), many translators and interpreters simply do not receive formal training. So, despite authors reporting success within the classroom setting, this will not filter through to all professionals. One way of potentially avoiding this pitfall is to return to the codes themselves. Tate and Turner (1997/2002) found that sign language interpreters in the UK often override the literal prescriptions of their code of practice, using their own judgment and 'intervening' in different ways (e.g. to clarify or correct misunderstandings). They instead proposed an "evolving 'case law' annex that would codify good new solutions [...] to dilemmas not adequately covered by the Code" (Setton and Prunč 2015: 147 in Pöchhacker). Lambert (2023), meanwhile, calls for a potential "post-code" approach, which envisages making wholesale changes to the way in which ethical guidance is offered to translators and interpreters, drawing inspiration from "outliers" in a contemporary corpus of codes that suggest the potential for accessible, client-facing, or scholarly based documents that deviate from the "traditional" approach of listing a handful of static values on an association webpage. At the very least, he calls for codes that do indeed tackle the issues that translators and interpreters care about. Unfortunately, however, the static nature of the codes suggests that implementing any sweeping changes will be a tough, time-consuming process.

Returning to a key criticism of codes of ethics from Inghilleri, she concludes that

> if notions like impartiality and neutrality are to persist as guiding principles for the role morality of interpreters ... they need not imply the neglect of personal and social responsibility toward others where questions of justice and fairness are concerned.
>
> (2012: 70)

While codes have not shifted towards this basis in personal or social responsibility, conversations around ethics in the translation profession certainly have, and this is a key focus in Chapter 8, where we examine emerging concerns that are not covered in codes of ethics, as well as extending our inward, personal focus to consider a final range of ideas relating to the individual "ethical" professional.

Discussion, Presentation, and Assignment Topics

1. Group presentation. Imagine you are the head of a new translation and/or interpreting association looking to develop a code of ethics. Drawing upon the discussions above, outline your approach to drafting this document.
2. To what extent do you think that it is realistic and/or desirable for translators and interpreters to follow all of the guidelines contained within a typical code of ethics?
3. Read Chesterman's "Hieronymic Oath" (mentioned in Chapter 2) and compare and contrast the topics and content covered with the codes outlined here (or a code in a specific field/country that you work in).

Note

1 Diriker and Donovan specifically refer to interpreting, but the same problem exists within translation.

Further Reading

In relation to translation specifically, **McDonough Dolmaya (2011a)** analyses, line by line, seventeen codes of ethics published by profession-oriented translation networks in order to determine what values are most commonly held by translators belonging to such networks. She also analyses forum entries on ethics and professionalism in order to uncover what issues were being discussed by translation professionals relating to their day-to-day practice. **Lambert (2023)** offers an updated snapshot of the state of codes of ethics in translation as well as asks how we can potentially improve codes of ethics, a topic that is also covered by **Lee and Yun (2020)**, who reflect on the potential of Chesterman's *telos* in this context, illustrating the potential for theoretical conceptions of ethics to inform more practical discussions.

For interpreting, **Hale (2007, Chapter 4)** analyses sixteen codes of ethics for interpreting from nine countries and draws up the range of principles covered, while **Phelan et al. (2020, Chapter 2)** offers an in-depth guide to codes of ethics in force in the context of public service interpreting. Her coverage includes a study of twenty current codes to capture common (and less common) principles covered, criticisms of codes in this specific context, and an illuminating section on advocacy, which she labels as "probably the most controversial issue" in public service interpreting (2020: 111). Particularly useful is the collection of case studies that demonstrate each of the codes' key principles in practice (ibid. 122–137). This is a rich source for classroom discussions and even assessment topics.

8 Ethical Professionals

> Key questions
> - What is a professional translator or interpreter?
> - What are the key issues facing professionals on both an individual and a global level?
> - How do considerations of elements such as rates of pay and technological advances affect our understandings of ethics in the profession?

Following on from Chapter 7's critique of codes of ethics, this chapter extends our direct enquiry into matters affecting professional translators and interpreters. It explains and acknowledges the constraining factors at work in the profession and examines a range of ethical questions and challenges facing professionals, looking both outwards to the wider world and inwards to consider very personal interests and impacts. Indeed, while Abdallah (2011: 131) suggests that translators are caught between two different ethical systems – "utilitarian business ethics" that requires the translator to forge a trusting relationship with the client and to work quickly in order to get paid and to make a profit, and the "translators' deontological ethics" as outlined in codes – we could add two further sides to this, each with its own complex areas of concern: wider social responsibility is one, our own personal needs is another. This includes discussions of industry workflows, rates of pay, the link between ethics and technology, and personal concerns over wellbeing, which is indicative of the incredibly broad nature of thought on ethics. As we saw in the previous chapter, two of the greatest sources of anxiety for professionals – technology and money – are not covered in codes in detail, necessitating this further exploration.

Professions and Professionals

Though Chapter 4 introduced various stakeholders involved in translation and interpreting project workflows within the context of consequentialist

DOI: 10.4324/9781003148265-9

and contractarian theories of ethics, an extended focus on this area in the professional context is necessitated by what has been described as the "Great Divide" (Jemielity 2018: 543) between theory and practice in translation and interpreting, where academic sources are not always considered to align with the practical demands of the profession. In the twenty-first century, an earlier general marginalisation of the professional domain has been "emphatically overturned" (Lambert 2021: 167), but ethics has been rather slow to follow suit. Consider, for instance, Ben van Wyke's entry on 'Translation and Ethics' in the *Routledge Handbook of Translation Studies* (2013). Here, we find no mention of professional translators or interpreters, which is indicative of 'traditional' areas of focus in TIS, where the "non-literary" domain was for a long time viewed apart from, or even in opposition to literary translation (Rogers 2015). However, that is not to say that the theoretical ideas in previous chapters are not relevant in a practical context, far from it. Indeed, many of them can provide real help with ethical decision-making in a practical context. Pym's ideas, for example, are a prime example of this, yet it is worth noting that he too considers many of his ideas as anathematic to received wisdom in TIS, placing him perhaps more on the 'practice' side of the divide. Elsewhere, not all are perfectly suited to the professional context. For instance, many translators and interpreters simply want to do a 'good' job and earn a decent living, something that sits in contrast to activist aims, to an extent. Importantly, professionals – and students – are often not exposed to, or cannot gain access to, many of these ideas (hence the vital importance of codes, in spite of the shortcomings we have explored, and the accessible nature of this book!). We begin by asking what exactly a professional is, and what it is that they do.

There is a complex and somewhat contested relationship between translation, interpreting, and professional status. Defining the professional translator is a challenging and yet important task, which risks detours into issues of status, context, and definitions of professionalism itself. Does a professional simply make a living through their work? Or is it a certain number of years' experience, qualifications, status, or membership to a particular institution or community that qualifies a translator as a professional? Perhaps even their adhesion to a code of ethics? While Schaffner (2020: 64) understands professional translation "as a paid occupation which requires a formal qualification", this definition precludes a large number of translators who work as professionals without formal qualifications. Indeed, as Lambert puts it (2021: 166):

> For the most part, anyone can call themselves a professional translator. That said, some translation agencies do require that their translators have certain qualifications or levels of experience, and academic and professional qualifications (for instances MAs and BAs or certification provided by professional associations), professional memberships, and demonstrable working experience do serve as guarantees to

potential clients more generally and thus indirectly correlate to perceived professionalism.

These are "traditional signals of professional status" (Pym et al. 2016: 34), but the professional translator works in a wide range of settings, has wide-ranging statuses, works on a wide range of materials, in a wide range of subject domains, and uses a wide range of tools in their practice. As such, a working definition of a professional can simply be translators or interpreters getting paid for translation, and this is enough to introduce a range of concerns in this chapter, as we consider the professional's place within their wider network. Indeed, how exactly do these professionals work?

In a professional context, we may work with a single end client directly – the person who requires translation or interpreting services – and we may come into contact with the end users of our translations (or, more likely, our interpreting work). However, this process is often facilitated by an LSP and a project manager or management team within that LSP, and there may be entire teams of editors, reviewers, and proofreaders checking our work. Moorkens and Rocchi (2021: 324) add LSP owners, language software developers, and other employees in LSPs to the list of people we may work with/for and, at the largest level, we also have a wider responsibility to society to consider (see below). As is hopefully abundantly clear by now, as language industry professionals (and human beings) we are always embedded within institutional, social, and political contexts that force us to balance a diverse range of (sometimes competing) duties, responsibilities, interests, and aims. Our considerations extend beyond texts and authors. It is also worth remembering that not all of these parties have our interests at heart. LSPs have their own interests and aims, for instance, and there are not equal levels of power and information available to each party (consider, for instance, Pym's stance on the need for trust – see Chapter 4 – that emerges from an asymmetry of information). Unfortunately, translators and interpreters also have relatively little say in the development of processes employed in translation projects and overall working conditions; see Moorkens and Rocchi (2021) for a more in-depth exploration of ethical issues in the translation industry, an account of the processes involved, and the complex power dynamics at work.

By definition, the focus here on professionals cuts off the sizeable domain of non-professional translation and interpreting. While this area is often negatively associated with amateur or novice practitioners, this unfairly reduces the scope of the field. Definitions are contested and areas such as crowdsourced translations – where translations are the product of multiple translators, often sourced for free – do indeed tend to be completed by inexperienced or untrained practitioners.[1] However, there is also significant overlap, or perhaps even a need to swap labels, between non-professional and **volunteer** translation or interpreting, which has as its defining feature an absence of payment and would be preferable as a term that places "the person, not the action" (Pym 2011: 108) as the centre of enquiry. This wider understanding of the non-professional domain has led to "increasingly less judgemental" attitudes, and serious consideration of the activity's status and social/political functions (Basalamah 2021: 228–229). Importantly, Basalamah (2021: 230) is at pains to point out "the changing status and role of professionals versus non-professionals, amateurs and volunteers in the last few decades", with volunteers being increasingly active and valued due to their engagement with ever more prevalent humanitarian disasters and digital initiatives, which have allowed non-professionals to gain "a foothold in their respective fields in such a way that they have demonstrated their indispensability" (ibid.).

Unfortunately, an in-depth exploration of these themes falls beyond the scope of this introductory textbook. For an initial exploration of volunteer translation and interpreting, see Basalamah (2021), and for a more in-depth focus on the challenges facing NGOs in crisis situations in relation to new technologies and practices such as crowdsourcing, see the volume *Translation in Cascading Crises* edited by Federici and O'Brien (2019). However, while non-professional translation is not at the heart of our explorations, this question of motivation (why are we translating?) and the link to wider societal and political events leads us neatly to a focus on social responsibility in the translation profession. In the following sections, we consider our relationship with this range of industry stakeholders by first looking outwards to consider our relationship with society and other players in the industry and then turning inwards to consider the importance of looking after ourselves.

? What do you consider to be the defining feature of "professional" translation and/or interpreting?
? What unites professionalism and ethics? For instance, are the workflows adopted in the industry and the degree of agency that professionals have in developing or negotiating these workflows an ethical issue?

Looking Outwards: Social Responsibility

In the last decade or so, the question of social responsibility has emerged as a key theme across translation and interpreting and has gained popularity as a potentially productive way of reimagining our ethical underpinnings. This area builds upon activism in a way (and indeed could be seen to encapsulate a range of ideas covered in Chapters 5 and 6) but does not necessarily involve political causes. Rather, it is more closely related to having the courage to challenge rather than being bystanders (we specifically alluded to the concept of translators as passive bystanders in Chapter 6).

Paying attention to social responsibility means that our focus shifts outwards, beyond T&I providers themselves or TIS as a discipline and, as opposed to the other accounts of responsibility we have considered, this area emphasises responsibility as socially distributed and a dynamic feature of translatorial activity, moving away from the text as the centre of our enquiry and deontological impositions. For Drugan and Tipton – the key proponents behind this school of thought – "'[r]esponsibility' is therefore understood here as action-oriented and dynamic, encompassing value judgements and decisions that may lead as much to resistance as to acceptance and commitment to sustain a form of social consensus." Importantly, "what constitutes socially responsible action for one person may be considered irresponsible by another, meaning that 'responsibility' can never be ideologically neutral and its invocation always confers an obligation to determine whose responsibility, to whom and for what" (Drugan and Tipton 2017: 121–122).

The basic premise here is perhaps familiar, moving beyond textual concerns and opening up a space for the non-neutral, subjective nature of ethical decision-making on a general level, and their framework is designed to create room for a wide range of viewpoints and methods. Research suggests that a focus on social responsibility in professional contexts has wide-reaching positive impacts including enhanced employee ethical attitudes (Drugan and Tipton 2017: 120). However, that loose nature also makes it a somewhat nebulous concept, and so Drugan and Tipton seek to narrow enquiry further. While corporate social responsibility is one of the more well-developed fields of social responsibility – and definitions such as Carroll's ('make a profit, obey the law, be ethical, and be a good corporate citizen') do apply to T&I professionals to an extent – there is little research into what being a 'good corporate citizen' means for the freelance translator or public service interpreter, for instance. As such, Drugan and Tipton argue that perhaps business is not the place for us to look for our ethical underpinnings. Instead, 'caring' professions such as medicine, social work, or teaching, which have a stronger tradition of considering social responsibility, represent their model of choice for T&I.

These 'caring' professions' focus on social responsibility during training and place an important emphasis on mitigating internal and external risks. Externally, there is the risk "to society if professionals are not conscious of their broad duties and responsibilities in their work" and internally there are "risks of consequences such as burnout, stress and vicarious traumatisation for professionals themselves" (ibid.). We will consider these internal risks in more detail later in this chapter. Ultimately, the hope is that a focus on social responsibility will encourage professionals to consider the impact of their work beyond the narrow professional sphere. In sum, **social responsibility as a framework, while somewhat nebulous, asks that we act in the best interests of our environment and society as a whole,** with a view to benefiting the community that will inherit the world we leave behind.

However, as important as these wider concerns are, translation and interpreting still happen in a competitive economic climate, and complex questions remain as to how we can marry utopian aims of cooperating for the best interests of the wider world with the need to pay the bills and to survive and thrive in a challenging business environment. Problematising this division, David Jemielity (2018: 535) discusses a potential ideological and behavioural "disconnect" between general translator culture and businessperson culture, pointing towards a "poverty cult" among translators, characterised by an "economically unambitious, arguably anti-capitalist approach". We now turn inwards to personal needs, first in relation to concerns over mental wellbeing and secondly in an economic context.

? How important is social responsibility in relation to your professional life?
? What is your priority when you are translating or interpreting?

Box 8.1 Environmental sustainability

A useful example of a way in which social responsibility can manifest itself in the translation world is environmental sustainability. Eco-translation is an emerging strand in TIS and, with translation and interpreting revolving around sharing and storing data electronically, many professionals are now considering their digital carbon footprint. In an article dedicated to this question in the ITI's professionally oriented magazine *The ITI Bulletin*, Stansfield offers several illuminating figures:

- Data centres, where information is stored and processed, now consume around 1% of the world's electricity.
- Every email we send is responsible for emitting at least four grams of CO_2, and that figure increases to 50g every time we send an attachment.
- All of the emails sent around the world in a year emit as much CO_2 as seven million extra cars on the road

(Stansfield 2022: 10)

In a world where the ICT industry is responsible for more CO_2 emissions than global aviation, we are now seeing some "carbon-negative" translation companies (companies who offset their carbon emissions by supporting reforestation projects, for instance) and calls for changes in the overall thrust behind translation and interpreting. Cronin (2017: 6) – a leading voice in the area – comments on the link between unsustainable energy dependency and the "ideology of boundless growth" that we find in localisation in particular, and he calls for a move away from translating everything for the sake of wealth creation. He shuns Weaver's envisaged machine translation purpose of complete "mutual intelligibility" (see below) and argues that diverse linguistic spaces are more resilient and viable (Moorkens and Rocchi 2021: 330). All of this is in the name of solidarity with global and future humans.

? What do you think about these issues?
? Is there an ethical responsibility for translators and interpreters to consider their digital carbon footprint?

Looking Inwards: Ethical Stress

While the previous section looks outwards, we now turn back in on ourselves. Over the course of the previous chapters we have seen that ethical dilemmas occur in a range of contexts and can be incredibly challenging for professionals to deal with. Whether we are working in a war zone, deliberating over a specific word choice that can do justice to a particular text, or struggling to negotiate a fair rate, ethical decision-making is hard work and this can take have a very real mental toll on the translators and interpreters (and students) working through these issues.

Ethical stress is an occupational stress "resulting from disparities in the ethical values and expected behaviour of employees" (DeTienne, Agle, Phillips and Ingerson 2012: 377–378) and is made up of disjuncture/dissonance (the painful feelings of inauthenticity when values and feelings do not align with actions) and ontological guilt (the specific guilt of not being able to act in accordance with your own values) (Hubscher-Davidson 2021: 417). While stress in general has traditionally been more closely linked with interpreting, very little work "has been carried out on the psychological repercussions for translators and interpreters of being enmeshed in ethical dilemmas, and no study has yet investigated the impact of ethical stress specifically on translator or interpreter performance" (ibid 2021: 416). And while there is evidence of a closer relationship with ethical stress and interpreting, in part due to the physical proximity of the interpreter and the use of the first person in interpreting, which "can intensify the embodiment of emotions and enhance its traumatic impact" (Hubscher-Davidson 2021: 424), **there is cause for all language professionals to consider the relationship between their work and their mental health.**

In general, translators and interpreters face a number of clear occupational stressors, many of which we have alluded to in this and previous chapters: time pressures, technology competition, the transitory nature of the profession, questions over low status, rates of pay, and so forth. Meanwhile, Hubscher-Davidson contends that translators and interpreters similarly face specifically ethical stressors and are discouraged from exercising their agency for three specific reasons:

- Lack of trust between involved parties (which leads to translators "playing it safe" – explaining choices, for instance);
- Lack of support for the translator (e.g. resources to support discussions and understandings of ethics);
- Lack of necessary information (important info being withheld).

(Hubscher-Davidson 2021: 418)

Questions of information asymmetry and a widespread lack of understanding of translation and interpreting are implicit factors in the first and third reasons, while the second is exemplified clearly in the translation profession. For instance, given that codes of ethics are unable to provide unproblematic, clear-cut answers when it comes to ethical dilemmas (as explored in Chapter 7) and there is little ethical training available on a large scale, translators are forced to contend with these tricky issues alone. Some translators do seek to concretise their ethical decision-making via other means such as other professionals' blog entries, translation forum posts, and social media discussions (resources that provide something of a window into the profession (McDonough Dolmaya: 2011b) in terms of ethical issues encountered), but there is no widespread, regulated release or standard practice when it comes to tackling these ethical issues.

When these clashes occur between the professional's own values and the context in which they are working, the aforementioned dissonance occurs. This is part of a cycle of ethical stress (Hubscher-Davidson: 2021: 424), which subsequently moves to a self-control/self-regulation stage, where the professional attempts to regulate their feelings, involving emotional labour. Määttä (2015) gives the example of interpreters intervening in the context of asylum interviews in Finland, for instance by correcting an error in a transcript. This intervention brings up a clash between professional expectations (neutrality) and individual values (the desire to assist a fellow human being), which may lead to "increased ethical stress, general work stress, and potential vicarious trauma" (Määttä 2015: 32). Indeed, this vicarious trauma (VC) is the next point in the cycle of ethical stress. VC is associated with poor peer support, doubts over professional competence, and changes in self-image and is said to result in "reduced respect and concern for others." Symptoms include "social withdrawal, aggression, greater sensitivity to violence, cynicism, numbness, sexual difficulties, eating disorders, helplessness, difficulty in relationships, etc." (Hubscher-Davidson 2021: 424), foregrounding the powerful and pervasive nature of the potential impact upon professionals. Bancroft, meanwhile, offers an interesting account of the tangible effects on interpreters:

> [I]nterpreters reported getting dizzy, nauseated or fearful after sessions with survivors. They had nightmares or disturbed sleep. Their concentration was disrupted during interpreting. They had difficulty getting certain stories or images out of their head [...] they might shake or tremble. Most distressing of all was the degree to which a number of interpreters simply burned out.
>
> (Bancroft 2017: 209)

Burnout occurs as a result of the repetition of these processes and may lead professionals to leave the field and fail to forgive themselves or others. Thankfully, however, it is not necessarily an irreversible endpoint. Even once we have suffered through this cycle there is also the possibility of vicarious transformation – "renewed hope, spiritual growth, and a greater appreciation for life" (ibid. 425). However, this cycle is something that is very real and "unchecked ethical stress may cause irreparable damage to their mental health and well-being" (ibid.).

Potential advice to avoid these worrying effects could be to simply remove ourselves from situations that may lead to these kinds of encounters, but it is not easy to anticipate when and where ethical dilemmas will arise. Furthermore, due to the economic demands placed on professionals, they may find themselves "making a trade-off between work they want to do and work they have to do" (Leiter and Maslach 2008: 501). We need support in place to assist us in our ethical decision-making and to maintain reasonable working conditions, and it is important to recognise that the translator is not simply an invisible channel but rather a human being who is impacted by the work and the words they deal with. This leads McAlester (2003: 226) to powerfully contend that **"ultimately, translators' responsibility is not to the author, or the reader, or the commissioner, or to the translating profession but to themselves"** (bold for emphasis). Educators, employers, and professional associations should help here, and we need to learn how to deal with these issues. Some support mechanisms could include:

1. Social support networks of peers
2. Role plays
3. Counselling sessions
4. Ethics consultations
5. Open discussions with clients and managers etc.

Adapted from Hubscher-Davidson (2021: 426)

A powerful related strand of thought is the importance of self-care. Costa et al. (2020: 36) contend that this is an ethical responsibility for interpreters, and that they must keep themselves "fit and well-prepared to perform interpreting assignments to the highest standards." Self-care "requires the deliberate practice of activities which keep a person healthy, engaged, and well-functioning" (2020: 40) and reduce susceptibility to vicarious trauma.

In their pilot study, they found that interpreters who received support sessions showed "an increase in their confidence, resilience, and effectiveness" (2020: 50), pointing to the importance of this additional support and the potential of training. Ultimately, the obligation to be emotionally and physically fit enough for the work we take on adds another interesting layer to the myriad responsibilities at work. They lament the lack of power that professionals and non-professionals have in their professional encounters and the lack of available outlets to provide relief from the toll their work takes, accentuating the risk of burnout and impacting their performance. They also discuss the jarring impact of expectations of neutrality and bemoan a lack of training in ethical decision-making, stress management, and self-care, as well as highlighting the prominence of self-care in codes for frontline workers in other domains, further accentuating the gaps that exist in interpreting contexts. Undoubtedly, this area warrants further exploration in the future.

Between social responsibility and concerns relating to ethical stress and self-care, there is something of a tension between internal concerns for selfhood and identity and wider social and economic concerns. For Drugan and Tipton (2017: 121),

> approaches informed by social responsibility make it possible to move beyond questions about what motivates translators and interpreters to supply their labour (whether waged and/or unwaged) based on individual notions of what is good for society or self interest, to questions about how translation can support better living together as an ethical goal.

This quote exemplifies a divide between individual ethical concerns and social responsibility, but arguably translators and interpreters must be sensitive to both sides of the equation. However noble the causes (e.g. living together better), if outward-looking viewpoints are conceived of in opposition to internal needs, there is a risk to the individual professional. Particularly in the challenging context of a changing professional world, translators and interpreters must look to protect not only their mental health, but also seek to guard the sustainability (both financial and existential) of their profession and career. These are areas we will explore in the next sections.

Box 8.2 The Railway Man – Ethical stress in T&I

The 1995 book *The Railway Man*, which was subsequently adapted into a film in 2013, not only provides a fascinating account of extreme hardship, recovery, reconciliation, and repentance, but also presents a shocking case of the mental toll of interpreting practice. The book tells the story of a former British Army officer, Eric Lomax, who was tortured as a prisoner of war at a Japanese labour camp during World War II. Military interpreter Takashi Nagase took part in Lomax's torture and, while never tried for any crime, the interpreter felt a profound burden of guilt.

Lomax describes the bipolar nature of the interpreter's role – sometimes detached and other times more actively involved. Even when delivering the news that Lomax has effectively been sentenced to death, Nagase does so with "so little inflection in his voice" but also betrays a "smug virtuous complicity" (1996: 135) and eventually gets "deeper into his role [...] as though he were enjoying it". At one point, when the interpreter ends up having a tangential conversation with Lomax, a Japanese NCO (non-commissioned officer) becomes suspicious and berates the interpreter, re-emphasising this bipolar role. As Lomax puts it, "the interpreter was simply meant to be a channel of communication, and when it got blocked or distorted, the NCO would shout at him too" (ibid.).

After fifty years of being haunted by what he had been through, Lomax discovers the identity of the interpreter and considers whether to exact some form of revenge. In the intervening years, Nagase had gone on to spend his life as an activist for post-war reconciliation and against Japanese militarism, criticising the oath of loyalty – or as he put it the "cult of obedience to authority" (1996: 272) that soldiers adhered to in following the Emperor's orders. Reading about Nagase's efforts to atone, Lomax first questions whether they are genuine but also realises that these events and memories have taken a toll on the interpreter: "he too had nightmares, flashbacks, terrible feelings of loss" (1996: 240). Upon meeting, Nagase explains that "[f]ifty years is a long time, but for me it is a time of suffering" (1996: 263) and even explains how he tried to persuade the NCO he was interpreting for that Lomax was not the leader of a group attempting to communicate outside of the camp.

This case questions the difference in intensity between translation and interpreting (and interpreting in war zones!), points to questions of responsibility (again), agency, and non-neutrality, and points out the utopian nature of activist aims – we are not always in a position where championing a certain cause is feasible or at least uncomplicated. Nagase is not an advocate, or at least he is for the state, perhaps, facilitating communication in line with a national agenda. However, he (presumably) does so for fear of his life – despite Lomax's comments that he seemed to enjoy it at times, his repentance appears genuine. Finally, the psychological impact of this role comes to the fore: this is obviously an extreme example, but the case points to the vicarious trauma experienced by interpreters and the inescapability of some situations – we have to make choices and we have to live by those choices.

? Can we justify Nagase's actions during the war? (See also Box 6.1).
? (How) could Nagase mitigate against the mental toll of his work?
? How can we atone for our mistakes?

Growing Concerns: Rates of Pay and Ethical Payment Practices

While some scholars argue that money is not an ethical issue (and this is sometimes used as a rationale for its absence in codes of ethics, as explored in Chapter 7), historically there is a strong link between money and ethics, from the Biblical allusion to money as the root of all evil to more recent critiques of capitalist culture and the endless accumulation of money described by Marx (1867) as "fetishism". And this link between the two areas seemingly extends to the context of translation. Rates of pay have been the subject of inadequate attention in both academic and professional literature in translation and interpreting for a number of reasons. While money remains a taboo topic in many parts of the world, the wide-ranging nature of the "profession" makes it difficult to carry out systematic studies or to make easy comparisons, and the decidedly economically unambitious mindset mentioned above complicates matters further. However, this represents one of the most pressing areas of concern to working translators and interpreters. In a 2020 survey, the UK-based Institute of Translation and Interpreting asked members which ethical dilemmas they had faced in the previous three years, and by far the largest proportion of answers, 42 per cent (the next highest was 28% and then 16%), related to "Rates/conditions asked to accept". Meanwhile, another 2020 survey of 1,510 freelance translators by Inbox Translation similarly found that "low rates of pay" was the leading challenge facing freelancers, with 59 per cent of respondents selecting this area, and many commenting on a general downward pressure on rates as a specific area of concern. **Generally, translators feel that they are not paid enough, and there is evidence of low, and decreasing rates being offered.**

This stems from a number of key sources, including **industry disruptors**, ongoing issues of **low status**, and a **lack of regulation** (this is not the place to get into an in-depth exploration of money in translation). For a more detailed picture of the current situation in relation to translation in the UK context, see Lambert and Walker (2022). In addition, the way that the translation industry works exacerbates issues. Employing an outsourcing model where either individual translations or LSPs will take care of translation on behalf of a client as the "recipients of expert services are not themselves adequately knowledgeable to solve the problem or to assess the service required" (Freidson 1983: 41, cited in Sharma 1997: 764). Within this model is information asymmetry, where one side of the market has more information than the other, resulting in "a market price lower than the fair price" (Chan 2017: 93). So, as our clients cannot assess our skills, or see or fully appreciate the process or the quality of the product of translation (think, for instance, of the ubiquity of imperfect tools such as Google Translate), translation itself is undervalued, translators are accorded less status and prestige than other comparable professions and, ultimately, pay is lower than it perhaps should be. Of course, this is a very quick rundown of what is an enormously complex area, but it suffices here to point out some of the underlying mechanisms of low pay.

In an ethical sense, we are forced to question whether we should insist upon higher pay as translators and interpreters? However, how willing would LSPs be to increase prices? Of course, the blame does not just fall on the LSPs, who are following the profit motive as many would in today's world, but there is a range of practices that are morally questionable. For instance, is it ethical to undercut other translator's/interpreter's/LSP's prices in order to gain work? Gouadec, for instance, has argued that translators have an ethical "obligation" to refuse unremunerated work and never knowingly to underbid for contracts (2007: 196). What about hiring unqualified translators (an area further problematised by the lack of regulation in the area!)? Is it ethical for LSPs to pay reduced rates for tech-assisted translations (see below) to benefit themselves? What are the ethical implications of clients paying late or not paying at all? And finally, what are the ethical implications of LSPs or clients asking for translators to complete free translation tests with the lure of potential future work? Some translators even report that unscrupulous clients have used this method to source entirely free translations, breaking texts up and presenting the individual parts to translators as a "test".

Ultimately this is a minefield. Information asymmetry, a lack of status, perceived unimportance, poor understandings, and perhaps even low self-confidence all inhibit translator's price-setting ability. To fight low rates, we need to perhaps hold our nerve and ask for rates that are appropriate (some codes do ask translators to do this, though this is not easy, particularly when you are just starting out in your career, hence, the need for more training and further reflection), but much is embedded within wider concerns of status. At this point, consider how much help the more theoretical ideas of ethics explored in chapters 2 to 6 offer here.

? What is your stance on rates of pay? Would you simply accept the rate offered by a client/LSP or would you negotiate and refuse rates that you consider to be lower than what the services are worth?
? How would you handle a situation in which a client refuses to pay for a translation that you have completed? How could you mitigate against situations such as this?

Box 8.3 How much should you charge?

Imagine that you have just started your career as a translator or interpreter and a potential new client asks you what you are going to charge. How would you respond? Drugan and Megone (2011: 195–197) offer something of a response to this question, exploring common ways in which translators come to calculate rates of pay and introducing the ethical dimension of this area. They note that rates are highly motivating but "often shrouded in mystery" and acknowledge the specific pulls felt by newly graduated students venturing into the profession. Rates vary enormously based on language pair, practice type, domain, and geographical location, and this makes blanket suggestions somewhat futile (searching online is a good place to start for concrete figures), but their range of models offers a useful map of considerations (see also Walker 2022, Chapter 6 for a breakdown of these factors from the perspective of project management):

1. **The same rate – or agreed range of rates – for every job,** which is the most common solution adopted in the profession;
2. **Client-dependent.** Translators may set rates depending on the nature of the client's business;
3. **Experience-dependent.** Translators often charge more for work in a field where they have gained a specialization or prior experience;
4. **Source text- / Domain-dependent.** Translators may vary their rates according to the complexity, length or format of the source text;
5. **Deadline-dependent.** An urgent deadline or requirement to work nonstandard hours (evenings, at weekends) will often incur a supplementary charge;
6. **Colleague or sector-dependent.** Translators in niche domains and specialised sectors such as subtitling typically know what the standard rate for their type of work is and set their rates accordingly, while avoiding potential legal issues with price fixing;
7. **As much as you think you can get away with.**
   Drugan and Megone question these approaches using concepts including **justice, fairness, generosity,** and **kindness**, which feed in at various points. We could also add the ubiquitous **profit motive** and a **personal need to survive** to these calculations.
   ? Which of the models above would you adopt and why?
   ? Which principle(s) above (if any) drives your decision-making?

Translation Technology and Ethics

A related area of pressing concern for professionals in both translation and interpreting, which not only impacts upon our relationship with money but feeds into a number of widespread ethical concerns, is the continued role of technological developments. **Technology is already and increasingly central to the way that translators and interpreters work (Doherty 2016, Zetzsche 2020), to the point that many argue that it has fundamentally changed our working habits.** Computer-assisted interpreting (CAI) tools continue to develop at pace, while in the context of translation, Pym (2013: 493) comments that "whereas much of the translator's skillset and effort was previously invested in identifying possible solutions to translation problems [...], the vast majority of these skills and efforts are now invested in selecting between available solutions". LeBlanc, meanwhile, contends that translation memory (TM) tools "render the translator's work more mechanical and, when misused, may lead to deskilling and may have an effect on the translator's professional satisfaction" (LeBlanc 2017: 48).

In recent years, this central role has been considered to a greater extent in relation to ethics, with the increased technologisation of both translation and interpreting forcing us to consider our positioning. Neural machine translation (NMT), which uses machine learning techniques to 'learn' over time – the more examples it has available, the better the quality – is reflective of the parallel between wider coverage of AI and technology and translation specifically. Importantly, this is very much a developing field, and the literature is still rather fragmented. As Bowker (2021: 262) puts it, "while there is a considerable body of work on the ethics of translation, as well as one on computer-aided translation (CAT) and MT, relatively little scholarly literature directly addresses the intersection of the two, though this is starting to change."

This lacuna is equally concerning in the profession where, as evidenced by the focus of codes of ethics in the previous chapter, consideration of ethics and technology remains marginal despite its wide-ranging impact. Indeed, many of the concerns within the domain of translation technology fall in line with wider ethical concerns. As Drugan notes, "[m]any of these questions about ethical aspects of new [translation] technologies are difficult to separate from broader sociocultural issues. Technological developments have occurred alongside, and played a part in, major ongoing shifts in social structures, migration patterns, trade, information and employment" (Drugan 2019: 250). In this section, we explore a number of these ethical concerns.

Types of translation technology

It is beyond the scope of this textbook to explore the precise nature of these technologies in detail (see Mitchell-Schuitevoerder 2020 for an accessible introduction to the wide range of computer-based tools that translators must be familiar with today), but it is worth quickly mentioning a few distinctions. CAT (computer-assisted translation) tools can be broken down into two vital areas that suffice for exploring the key ethical issues below: **Translation Memory (TM) tools** and **Machine Translation (MT)**.

TMs provide a database of matching source and target segments of text, generally entered by human translators. The TM software analyses the source text and splits it into segments, compares and matches each segment in the ST with the database of SL/TL pairs as the translator translates, and stores new source and target segment pairs for subsequent use. The idea is that this database of existing translations will improve consistency and speed/productivity and facilitate terminology searches, while the CAT tool can also handle complex formatting for the user.

MT systems, on the other hand, are specifically designed to automatically translate text (or speech) from one language into another. The most famous example of an MT system is perhaps Google Translate, which launched in 2006 and is now reported to have over 500 million daily users translating over 100 languages. To muddy the waters slightly, it is worth noting that CAT tools incorporating TM can also incorporate MT add-ons to allow translators to leverage automatically generated translations in their work but, primarily, a TM tool can be seen as providing machine-assisted human translation rather than carrying out the translation fully for you.

MT research started around World War II, but the relationship between technology and translation really transformed in the 1990s with the introduction of TM systems. Now, translators use a wide array of tech in their work and, with advancements in MT and free online translation available, tech is now used regularly by people outside the translation profession, too (see Bowker and Buitrago Ciro 2019). Indeed, MT pioneer Warren Weaver envisaged the new tool as necessary for "the constructive and peaceful future of the planet" (Weaver 1947: 1), a nod to the ideas of social responsibility mapped out above. Now, MT is at the centre of our discussions of technology and ethics and, in the context of interpreting, MT continues to generate debate and is likely to continue to impact upon working methods (see, for instance, Haddow, Birch, and Heafield (2021) for a fascinating overview of the usage of MT in healthcare settings).

? Have you used any CAT tools in your translation or interpreting work? Can you anticipate any ethical questions that may come up, perhaps in relation to rates, privacy, or commoditisation?
? What positive or negative impacts might the democratisation of MT tools to non-translators around the world have on professional translation and interpreting?

Machine translation post editing and professional status and sustainability

Inherent in translation automation is a perceived threat to human translators, and these concerns have become more acute as MT output has continued to improve. However, despite leaps in technology and MT quality in an ever-growing range of languages and domains, human parity seems a distant dream, and one that is perhaps not even desirable. In reality, rather than simply replacing human translation, the relationship between technology and translation has been more nuanced, with advancements harnessed to allow evolutions in the roles carried out by professionals. One of the clearest ways in which MT has impacted upon the translation world in recent years is the advent of Machine Translation Post-Editing (MTPE). This is the process during which a text that has been pre-translated using MT is corrected by human linguists/editors rather than translated from scratch, with the aim of saving time and money. It should be noted that rates for post-editing tend to be significantly lower than for 'full' translation. For this reason, MTPE has become increasingly appealing to clients and employers, and Garcia (2010: 19) even contends that students at his own university produced better (English-Chinese and Chinese-English) translations when they post-edited SMT output than when they translated from scratch. This finding is then used to motivate the question of whether translators should consider post-editing as a viable alternative to conventional translation. Related to this, the increasing prevalence of post-editing also leads to a dilemma in the classroom. Should we focus on improving human translations or, if MTPE is going to lead to better results, should we focus on teaching this instead?

In the profession, there is a wide range of attitudes towards MTPE. Many hold a decidedly negative view of the practice: For instance, Nataly Kelly (2014) describes post-editing as "linguistic janitorial work", arguing that the practice is condescending, does a disservice to colleagues, and is bound to feed into professional satisfaction, while Moorkens and O'Brien (2017: 109) call it "boring and demeaning." Dyson (2003: 11) suggests that, for translation tool users, "their technology will label them as bottom feeders, not premium market contenders" and this assertion points to a dual model of translation service provision, with a dividing line between **premium and bulk translations.** For Bowker (2021: 269),

> [t]he general premise is that premium services, carried out principally by skilled human translators, can command higher prices for their quality-focused work. Meanwhile, the bulk services carried out with the help of MT or CAT tools offer a comparatively low-cost, quick-and-dirty solution that encourages technology-dependent translators to focus on processing large volumes of text to earn a living.

This leads to concerns over the "lower end" of the marking forcing rates down and shifting quality expectations. Other scholars recognise the idea that translations only need to be "fit for purpose" and see post-editing as a very attractive proposition for some translators.

From an ethical perspective, is it acceptable to go for "good enough" quality? Consider, for instance, Chesterman's Oath guideline stipulating that "I will always translate to the best of my ability" (2001: 153). Bowker also questions the issues of professional esteem that go hand in hand with labels such as "linguistic janitorial work", commenting on how translators reading these "condescending" descriptions are sure to suffer from low job satisfaction and question their professional identity, asking whether it should "be shameful to produce a translation that meets the specifications provided?" (Bowker 2021: 269).

As a practice itself, a number of authors also argue that using CAT tools and the practice of MTPE "risks concealing, overshadowing or downgrading the translator's contribution" (Bowker 2021: 267), being relegated to a word-replacement activity. As we know, this is something that translation already struggles with, with limited wider understandings of translation mentioned above. By shifting the translator's role to that of an editor who tweaks automated output, these wider misunderstandings of translation risk becoming even more pervasive, something that Stupiello refers to as a "hidden ethical cost" (2008) of technology usage, forcing translators to balance increases in productivity and consistency against issues such as the risk of further misunderstandings of what their role entails among the general public.

? What are your thoughts on MTPE? Does the practice appeal to you?
? Should you always seek to achieve optimal quality when translating or interpreting?

Money

As alluded to in the section above, remuneration is closely linked to technological advancements, with new systems, workflows, and practices leading to a battle over the range of leverage these advancements offer. However, though it is abundantly clear that there is a strong link between these issues, the two areas stand out as notable absences from codes of ethics (see Chapter 7) and discussions of ethics more widely. CAT tool usage is regularly based on aims of boosting productivity and minimising costs. SDL (the former owners of industry-leading CAT tool Trados), for instance, touted MTPE as yielding a 140 per cent productivity increase in relation to pure human translation, with a leap from 2,500 to 6,000 words per day. However, as noted above, there are hidden costs associated with this supposed gain. CAT tools require other investments that offset benefits like time and money spent on buying and learning to use the tools. Clients will also regularly capitalise on any increases in productivity by paying lower rates or even not paying at all for translations, depending on the match percentage – that is, if a translation already exists in a TM, the client will often offer no payment (Marshman 2014: 381).

It is very common for clients to request discounts for machine-translated segments or repetitions based on TM matches, often adopting a sliding scale whereby no match would pay 100 per cent of the translator's full rate and a 100 per cent match would not be paid at all. This can lead to translators being paid only a fraction of the "full" word count for a text, despite having to, at the very least, check those matches to ensure that the translations are correct. In this way, productivity and consistency benefits are reaped by LSPs rather than translators, recalling the debates over "business-mindedness" touched upon earlier in this chapter and foregrounding concerns over the gulf between LSP profits and stagnating rates for translators and interpreters (see Lambert and Walker 2022). This is a practice that understandably riles many student and professional translators, but is one that is seemingly becoming more widespread. Again, think about how this impacts upon our relationships with codes of ethics or traditional understandings of ethics that we have covered. TMs and MT can be discussed in terms of rates. Above, we considered the idea of rates commensurate with our abilities, or fair, dignified rates but, unfortunately, many current MT-modified pay structures appear questionable at best.

Sharing and commoditisation of translation resources

Given that TMs are used to leverage existing translations as a time-/money-saving measure, another ethical issue that has been raised relating to technology is the question of whether TM databases should be shared. As Topping (2000) reported, some translators attempt to maximise productivity "by expanding their TM database collection as quickly as possible, and so they advocated for TM database exchange" (Bowker 2021: 265). LSPs, however, have argued that this sharing of resources would mean that different clients end up with translations that employ similar or the same style and terminology, breaching their intellectual property rights and nullifying their investments. This debate conceptualises TMs and terminology databases as assets (Zetzsche 2005), and many clients are abundantly aware of their value, allowing them to both ensure consistency and pay less for translations. In the profession, it is common for clients to want translators to send them updated TMs and term bases upon completion of a project and to insist on using them in future projects (Bowker 2021: 266). But, translators cannot in turn use them with other clients. Still today, translators do not have any significant control over TM resources (Moorkens and Lewis 2020) and the fast pace of change means that copyright legislation is struggling to keep up with the changes in the profession.

Ultimately, the question of who exactly owns and controls these resources is still contested, and the way in which content is used and re-used requires further attention.

Privacy and confidentiality

The issues of resource sharing above also allude to concerns around confidentiality: should we share translations that have been prepared for a specific client? Indeed, this aspect is felt even more keenly in the context of MT. According to Kamocki and O'Regan (2016: 4461), using free online MT may entail privacy risks of which users may be unaware and of which MT service providers may be tempted to take advantage. When you use free online translators such as Google Translate, that data does not simply disappear. Many providers use it for training data or to expand their corpora, subsequently training their systems further, and there is huge potential for issues. Say, for instance, that a translator inputs sensitive company information into the system. Common Sense Advisory's Don DePalma warns that "employees and your suppliers are unconsciously conspiring to broadcast your confidential information, trade secrets, and intellectual property (IP) to the world" (DePalma 2014). For this reason, some LSPs will specifically state that you cannot use MT when translating and in Trados; for instance, project managers will be able to see if you have used automatic translation, though there are ways around this via add-ons – another ethical grey area (for more on this, see Moorkens and Lewis 2020).

While Google states in its policies that it "does not claim any ownership in the content that you submit or in the translations of that content returned by the API", later terms reveal that

> [w]hen you upload or otherwise submit content to our Services, you give Google (and those we work with) a worldwide license to use, host, store, reproduce, modify, create derivative works (such as those resulting from translations, adaptations or other changes we make so that your content works better with our Services), communicate, publish, publicly perform, publicly display and distribute such content.
>
> (cited in DePalma 2014)

The license to use the data also continues even after a user ceases to use the service.

All of this potentially impacts upon our relationships with ethics and codes of ethics. While confidentiality is universally present in codes, none engage specifically with issues relating to technology usage and, though Drugan and Babych (2010) claim that codes can help with some of these issues, I would argue that this help is extremely limited. Indeed, as noted in Chapter 7, many codes include no mention of technology at all, driving translators to discuss these issues with peers online (Bowker 2021: 269).

Collaboration, quality, and fidelity

One further significant way in which technologies have changed the translation profession, which again forces us to rethink a principle that is regularly codified, is by facilitating group work. This is both a positive move and a challenge, dissolving boundaries between collaborators while also engendering important changes to the way we conceptualise translation. Collaborative working means that the notion of fidelity is arguably no longer applicable at all – or must be rearticulated – as no one translator is 'in charge' of the final product. Consider, for instance, crowdsourced translations, where content is outsourced to many participants: Who is responsible for the final text in this case? In addition, crowdsourcing often involves the participation of non-professional translators; see Basalamah (2021) for an exploration of this domain.

As with the concerns over MTPE mentioned above, TMs prioritise "consistency and efficiency and instead force translators to reduce translation to the most primitive sense of fidelity imaginable: fidelity to words at the sentence or even the subsentence level (because of segmentation)" (Bowker 2021: 267); and this again raises a tension between quality, time pressures, and 'traditional' ethical values in translation. Translators working with TM tools stand to benefit from working as quickly as possible, accepting existing solutions, and potentially even producing renderings that will work in multiple future instances. For LeBlanc (2017: 45),

> [i]n the eyes of many translators, some of the new guidelines – most notably, those pertaining to the establishment of productivity requirements and the enforced recycling of previous translations – represent a radical departure from what was done beforehand, and, more importantly, may have an effect on translators' professional autonomy and their overall professional satisfaction.

Ultimately, current practices and workflows have not only changed translation almost unrecognisably in some cases, but these changes are also having far-reaching impacts upon those who work in the field, and will continue to do so. While changes in interpreting have arguably been less radical to date, this area has also seen considerable technological adoption in recent years, not least with the massive rise in remote interpreting, in part fed by the COVID-19 pandemic.

Cultural hegemony

One final area of consideration in relation to technology revolves around a paradox inherent in MT usage. Moorkens (2022: 121) reminds us that MT and technology are "not ethically neutral, but rather [reflect] the values of those behind [their] development"; and MT's stated aim of overcoming barriers in communication risks marginalising certain languages, cultures, and people. Translation is available on an ever-wider level and between an ever-increasing number of languages, but it can also be seen to accentuate current issues rather than promoting diversity. For instance, the status of English as the dominant *lingua franca* of our time and wider usage of MT are leading to more material being translated both into and out of English, further entrenching the position. Quality is also higher for languages with larger corpora, consolidating the place of English while increasing challenges for less-common languages, despite efforts to promote/preserve them, that is, English MT output is often excellent while minority language content is weaker, strengthening that position of dominance.

In recent years, attention has also turned to the way in which neural machine translation's (NMT) makeup can strengthen biases. Most current NMT systems do not take context into account but select the option that is statistically the most likely variant, and this has been found to perpetuate a male bias. Google Translate, for instance, was found to generally use masculine pronouns for words like "strong" or "doctor" and feminine pronouns for "beautiful" and "nurse" (Bowker 2021: 273). Though Google later publicised efforts to reduce this bias, it remains unclear how far/successfully this has been implemented as similar examples have been reported in other languages since the publication of Google's response. For example, as of May 2022 this bias persists in Finnish, which does not have gendered third-person singular pronouns (he and she) but rather one gender-neutral pronoun, Hän. As shown in Figure 8.1, the gender-neutral source text (the same pronoun 'hän' is used in each sentence) demonstrates a clear bias in the English target text.

Ultimately, there is a range of perspectives on the future of translation – uncertainty and optimism among them – and a need for more concrete ethical guidance in relation to technology underpins many concerns. MT is reliant upon human translations to keep improving, but tensions exist. What is certain is that technological change is continuing at pace and translation is not the only field affected. Authors, journalists, musicians, and artists are also susceptible to having "the fruits of their intellects and imaginations" treated "as fragments to be given without pay to the hive mind" (Lanier 2010: 57).

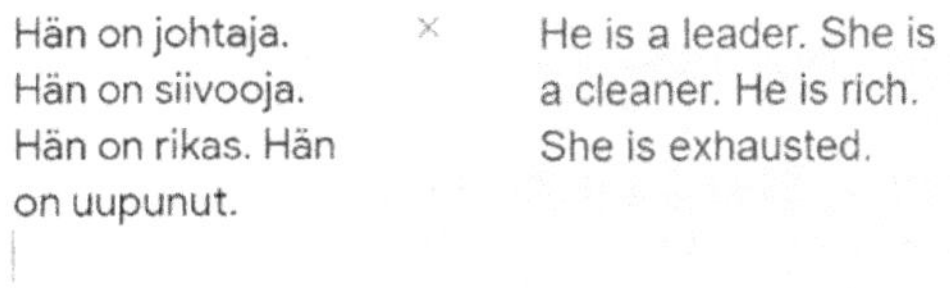

Hän on johtaja.   ×   He is a leader. She is
Hän on siivooja.   a cleaner. He is rich.
Hän on rikas. Hän   She is exhausted.
on uupunut.

Figure 8.1 Gender Bias in Google Translate.

How we will deal with these issues is still unclear, but this is not going away. There is a worrying push to laud the progress made by CAT and MT tools, which risks harming perceptions of translation – it becomes something that is quick and cheap while masking hidden costs. As Bowker again notes, "[t]ranslators may try to explain to the customer that high-quality translation requires time and money. However, they will likely seek someone who is happy to deliver unpolished computer-aided translations for a cheaper price and in a shorter turnaround time" (2021: 270). Education is vital: students, trainers, clients, authors – all of the stakeholders mentioned before – and so is the image we share of translation. The future is not easy to predict but this is fertile ground for future research with lots of pertinent questions to ask.

> **Box 8.4 Technology, money, and ethics**
>
> Imagine that you have been asked to translate a large user manual (over 20,000 words) for an end client. When you run an analysis in your usual CAT tool, you realise that there is a high percentage of repetition (over 10,000 words). The LSP who has approached you with the project does not use any CAT tools and they have not asked you about discounts. In fact, they are entirely ignorant about CAT tools and how they work.
>
> ? What should you do in this situation? Why?
> ? If the LSP's pay structure included discounts for matches (for instance, paying zero for 100% matches) what would you do?
>
> Though many translators are initially surprised by this payment practice, there are also many who do accept it, as they often have very little room to negotiate – in common language pairs in particular, a client will simply go to another translator if you refuse their rates. And while a general principle of business ethics is the right to make a profit, the downward pressure on translation rates of pay raises important ethical questions relating to translator's agency and the long-term sustainability of the profession.

Conclusion

While we have, above, somewhat separated internal and external concerns, there is no need for such a stark dividing line. While wider social causes will not always align with internal needs (and indeed there are tensions within these domains, too – consider clashes between payment and mental health, for instance), the need to prioritise individual wellbeing, environmental sustainability, and financial flourishing, for instance, can be harmonised with "socially responsible" viewpoints aiming to live better together. It is also worth noting that these issues are not only of concern to professionals, but to clients and end users too. What is required as a starting point is for "ethical" professionals to be aware of, and become engaged in, these debates.

This is one of the most compelling calls within the broad framework of social responsibility, specifically, the need to consider ideas beyond our relatively narrow field of translation and interpreting, to consider our role in promoting social and procedural justice, particularly "in relation to vulnerable groups and relevant inter-professions" (Drugan and Tipton 2017: 123). Of course, this sits implicitly at the heart of the ideas covered in Chapters 5 and 6, but is well worth reiterating in the professional sphere.

In terms of technology, meanwhile, translators and interpreters are empowered by continued developments, but these are not without their risks and challenges. While they have created a space for participatory cultures, providing networks and platforms to everyone from amateurs to activists, there is an array of ethical considerations to bear in mind, and evolving questions in relation to sustainability – of both the environment and the profession. However, the nature of translation, current global developments, and MT's underlying need for human translations suggest that the future of human translation is in no way in doubt.

Money is also a common underlying theme to many of these concerns – translators and interpreters find themselves marginalised because of poor understandings of what their work entails, poor status and perceptions of their work, and a lack of regulation that allows anyone to enter the market. Technological developments risk further exacerbating the situation by acting as "disruptors", introducing practices such as *Uberisation* in the translation industry (Fırat 2021), providing quasi-legitimate platforms for amateur translators to join the body of practicing translators, and allowing (unscrupulous) LSPs to push rates down further through divisive practices such as discounts for matches. This anxiety around finance leads to (ethical) stress among translators and interpreters, to the extent that the importance of practicing financial self-care has entered the professional discourse in recent years. Considering how we can promote the practices of translation and interpreting, improve wider perceptions, and subsequently ensure fairer pay commensurate with the work involved, all while respecting our own and our society's ethical needs and ideals, are key ethical questions that professionals continue to battle with.

The complex interplay between all of the factors considered in this chapter (and beyond) is worth noting. Indeed, they are not discrete entities, but rather interact with one another. For instance, technological developments feed into environmental concerns, which in turn can damage an individual's mental health in the form of climate anxiety. This complex web of competing concerns and considerations makes ethics an incredibly challenging area to engage with, and I attempt to bring together some further diffuse threads in the final chapter.

Discussion, Presentation, and Assignment Topics

1. In what way are technological advances in translation and interpreting impacting upon our understandings of ethics in the domain, and what do you consider to be the most pressing areas to address?
2. Should wider social responsibility or personal interests (mental health, financial wellbeing) be the overriding considerations behind decisions we make as a translator or interpreter?
3. Group project: in small groups, come up with an agreed definition of an "ethical professional" in translation and/or interpreting.

Note

1 Anastasiou and Gupta define crowdsourcing as "the process by means of which organisations can tap into the wisdom of their dedicated external community and use the wisdom for their benefit, i.e. with low cost, for more languages, and within the specified time frame" (2011: 2).

Further Reading

As is the case for many of the other chapters in this textbook, *The Routledge Handbook of Translation and Ethics* (Koskinen and Pokorn 2021) is a rich source for further reading in this domain. **Lambert's** chapter explores professional translator ethics in general, **Hubscher-Davidson** explores ethical stress in more detail, while **Bowker** provides an incisive image of the range of concerns in relation to ethics and technology. Elsewhere, **Moorkens (2022)** offers a rich and accessible exploration of ethics and technology, full of 'real life' case studies; **Lambert and Walker (2022)** explore the complex relationship between translation, rates, and professional status; and **Drugan and Tipton's 2017** special issue of *The Translator* groups together a fascinating range of articles illustrating the many and varied research trajectories that a basis in social responsibility can offer.

9 Other Viewpoints

> **Key questions**
> - What emerging topics are currently occupying scholars, professionals, and students, and what does the future hold for research in translation and interpreting ethics?
> - Can we legitimately consider our own interests as a valid part of our ethical decision-making?
> - Who can, may, or should translate or interpret?

It is abundantly clear from our discussions in this textbook that ethics in translation and interpreting is a multi-dimensional, complex, and evolving area of discussion. While we have delved into many of the most prominent areas of research, past and present, it is only right that we now consider 'what next', giving voice to emerging or otherwise less visible strands of thought on the topic. The broad and arguably growing nature of discussions on ethics precludes an in-depth review of every emerging theme in this chapter so I therefore highlight two particular cases while alluding to several other potential lines of enquiry. These cases are selected, not as the most prominent in the area, but rather because of their contrasting approaches to the self and Others – a recurring concern throughout this textbook, perhaps unsurprisingly given the belief that "translation represents the quintessential ethical situation of the encounter with the other" (Goodwin 2010: 19). They illustrate the wealth of contrasting potential ethical paths available to us and foreground the dynamic nature of discussions, where different themes rise to prominence and fade away in different times, regions, languages, cultures, and communities. I then return to the thorny question of responsibility, bringing together the vast array of concerns that we have covered in this textbook, encouraging readers to reflect on their positioning in light of this range of 'pulls' and to consider how these often-competing interests interact with one another. To finish, I point to a number of potential future research strands, which once again illustrate the incredibly broad nature of questions

162 *Other Viewpoints*

of ethics in the domain, and will hopefully inspire further exploration of this fascinating area.

Looking Further Afield

Beyond the key themes introduced in this textbook, there remains a plethora of viewpoints, literature, and studies to be explored across the dynamic and wide-ranging field of ethics for those interested in doing so. For instance, ethical exploration shares certain ties with thought in **post-colonial translation studies**, several of which have built upon the German Romantic ethics of difference to forward an "ethos of anticoloniality/decoloniality" that seeks to reflect and represent the foreignness of an ST (see Robinson 2021). **Gender studies,** to name another field, challenges – among other things – concepts of fidelity and raises questions of borders, (inter)subjectivity, and solidarity (on feminist translation ethics see, for instance, Ergun 2021). There are also numerous studies exploring the ethical and ideological implications of **censorship in translation** (see, for instance, McLaughlin and Muñoz-Basols 2021), which force us to re-assess our thinking on issues such as truth, representation, and our socially embedded role. Further still, emerging conversations have covered topics that include **child language brokering** (Angelelli 2021), questions of **accessibility** (Hirvonen and Kinnunen 2021), and **research ethics** (Mellinger and Baer 2021). As noted in the 'Further Reading' section at the end of this chapter, *The Routledge Handbook of Translation and Ethics* is a rich source for many of these themes, and indeed for additional coverage and renewed perspectives on the topics covered in previous chapters (as are the previous 'Further Reading' sections and the Bibliography, of course!).

Other edited volumes on ethical issues (which have appeared in a range of journals across TIS) also point to important potential areas of further consideration. Within Pym's (2001) special issue of *The Translator* entitled 'The Return to Ethics', for instance, Salah Basalamah investigates **ethical copyright in translation,** David Katan and Francesco Straniero-Sergio delve into **the ethics of entertainment** and talk show interpreting, and Alev Bulut and Turgay Kurultay focus on community interpreting in the process of **disaster management.** Drugan and Tipton's (2017) special issue of *The Translator*, meanwhile, which foregrounds the theme of social responsibility (see Chapter 8), includes contributions that explore topics as diverse as **collaboration, flows, and policies in crowd-sourced translation** (McDonough Dolmaya 2017), **the importance of interpreters' pragmatic competence in police investigative interviews** (Gallai 2017), and **the role and impact of volunteer interpreters working with survivors of domestic abuse** (Tipton 2017).

Elsewhere, Greenall et al. (2019) draw together an array of fascinating contributions on voice, ethics, and translation, including papers on **the ethics of publishing** and **translators' copyright.** In their special issue of *Translation and Interpreting Studies,* Monzó-Nebot and Wallace (2020) explore **the** ethics of non-professional translation and interpreting, while Moorkens, Kenny, and do Carmo (2020) reflect on **paths towards ethical, sustainable Machine Translation** in *Translation Spaces*. Even more recently, *The Translator* dedicated another special issue to ethics in 2021 – 'Translation and the Ethics of Diversity' (ed. Hutchings 2021) – with contributions ranging from **the ethics of translation in Cold War espionage** (Tyulenev 2021) to **the ethical dimension of the translation of post-conflict literature** (Rossi 2021). All of these areas would undoubtedly warrant further research in the future, and it is noteworthy that so many of these special issues have appeared in the last few years: a testament to the prominent current place of ethics in TIS and the ever-broadening research in the area.

Arguably, there remains much work to be done to explore traditions and currents of thought from other countries, cultures, and languages too, with a developing body of work on ethics related to Chinese philosophy (for instance Li and Chen 2018) and non-Western viewpoints more generally. Indeed, though I provided some coverage of **the Chinese tradition** in this textbook (see Chapter 2 in particular), there is also increasing interest in **socialist translation theories** (see Baer and Schäffner 2021), for example, where translators have served a different purpose to that in the West, prioritising the interests of the working class and the socialist state – though this did not happen through active intervention (as would be the case with activist ethics, covered in Chapter 6), but rather through censorship and self-censorship, another fascinating area for consideration, as alluded to above. Other traditions, meanwhile, have received scant attention, though interestingly (and somewhat surprisingly), Koskinen and Pokorn (2021: 5) contend that the development of TIS thought on ethics to date "may offer an argument for universalist ethics." Indeed, there is a strikingly similar basis to ethical principles across the globe, either suggesting a proliferation of European ideas, a homogeneous understanding of translation across an array of cultures, or a need to continue working to uncover these new and contrasting theoretical bases and viewpoints, which have so far been neglected or marginalised.

Conceptually, too, there are numerous strands of further exploration, including within the philosophical bases that we explored in Chapter 1. Though there are several philosophically driven perspectives on translation ethics that have garnered significant attention (see, for instance, Pokorn and Koskinen (2021) on **the ethics of linguistic hospitality** in the work of Jacques Derrida and Paul Ricoeur), an explicit focus on many strands of moral theory specifically (see Chapter 1) is curiously underrepresented. Wolf (2015), for instance, provides a fascinating account of ethics based within the idea of a "love command", which eschews a supposed secular bias in translation studies and adopts **a religious perspective on ethics** in an attempt to move beyond deontological and relativist approaches. Elsewhere, and as readers may have noted, there are a number of references to the importance of the self across contemporary contributions to translation and interpreting ethics, which allude to the potential of egoism – a moral theory that variously places self-interest at the heart of morality. Below, I explore this thread in some more detail before exploring another pressing contemporary question. These two 'case studies' (on the self and representation and representativeness below) are designed to be somewhat competing but nevertheless equally illustrative of the diverse and innovative ways in which scholars and practitioners continue to reconceptualise and reframe ethics.

> **Box 9.1 How far do questions of ethics extend? Gender-inclusive language and ethics**
>
> In 2022, the UX Content Collective – who offer training in user experience content design – released an international guide to gender-inclusive writing (UX Content Collective 2022). While gender inclusivity is by no means a new topic, initiatives such as this mark its place at the forefront of current shifting practices in workplace equality and, arguably, a more general increase in public consciousness of the topic. Indeed, it is only in recent years that there has been a more widespread acceptance of the practice of (and indeed the option of) adding pronouns to email signatures, social media profiles, and so forth.
>
> The guide includes advice on gender-neutral language (for instance, the neutral pronoun "they" in English) and even notes on how languages are changing at their very source. For example, the emerging use of inclusive suffixes – for example, usuário(a); produtor(a) in Portuguese, or the gender-neutral plural 'ami·e·s' in French to reflect both masculine and feminine endings – or neologisms – such as the English neutral pronoun 'hir' or the Italian 'ragazz@' or 'ragazz*' in the place of the typical masculine usage of 'ragazzi'.
>
> This case presents a confrontation between ethical and ideological thought and showcases the dynamic, constantly developing nature of language within the frame of representations and respect for the Other. It also offers an indication of the way in which the pace and nature of change is geographically varied, not only due to linguistic constraints but also the pace of change in terms of prevailing narratives (see Chapter 6). Issues that were deemed unworthy of consideration by many can soon become a moral priority while previously acceptable beliefs may become outdated. Consider the following questions:
>
> ? What linguistic resources are available in your language(s) to account for gender neutrality? Or, how gender-neutral/biased is your language?
> ? Are there any particular ethical currents of thought that have recently risen to prominence in your social/geographic/professional

context? For example, attention to the gender, sexuality, the use of AI or autonomous technology, misinformation, environmental sustainability, and so forth.
? (How) can we anticipate and adapt to the dynamic nature of ethics?

The Self: Egoism and Self-Interest

While in Chapter 8 we noted several productive calls for a prioritisation of the self in the profession, particularly in relation to concerns over mental health, where self-care (Costa et al. 2020) and a re-situation of our underpinnings (McAlester 2003) are forwarded, this allusion to the potential of self-interest has also appeared in literary (and other) contexts. It is useful to recall at this stage that any recourse to self-interest sits in direct contradiction to the stipulations of many codes of ethics. For instance, the ITI code states that members should not allow themselves to be "improperly influenced by self-interest" (ITI 2016: 5), and this is representative of a generally negative traditional attitude to this area.

Rather than having an ultimate "good", egoism is based around a contingent "good-for-you". A major problem, however, arises because this ability to prioritise your own self-interest has been linked to an indulgent selfishness. This, in turn, has led to egoism often being treated with condescension bordering on contempt and derided as "a wicked view" or even "a preposterous" ethical theory (Burgess-Jackson 2013: 530). In Venuti (2013), this use of egoism occurs when discussing degrees of freedom in poetic translation, following Paterson's notion of a "versioning" poet, who openly admits to plagiarism from earlier "unimprovable" lines, and describes a translation methodology that involves "mangling", "omission", and "deliberate mistranslation", selecting or constructing interpretations that "answer to a personal preference".

> As Paterson explained, "the only defensible fidelity is to the entirely subjective quality of 'spirit' or 'vision', rather than to literal meaning" … The version would thus seem to assume **an ethics of sheer self-interest**, where poetic license has been redefined as the privileging of a poet's interpretation according to the strength of its originality.
>
> (Venuti 2013: 177)

These ideas sit in stark contrast to conceptions of fidelity discussed earlier in this book and could undoubtedly be cause for concern. However, there are ways of softening this stance. Lambert (forthcoming) argues for the concept of **enlightened egoism** (see Box 9.2 below) as a means of doing just this. In this form, self-interest is made up of a complex network of competing elements that require careful and sensitive appraisal, as opposed to being understood as a one-dimensional pursuit of immediate, selfish goals. Though immediate, realisable consequences are easy to spot, longer-term consequences are to be accorded just as much value. For translators, this can be used to implicate them within a wider context. The translator is (indirectly) tied to their profession, their fellow translators, their client, and so forth, and is to consider general ethical norms and guidelines, and notions of justice and legality in their ethical decision-making. But we also allow space for our own personal need to survive: the need to pay the rent, to increase our productivity, to decide where we stand on global issues and where the balance lies in terms of personal gain and sacrifice, which can sometimes clash with wider ideological beliefs. The shift lies not within telling the translator what to do, but rather the translator being trusted to critically consider the choices available, to decide upon a course of action, and to be accountable for that decision. There is a call to dialogue and opening, and an active empowered role that can help us to shape understandings of translation. We must also accept that there are limits to a translator's agency, but when it comes to rates or payment practices, gendered language, representation and demographics, recognition, roles, copyright and legal status projects, and technological terms and conditions, we stand for or against certain practices together, and solidarity as a professional group can act as a valuable tool in ensuring that we survive and thrive in the long term.

Ultimately, this focus on the emergence of selfhood as a criterion for concern within translation and translator ethics is not the only new strand of thought in the area, but is indicative of the potential for new lines of thought from previously overlooked or maligned theories, of the potential of injecting new impetus in debates at both micro-, textual levels, and overarching societal levels, and of the overwhelmingly dynamic nature of ethics, with new ideas developing and occupying positions of strength and weakness at various points and in various cultures, languages, and domains. Box 9.1 above further emphasises this dynamic nature of ethics in the context of gender-inclusive language, a domain of thought that could be seen as running counter to a focus on the self, a deliberately challenging juxtaposition and a transition to the topics covered in the next section.

? Do you feel that translators and interpreters can and/or should consider their own personal needs in ethical decision-making, or do other factors (e.g. social responsibility, fidelity to the ST, a client's wishes) take priority?
? How do we handle the relativism (or even, when taken to its extreme, the subjectivism – "well, that's just your opinion") that can stem from ideas prioritising self-interest? Do we still need deontological rulings?

Box 9.2 Enlightened egoism

The following example briefly illustrates the difference between traditional conceptions of egoism as a one-dimensional pursuit of immediate, selfish goals and enlightened egoism, which posits self-interest as being made up of a complex network of competing elements:

> Suppose that Alex receives a job offer on the other side of the country and he asks his friend Bill for advice as to whether he should accept it. Bill recognizes the offer as an excellent opportunity for Alex, the net effect of which will significantly enhance Alex's overall well-being. Bill also realizes, however, that Alex's relocation would result in the loss of many features of their friendship that Bill enjoys.
>
> (Burgess-Jackson 2013: 535–536)

While traditional understandings of egoism would argue that Bill would (or indeed should, or can only) advise Alex to stay, in the context of enlightened egoism, saying that Bill would simply ask his friend to stay reveals "an extremely superficial understanding of the nature of self-interest and of the nature of love" (Smith 2005: 270). Indeed, Alex's happiness and well-being form a part of Bill's self-interest and, if nothing else, if his friend realised that Bill had offered the advice based purely on his own needs, that decision itself would risk jeopardising the friendship.

? What is your take on this scenario?
? (How) can we apply these ideas to the context of translation? Could this model be used to allow space for personal needs and desires, without sacrificing more global needs or are the two mutually exclusive?

Handling Others: Representation and Representativeness

The question of **who can, may, or should translate** has remained rather implicit in our discussions up to this point, but is one that has come into sharp focus in recent TIS literature and public debates in translation. While we have viewed translation and interpreting ethics as being irrevocably intertwined with concerns of responsibility, the related questions of representation and identity cannot be overlooked. Discussing the implicitly ethical nature of translation, Washbourne (2019: 399) reminds us that "[f]undamentally, translation contends with the spectre of appropriation, the issue of who can speak for another, how translation may speak, and whether translation is a speaking for or a speaking with." When we translate or interpret, we may be standing in for or alongside somebody else, being their voice, or at least sharing their ideas with a new audience, and this ontology of dual authorship – or even the paradox of sameness-in-difference – is central here (see Chapter 2). Given the plurality of experiences, knowledge, beliefs, and desires – which has led us to explore issues such as the subjective nature of ethics and the complexity of neutrality and impartiality – can we unproblematically step in for anyone in any situation, or are there cases in which the interpreter/translator's knowledge, life experience, viewpoints, and so forth are too markedly different from our client's, speaker's, author's own to render this problematic? Of course, (professional) models of impartiality and neutrality would suggest that our individual identity has no bearing on our ability to translate or interpret, and the question of representation offers yet another opportunity to problematise these fundamental ethical assumptions.

Kotze and Strowe (2021) astutely divide this issue of who can, may, or should translate between the local and the structural. On the local level we explore the questions of whether the individual translator is able to engage with, inhabit, and represent others' knowledge and whether they have the right to do this. Essentially, this is a debate over whether and indeed how we can acquire and transmit experiential knowledge: the question of **representation**. On the structural level, meanwhile, we explore who is given this opportunity in the first place. Indeed, purely asking whether a translator/interpreter can work in a given situation risks overlooking the important question of how "translation tasks are allocated, distributed, and recognised" (Kotze and Strowe 2021: 352). This question of **representativeness** relates to the structural inequalities in society (in this case, the authors are specifically referring to publishing) and the underrepresentation of minority/minoritised groups, which is a well-known feature of the translation industry. As Kotze and Strowe eloquently put it, "we also need to consider which social, economic, political, and institutional forces and agents are involved in *choosing* who will translate" (Kotze and Strowe 2021: 352). For them, this is perhaps the most pressing dimension of all, arguing that the very question of who can translate arises because of a lack of industry representativeness and a lack of opportunities for access to the industry for certain groups. Worryingly, Kotze and Strowe argue that "the experiential knowledge of marginalised groups is often seen as a type of knowledge that can be acquired by anyone" (ibid. 353), thus legitimising this inequality. This fascinating new perspective expands the question of who *should* translate beyond questions of responsibility (to texts, authors, clients, etc.) to consider notions of industry-wide equitability and how we can question and change existing structures and assumptions. The case that prompted Kotze and Strowe's piece and a whole host of other reflections on these questions of representation and representativeness is outlined in Box 9.3.

Beyond this more academic context, elements of these questions, too, have been the subject of debate in professional circles in recent times (albeit again in the domain of literary translation, which is often viewed as holding distinct challenges to its non-literary counterpart – inevitably raising the spectre of domain-specific ethical challenges). In the ITI's professional magazine, *The ITI Bulletin*, for instance, Tony McNicol has reflected on his experience of translating the memoir of a Japanese Buddhist monk, make-up artist, and LGBTQ activist, Kodo Nishimura. Aside from the linguistic challenges that the text posed, as a white, male, UK-based translator who does not identify as LGBTQ, McNicol queried his suitability as a translator for this project, which shared a raw and personal lived experience (2022: 11). His conclusion was in fact that his "reason – perhaps a selfish one – for translating the book was that Kodo is so different from me", offering another implicit link to the presence of self-interest in translatorly decision-making and hinting at an industry model that does not place a particularly heavy focus on the exclusivity (or importance perhaps?) of experiential knowledge.

? Is there any work that you feel you would/should refuse for reasons related to identity, representation, or experiential knowledge? Why?
? How representative are the contexts that you work in? Do you work with people from a range of backgrounds? Does everybody have an equal chance to voice their beliefs or to take on new opportunities? What do you feel is the impact of this presence or lack of diversity?

Box 9.3 A case study: Amanda Gorman's Dutch translator

Amanda Gorman, an American poet and activist and (importantly here) a young, black, female spoken-word artist, became an international sensation after reading her poem 'The Hill We Climb' at US president Joe Biden's inauguration in January 2021. Shortly after the inauguration, publishers scrambled to distribute the poem worldwide with a host of translations soon commissioned. In March 2021, Dutch publisher Meulenhoff announced that acclaimed poet and Booker Prize-winning novelist Marieke Lucas Rijneveld would be the Dutch translator of the poem, leading to a wave of criticism. Journalist and activist Janice Deul led critics asking why Meulenhoff had not chosen a translator who was, like Gorman, a spoken-word artist, young, female, and unapologetically Black. Kotze and Strowe (2021: 352), meanwhile, added that the publisher even conceded that Rijneveld was not particularly good at English and had never published a translation, leading them to conclude that the choice "would seem to be based not on subject knowledge (experiential or otherwise), genre expertise, or translation expertise, but on marketability" (a vivid reminder of the conflicting interests at work in translation projects). For their part, Meulenhoff appealed to similarities between Gorman and Rijneveld, both being young writers who had come to fame early.

Following the backlash, Rijneveld said they decided to step down because they were "able to grasp when it is/isn't your place" (*The Guardian* 2021). Rijneveld subsequently published their own poem – *Everything inhabitable* – as a response to the reaction and, while noting that they were "shocked by the uproar surrounding my involvement in the spread of Amanda Gorman's message" and "understand the people who feel hurt by Meulenhoff's choice to ask me" (Flood 2021), nevertheless conceded that they "had happily devoted myself to translating Amanda's work, seeing it as the greatest task to keep her strength, tone and style. However, I realise that I am in a position to think and feel that way, where many are not."

Though responses varied wildly, most criticism did not revolve around arguments stating that all literary translators must share the exact same identity as the author (the question of representation), but rather that the publisher had made this choice against a backdrop of systemic racism (representativeness). However, the question of required experiential knowledge rages on – and translators and interpreters' backgrounds will undoubtedly affect the choices that they make – and the clash between profit, marketability, and ethics ties into a number of other threads.

? Was the translator right to turn down the work in this case? Why?
? Can/should publishers consider the profit motive over questions such as representation, access, and power?

So, Where Does Our Responsibility Lie?

Returning to discussions at the start of this textbook once again, we reflect for a final time on Chesterman's (2016: 168) neat divide between macro-ethical and micro-ethical matters. Over the course of this textbook, we have explored a broad spectrum of concerns and hopefully at this point you have developed a strong sense of the range of ethical questions at stake when you translate or interpret. Responsibility has been at the heart of so many of the discussions throughout this textbook, that it is only fitting that this is where we draw our discussions to a close. Figure 9.1 attempts to capture the complexity of the area in graphic form by drawing together a wide range of viewpoints that we have considered throughout this textbook.

The four black boxes below our confused figure in the centre represent overarching drivers for ethical action. As noted in Chapter 8, Abdallah

Other Viewpoints 171

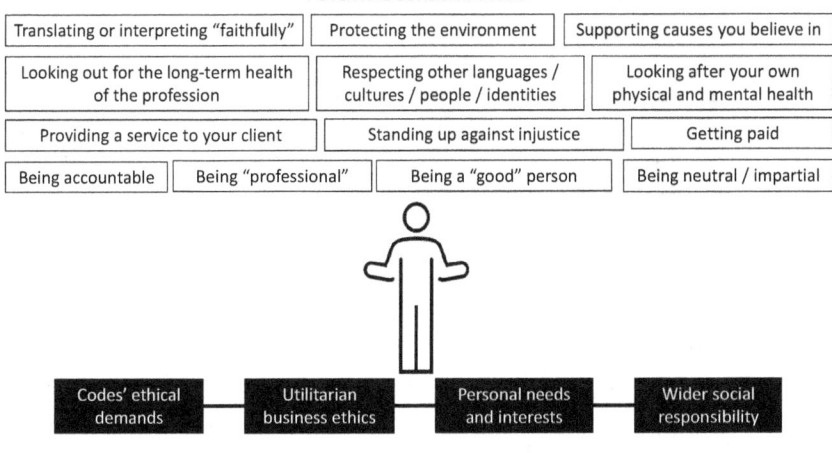

Figure 9.1 Potential reflections on responsibility in translation and interpreting.

raises the tension between deontological codes and utilitarian business ethics, while we added another two wide-ranging drivers – personal needs and interests and wider social responsibility. Above the figure is a multitude of potential considerations that can be derived from these overarching drivers, ranging from more narrow, textual concerns for fidelity (as explored in Chapters 2 and 3) all the way to the importance of protecting the environment and/or your own physical and mental health (see Chapter 8). This range of potential considerations is by no means exhaustive, though it does encapsulate many of the discussions from previous chapters and serves as a useful illustration to demonstrate how complex ethical decision-making is. Of course, many of these considerations can contradict one another (Can we always stand up against injustice while being "professional", for instance?) or be mutually dependent (Can we be a "good" person without respecting other people?). It also draws attention to the inescapably personal nature of ethics and the inescapably context-dependent nature of our decisions. There is no one "right" answer in all situations.

? Using Figure 9.1, which overarching drivers do you feel are the most helpful and/or important in terms of your ethical decision-making overall?
? Again using Figure 9.1, which potential considerations would you say are most important to you in a typical translation or interpreting assignment? Try to highlight 2–3 and compare and contrast with others.

Importantly, there is scope to explore each of these areas further (and others besides!), and one of the aims of this illustration is to serve as a quick-glance inspiration for future projects of all kinds. Practically all of the areas covered in this book arguably warrant further exploration, whether examining underlying theoretical bases or applying ideas to new languages, practices, and contexts. The list below aims to go one step further by providing some more specific, unanswered questions relating to various domains of responsibility, as covered throughout this textbook. In spite of the significant attention paid to ethics in the last few decades, its vast overarching nature means that there is considerable scope for further exploration in undergraduate and postgraduate essays, group presentations and dissertations, at doctoral or even post-doctoral levels. Indeed, information in so many of these domains remains rather fragmentary and there is space for much more ethically focused research across the entire range of topics.

Textual fidelity

? To what extent do different text types require differing levels of fidelity or approaches to ethics?
? Which particular elements of texts are most ethically problematic, and does this vary according to place, time, and language?
? How is technology shaping our relationship with texts and speakers?

Responsibility

? Can we make a case for a specific type of responsibility in translation and interpreting (or indeed translation *or* interpreting)?
? Are there any layers of responsibility that have not been covered to date?

New perspectives

? Are there any insights that can be drawn from your specific language pair(s), or do any of the ideas discussed fail to apply to those contexts requiring renewed ethical enquiry?
? Are there any cultural/ethical/political viewpoints not covered in the literature that would bring new impetus to discussions of ethics?
? How do the ideas covered relate to specific geographic locations, or specific groups of people? Are notions of ethics representative of different groups and viewpoints?
? What distinct ethical issues arise in other parallel practices such as subtitling, dubbing, and localisation, or variations such as remote interpreting or sworn translation?

Codes of ethics

- ? What gaps must be addressed in codes of ethics?
- ? Are there other ways of codifying ethics that would lead to more productive engagement with the domain?

Professionals

- ? How can we ensure the future sustainability of the translation profession in light of the various threats facing translation and interpreting?
- ? What ethical responsibilities do we have in relation to considerations of money?
- ? How can we reconcile phenomena such as climate anxiety with our personal need to survive, and what impact does this have upon our professional roles?

Society

- ? In what way are translation and interpreting impacting upon various crises in today's globalised world? For example, environmental, health, humanitarian crises.
- ? How can we make the languages industry more representative?
- ? How can translation and interpreting be harnessed to elicit societal change?

And, more generally

- ? What gaps do you feel require further attention?
- ? What interests you in relation to ethics?
- ? Do you strongly disagree with any of the ideas outlined in this textbook?
- ? Has your further reading brought up any prominent gaps in the literature?

Ethics is a broad and multifaceted domain, and part of what makes it so dynamic and so exciting is that it can be used as the catalyst for explorations of so many areas in TIS – there are always ethical underpinnings to our work and ideas. As we saw in chapters 7 and 8, however, ethics remains a relatively marginal topic in the professional domain in explicit terms and there is little immediate sign of this changing drastically. That said, ethics is slowly becoming a more prominent topic in the translation classroom and translation associations do continue to tweak and improve their ethical provision, which may elicit changes on a wider level. It is clear that there are several key ethical issues currently weighing on translators' and interpreters' minds, and these are not always the questions at the centre of existing ethical provision. For instance, as we have seen, technological advances continue to permeate and reconfigure professional workflows, while LSP practices, non-professional translation, and these very technological advances continue to apply downward pressure on rates. Meanwhile, wider environmental, health, and financial crises continue to punctuate our personal and professional lives. All of these inevitably have an impact upon the professional's mental health, hence the vital importance of not only looking outwards to consider how, where, and why we can focus our attentions, but also reflect inwards on our own wellbeing.

Factoring in this vast range of concerns, ethics arguably looks more prominent now than ever before, and merits further discussion and exploration among professionals, students, associations, and academics alike. Importantly, we all stake out a position in the world and, in order to negotiate, shape, and challenge understandings, we must embrace our agency rather than accepting an invisible, neutral conduit role. We need to be empowered to consider and forward our individual and collective interests and trusted to reflect critically on the impact that our decisions have.

Further Reading

As mentioned above, there are a number of fascinating areas that fall beyond the scope of this introductory textbook and a key source that captures a number of these areas is ***The Routledge Handbook of Translation and Ethics*** (Koskinen and Pokorn 2021). This fantastic volume has been cited at numerous points throughout this textbook, but it is worth reiterating that this represents an ideal next step for anyone looking to explore topics in this textbook (and topics not in this textbook!) from a different perspective and, of course, in greater detail. Readers are also invited to use this book's **Bibliography** as a guide to further reading – the citations used throughout this textbook come from leading voices in each of topic areas covered and the sources used are by and large the most authoritative ones available.

Bibliography

Journal Articles

Abdallah, Kristina. 2011. "Towards Empowerment: Students' Ethical Reflections on Translating in Production Networks." *The Interpreter and Translator Trainer* 5, no. 1: 129–154. http://dx.doi.org/10.1080/13556509.2011.10798815.

Anastasiou, Dimitra, and Rajat Gupta. 2011. "Crowdsourcing as Human-Machine Translation (HMT)." *Journal of Information Science* 20, no. 10: 1–15. DOI: 10.1177/016555150nnnnnnn.

Annas, Julia. 2004. "Being Virtuous and Doing the Right Thing." *Proceedings and Addresses of the American Philosophical Association* 78, no. 2: 61–74. https://doi.org/10.2307/3219725.

Awad, Edmond et al. 2018, October. "The Moral Machine Experiment." *Nature* 563, no. 7729: 59–64.

Baixauli-Olmos, Lluis. 2017. "Ethics codes as tools for social change in public service interpreting: Symbolic, social and cultural dimensions." *JoSTrans*, 28: 250–272.

Baker, Mona. 2005. "Narratives in and of Translation." *SKASE Journal of Translation and Interpretation* 1, no. 1: 4–13. www.skase.sk.

Baker, Mona. 2008. "Ethics of Renarration: Mona Baker Is Interviewed by Andrew Chesterman." *Cultus* 1, no. 1: 10–33.

Baker, Mona and Carol Maier. 2011. "Ethics and the Curriculum: Critical Perspectives." *The Interpreter and Translator Trainer* 5, no. 1: 1–14.

Basalamah, Salah. 2001. "The Thorn of Translation in the Side of the Law: Toward Ethical Copyright and Translation Rights." In *The Translator* 7, no. 2: 155–168. https://doi.org/10.1080/13556509.2001.10799098.

Bulut, Alev, and Turgay Kurultay. 2001. "Interpreters-in-Aid at Disasters: Community Interpreting in the Process of Disaster Management." In *The Translator* 7, no. 2: 249–264. https://doi.org/10.1080/13556509.2001.10799104.

Burgess-Jackson, Keith. 2013. "Taking Egoism Seriously." *Ethical Theory and Moral Practice*, 16, no. 3: 529–542. DOI: 10.1007/s10677-012-9372-5.

Chan, Andy Lung Jan. 2017. "An Economist's Proposal for the Study of the Translation Profession in Southeast Asia." *Manusya: Journal of Humanities* 20, no. 3: 85–97. https://doi.org/10.1163/26659077-02003005.

Charron, Marc. 2001. "Berman, Unfaithful to Himself?" *TTR* 14, no. 2: 97–121. https://doi.org/10.7202/000571ar.

Chesterman, Andrew. 2001. "Proposal for a Hieronymic Oath." *The Translator* 7, no. 2: 139–154.

Costa, Beverley, Raquel Lázaro Gutiérrez and Tom Rausch. 2020, June. "Self-care as an ethical responsibility: A pilot study on support provision for interpreters in human crises." *Translation and Interpreting Studies* 15, no. 1: 36–56. https://doi.org/10.1075/tis.20004.cos.

DeTienne, Kristen Bell, Bradley R. Agle, James C. Phillips and Marc-Charles Ingerson. 2012, February. "The Impact of Moral Stress Compared to Other Stressors on Employee Fatigue, Job Satisfaction, and Turnover: An Empirical Investigation." *Journal of Business Ethics* 110, no. 3: 377–378. DOI: 10.1007/s10551-011-1197-y.

Doherty, Stephen. 2016. "The impact of translation technologies on the process and product of translation." *International Journal of Communication* 10: 947–969.

Donovan, Clare. 2011, February. "Ethics in the Teaching of Conference Interpreting." *The Interpreter and Translator Trainer* 5, no. 1: 109–128. http://dx.doi.org/10.1080/13556509.2011.10798814.

Drugan, Joanna, and Bogdan Babych. 2010. "Shared Resources, Shared Values? Ethical Implications of Sharing Translation Resources." *JEC*, 3–10. https://aclanthology.org/2010.jec-1.2.

Drugan, Joanna, and Chris Megone. 2011. "Bringing Ethics into Translator Training: An Integrated Inter-disciplinary Approach." *The Interpreter and Translator Trainer* 5, no. 1: 183–211. https://doi.org/10.1080/13556509.2011.10798817.

Drugan, Joanna, and Rebecca Tipton. 2017, May. "Translation, ethics and social responsibility." *The Translator* 23, no. 2: 119–125. https://doi.org/10.1080/13556509.2017.1327008.

Dyson, Steve. 2003. "A Strategic Point." Letters, *Multilingual Computing and Technology* 14, no. 3: 11.

Fırat, Gökhan. 2021. "Uberization of Translation: Impacts on Working Conditions." *The Journal of Internationalization and Localization* 8, no. 1: 48–75. https://doi.org/10.1075/jial.20006.fir.

Gallai, Fabrizio. 2017. "Pragmatic competence and interpreter-mediated police investigation interviews." In *The Translator* 23, no. 2: 177–196. https://doi.org/10.1080/13556509.2017.1327317.

Garcia, Ignacio. 2010. "Is machine translation ready yet?." *Target. International Journal of Translation Studies* 22, no. 1: 7–21. https://doi.org/10.1075/target.22.1.02gar.

Goodwin, Phil. 2010. "Ethical Problems in Translation: Why we might need Steiner after all." *The Translator* 16, no. 1: 19–42. https://doi.org/10.1080/13556509.2010.10799292.

Gouanvic, Jean-Marc. 2001. "Ethos, ethics and translation: Toward a community of destinies." *The Translator* 7, no. 2: 203–212. https://doi.org/10.1080/13556509.2001.10799101.

Greenall, Annjo K., Cecilia Alvstad, Hanne Jansen, and Kristiina Taivalkoski-Shilov. 2019. "Introduction: voice, ethics and translation." *Perspectives* 27, no. 5: 639–647. https://doi.org/10.1080/0907676X.2019.1631862.

Hale, Sandra. 2008. "Controversies over the role of the court interpreter." *Benjamins Translation Library* 76: 99–121. https://doi.org/10.1075/btl.76.06hal.

Hutchings, Stephen ed. 2021. "Translation and The Ethics of Diversity." *The Translator* 27, no. 4. https://doi.org/10.1080/13556509.2022.2062108.

Inghilleri, Moira. 2008. "The ethical task of the translator in the geo-political arena." *Translation Studies* 1, no. 2: 212–223, DOI: 10.1080/14781700802113556.
Katan, David, and Francesco Straniero-Sergio. 2001. "Look who's talking: The ethics of entertainment and talkshow interpreting." *The Translator* 7, no. 2: 213–237. https://doi.org/10.1080/13556509.2001.10799102.
Ko, Leong. 2006. "Fine-tuning the Code of Ethics for Interpreters and Translators." *Translation Watch Quarterly* 2, no. 3: 45–57. https://doi.org/10.1163/978900 4299245_021.
Kopp, Ruth Katharina. 2012, December. "Skopos Theory and Ethics: A Paradox?." *mTm. Minor Translating Major-Major Translating Minor-Minor Translating Minor* 4: 145–166.
Kotze, Haidee, and Anna Strowe. 2021, September. "Response by Kotze and Strowe to "Representing experiential knowledge"." *Translation Studies* 14, no. 3: 3503–3554. https://doi.org/10.1080/14781700.2021.1972039.
Kruger, Haidee, and Elizabeth Crots. 2014. "Professional and personal ethics in translation: a survey of South African translators' strategies and motivations." *Stellenbosch Papers in Linguistics Plus* 43, no. 1: 147–181. https://hdl.handle.net/10520/EJC157652.
Lambert, Joseph. 2018. "How ethical are codes of ethics? Using illusions of neutrality to sell translations." *The Journal of Specialised Translation* 30: 269–290.
Lambert, Joseph, and Callum Walker. 2022. "Because We're Worth It: Disentangling freelance translation, status, and rate-setting in the United Kingdom." *Translation Spaces*, 1–26 https://doi.org/10.1075/ts.21030.lam.
Lee, Hyang, and Seong Woo Yun. 2020, November. "How can we improve the codes of ethics for translators?." *Babel* 66, no. 4-5: 706–718. https://doi.org/10.1075/babel.00190.yun.
Leiter, Michael P., and Christina Maslach. 2008, May. "Early Predictors of Job Burnout and Engagement." *Journal of Applied Psychology* 93, no. 3: 498–512. https://psycnet.apa.org/doi/10.1037/0021-9010.93.3.498.
Li, Hanji, and Haiqing Chen. 2018, March. "The construction of a new translation ethics from the perspective of Chinese philosophy." *Philosophy* 8, no. 3: 119–124. http://dx.doi.org/10.17265/2159-5313/2018.03.003.
Määttä, Simo K. 2015, January. "Interpreting the Discourse of Reporting: The Case of Screening Interviews with Asylum Seekers and Police Interviews in Finland." *The International Journal of Translation and Interpreting Research* 7, no. 3: 21–35. http://dx.doi.org/10.12807/ti.107203.2015.a02.
Maitland, Sarah. 2016. "'In-between' a rock and a 'third space'? On the trouble with ambivalent metaphors of translation." *Translation Studies* 9, no. 1: 17–32. https://doi.org/10.1080/14781700.2015.1085432.
Marshman, Elizabeth. 2014. "Taking Control: Language Professionals and Their Perception of Control When Using Language Technologies." *Meta* 59, no. 2: 380–405. https://doi.org/10.7202/1027481ar.
Martin Ruano, M. Rosario. 2015. "(Trans)formative theorising in legal translation and/or interpreting: a critical approach to deontological principles." *The Interpreter and Translator Trainer* 9, no. 2, 141–155. https://doi.org/10.1080/1750399X.2015.1051767.
McDonough Dolmaya, Julie. 2011a. "Moral ambiguity: Some shortcomings of professional codes of ethics for translators." *The Journal of Specialised Translation* 15: 28–49.

McDonough Dolmaya, Julie. 2011b. "A Window into the Profession." *The Translator* 17, no. 1: 77–104. https://doi.org/10.1080/13556509.2011.10799480.

McDonough Dolmaya, Julie. 2017. "Expanding the sum of all human knowledge: Wikipedia, translation and linguistic justice." In *The Translator* 23, no. 2: 143–157. https://doi.org/10.1080/13556509.2017.1321519.

Mikkelson, Holly. 2000. "Interpreter ethics: A review of the traditional and electronic literature." *Interpreting* 5, no. 1: 49–56. https://doi.org/10.1075/intp.5.1.05mik.

Monzó-Nebot, Esther, and Melissa Wallace. 2020. "New societies, new values, new demands." *Translation and Interpreting Studies* 15, no. 1: 1–14. https://doi.org/10.1075/tis.00046.int.

Moorkens, Joss, Dorothy Kenny, and Félix do Carmo. 2020. "Fair MT: Towards ethical, sustainable machine translation." *Translation Spaces* 9, no. 1: 1–11. https://doi.org/10.1075/ts.00018.int.

Moster, Stefan. 2003. "Birthday Blues." *Books from Finland* 1: 59–60. http://www.finlit .fi /booksfromfinland /bff /103 /moster .html.

Nord, Christiane. 2001. "Loyalty Revisited." *The Translator* 7, no. 2: 185–202. https://doi.org/10.1080/13556509.2001.10799100.

Nouss, Alexis. 2001. "Antoine Berman aujourd'hui." *TTR* 14, no. 2: 9–10. https://doi.org/10.7202/000564ar.

Ozolins, Uldis. 2014. "Rewriting the AUSIT Code of Ethics – principles, practice, dispute." *Babel* 60, no. 3: 347–370. https://doi.org/10.1075/babel.60.3.05ozu.

Prunč, Erich. 1997. "Translationskultur (Versuch einer konstruktiven Kritik des translatorischen Handelns)." *TextConText Neue Folge* 1: 99–127.

Pym, Anthony. 1996. "Venuti's Visibility." *Target* 8, no. 2: 165–177. http://dx.doi.org/10.1075/target.8.1.12pym.

Pym, Anthony. 2001. "The Return to Ethics." *The Translator* 7, no. 2: 129–138. https://doi.org/10.1080/13556509.2001.10799096.

Pym, Anthony, David Orrego-Carmona, and Ester Torres-Simón. 2016. "Status and Technology in the Professionalisation of Translators." *The Journal of Specialised Translation* 25: 33–53.

Pym, Anthony. 2017. "Translation and economics: inclusive communication or language diversity?" *Perspectives* 25, no. 3: 362–377. DOI: 10.1080/0907676X.2017.1287208.

Pym, Anthony. 2021b. "Cooperation, risk, trust: A restatement of translator ethics." *STRIDON: Studies in Translation and Interpreting* 1, no. 2: 5–24. https://doi.org/10.4312/stridon.1.2.5-24.

Ramírez Giraldo, Juan. 2014. "Translation Right or Wrong." *The Translator* 20, no. 2: 249–253. https://doi.org/10.1080/13556509.2014.960654.

Rossi, Cecilia. 2021. "Writers and translators working together: the ethical dimension of the translation of post conflict literature." *The Translator* 27, no. 4: 384–399.

Schweda-Nicholson, Nancy. 1994. "Community Interpreter Training in the United States and the United Kingdom: An Overview of Selected Initiatives." *Hermes, Journal of Linguistics* 12, no. 7: 127–140. https://doi.org/10.7146/hjlcb.v7i12.24930.

Sharma, Anurag. 1997. "Professional as agent: Knowledge asymmetry in agency exchange." *Academy of Management Review* 22, no. 3: 758–798. https://doi.org/10.5465/amr.1997.9708210725.

Skaaden, Hanne. 2019. "Invisible or invincible? Professional integrity, ethics, and voice in public service interpreting." *Perspectives* 27, no. 5: 704–717. DOI: 10.1080/0907676X.2018.1536725.

Stupiello, Érika N.A. 2008. "Ethical Implications of Translation Technologies." *Translation Journal* 12, no. 1. http://translationjournal.net/journal/43ethics.htm.

Tack, Lieven. 2001. "Review of Beyond Ambivalence." *The Translator* 7, no. 2: 297–321.

Tipton, Rebecca. 2017. "Contracts and capabilities: Public service interpreting and domestic violence services." In *The Translator* 23, no. 2: 237–254. https://doi.org/10.1080/13556509.2017.1280875.

Topping, Suzanne. 2000. "Sharing Translation Database Information." *Multilingual Computing and Technology* 11, no. 5: 59–61. http://dx.doi.org/10.5281/zenodo.6759984.

Tyulenev, Sergey. 2021. "In a wilderness of mirrors: the ethics of translation in Cold-War espionage." *The Translator* 27, no. 4: 368–383. https://doi.org/10.1080/13556509.2021.1992892.

Wang, Dongfeng. 2004. "The Deconstruction of 'Fidelity' and the Demythologization of Translation." *Chinese Translators Journal*, no. 6: 3–9.

Wang, Jie, and Yuanyuan Li. 2019. "Incorporating Ethics-Awareness Competence in China Translator-Training Programme." *International Journal of Linguistics, Literature and Translation* 2, no. 4, 164–170. DOI: 10.32996/ijllt.2019.2.4.16.

Wecksteen, Corinne. 2000. "*Pour une éthique du traducteur.*" *The Translator* 6, no. 1, 125–129. https://doi.org/10.1080/13556509.2000.10799059.

Wilensky, Harold L. 1964. "The professionalization of everyone?" *American Journal of Sociology* 70, no. 2: 137–158.

Wolf, Alain. 2015. "A Religious Ethics of Translation: The Love Command." *Journal of Translation* 11, no. 1: 61–73.

Zetzsche, Jost. 2005. "Translation Memories: The Discovery of Assets." *Multilingual Computing and Technology* 16, no. 4: 43–45.

Zhou, Meng. 2022, January. "Educating translation ethics: a neurocognitive ethical decision-making approach." *The Interpreter and Translator Trainer*: 1–18. https://doi.org/10.1080/1750399X.2022.2030534.

Chapters in a Collection

Angelelli, Claudia V. 2021. "Ethics in Child Language Brokering." In *The Routledge Handbook of Translation and Ethics*, edited by Kaisa Koskinen and Nike Pokorn, 383–397. Abingdon: Routledge.

Asimov, Isaac. 1950. "Runaround." In *I Robot*, 40. New York: Doubleday.

Bancroft, Marjory A. 2017. "The Voice of Compassion: Exploring Trauma-Informed Interpreting." In *Ideology, Ethics and Policy Development in Public Service Interpreting and Translation*, edited by Carmen Valero-Garcés, and Rebecca Tipton, 195–215. Bristol: Multilingual Matters.

Baker, Mona. 2009. "Resisting state terror: Theorizing communities of activist translators and interpreters." In *Globalization, Political Violence and Translation*, edited by Esperanza Bielsa and Christopher Hughes, 222–242. London: Palgrave Macmillan.

Basamalah, Salah. 2021. "Ethics of Volunteering in Translation and Interpreting." In *The Routledge Handbook of Translation and Ethics*, edited by Kaisa Koskinen and Nike Pokorn, 227–244. Abingdon: Routledge.

Berman, Antoine. 2000. "Translation and the trials of the foreign." In *The Translation Studies Reader*, edited by Lawrence Venuti, 247–260. London/New York: Routledge.

Boéri, Julie, and Carmen Delgado Luchner. 2021. "Ethics of activist translation and interpreting." In *The Routledge Handbook of Translation and Ethics*, 245–261. London: Routledge.

Chesterman, Andrew. 2009. "An Ethical Decision." *In Translators and Their Readers: In Homage to Eugene Nida*, edited by Rodica Dimitriu, and Miriam Shlesinger, 347–354. Brussels: Éditions du Hazard.

Cicero, Marcus Tullius. 46 BCE/1960 CE. "De optimo genere oratorum." In *Cicero De inventione, De optimo genere oratorum, topica*, translated by H. M. Hubbell, 347–373. Cambridge, MA: Harvard University Press.

Dancy, Jonathan. 2013. "An Unprincipled Morality." In *Ethical Theory: An Anthology*, edited by Russ Shafer-Landau, 772–775. Oxford: John Wiley.

Drugan, Joanna. "Ethics." In *The Routledge Handbook of Translation and Philosophy*, edited by Piers Rawling and Philip Wilson, 243–355. Abingdon: Routledge.

Ergun, Emek. 2021. "Feminist Translation Ethics." In *The Routledge Handbook of Translation and Ethics*, edited by Kaisa Koskinen and Nike Pokorn, 114–130. Abingdon: Routledge.

Guangqin, Xin. 2021. "Translation Ethics in the Chinese Tradition." In *The Routledge Handbook of Translation and Ethics*, edited by Kaisa Koskinen and Nike Pokorn, 25–41. Abingdon: Routledge.

Haddow, Barry, Alexandra Birch and Kenneth Heafield. 2021. "Machine translation in healthcare." In *The Routledge Handbook of Translation and Health*, edited by Şebnem Susam-Saraeva, and Eva Spišiaková, 108–129. London: Routledge.

Hebenstreit, Gernot. 2021. "Functional Translation Theories and Ethics." In *The Routledge Handbook of Translation and Ethics*, edited by Kaisa Koskinen and Nike Pokorn, 58–71. Abingdon: Routledge.

Hermans, Theo. 2018. "Schleiermacher." In *The Routledge Handbook of Translation and Philosophy*, edited by Piers Rawling and Philip Wilson, 17–33. Abingdon: Routledge.

Hirvonen, Maija and Tuika Kinnunen. 2021. "Accessibility and Linguistic Rights." In *The Routledge Handbook of Translation and Ethics*, edited by Kaisa Koskinen and Nike Pokorn, 370–383. Abingdon: Routledge.

Hubscher-Davidson, Severine. 2021. "Ethical stress in translation and Interpreting." In *The Routledge Handbook of Translation and Ethics*, edited by Kaisa Koskinen and Nike Pokorn, 415–430. Abingdon: Routledge.

Hursthouse, Rosalind, and Glen Pettigrove. 2018. "Virtue Ethics." In *The Stanford Encyclopedia of Philosophy*, Winter 2018 edition, edited by Edward N. Zalta. https://plato.stanford.edu/archives/win2018/entries/ethics-virtue/.

Inghilleri, Moira, and Carol Maier. 2011. "Ethics." In *The Routledge Encyclopaedia of Translation Studies*, edited by Mona Baker and Gabriela Saldanha, 100–104. Abingdon: Routledge.

Israel, Hephzibah. 2021. "Ethics of Translating Sacred Texts." In *The Routledge Handbook of Translation and Ethics*, edited by Kaisa Koskinen and Nike Pokorn, 441–457. Abingdon: Routledge.

Jemielity, David. 2018. "Translation in Intercultural Business and Economic Environments." In *The Routledge Handbook of Translation and Culture,* edited by Sue-Ann Harding and Ovidi Carbonell Cortés, 533–557. Abingdon: Routledge. https://doi.org/10.4324/9781315670898-30.

Jerome, E. H. (St Jerome) (395 CE/1997) 'De optime genere interpretandi' (Letter 101, to Pammachius), in Epistolae D. Hieronymi Stridoniensis, Rome: Aldi F., (1565), pp. 285–291, translated by P. Carroll as 'On the best kind of translator', in *Western Translation Theory: From Herodotus to Nietzsche,* edited by Douglas Robinson (1997b), 22–30. Abingdon: Routledge.

Kadric, Mira, and Klaus Kaindl. 1997. "*Astérix* - Vom Gallier zum Tschetnikjäger: Zur Problematik von Massenkommunikation und übersetzerischer Ethik" In *Translation as Intercultural Communication: Selected papers from the EST Congress, Prague 1995,* 135–145. Amsterdam and Philadelphia: John Benjamins Publishing.

Kamocki, Pawel, and Jim O'Regan. 2016. "Privacy Issues in Online Machine Translation Services: European Perspective." In *Proceedings of the Tenth International Conference on Language Resources and Evaluation* (LREC 2016), edited by Nicoletta Calzolari et al., 4458–4462. Paris: European Language Resources Association. https://aclanthology.org/L16-1706.

Koskinen, Kaisa, and Nike K. Pokorn. 2021. "Ethics and Translation: An Introduction." In *The Routledge Handbook of Translation and Ethics*, edited by Kaisa Koskinen and Nike Pokorn, 1–12. Abingdon: Routledge.

Lambert, Joseph. 2021. "Professional Translator Ethics." In *The Routledge Handbook of Translation and Ethics*, edited by Kaisa Koskinen and Nike Pokorn, 165–179. Abingdon: Routledge.

Lambert, Joseph. 2023. "From Stagnation to Innovation: Codes of Ethics and the Profession Today." In *Ethics and Professional Codes of Practice for Translators and Interpreters: New Contexts in the Profession and Training.* Granada: Editorial Comares.

Laaksonen, Jenni and Kaisa Koskinen. 2021. "Venuti and the Ethics of Difference." In *The Routledge Handbook of Translation and Ethics*, edited by Kaisa Koskinen and Nike Pokorn, 131–146. Abingdon: Routledge.

Leblanc, Matthieu. 2017. "'I can't get no satisfaction!' Should we blame translation technologies or shifting business practices?" In *Human Issues in Translation Technology,* edited by Dorothy Kenny, 63–80. London: Routledge.

Ko, Leong. 2015. "Training ethical translators and interpreters." In *Translation and Cross-Cultural Communication Studies in the Asia Pacific,* edited by Ko Leong and Ping Chen, 337–350. Leiden: Brill-Rodopi.

Lin, Yutang. [1993] 2009. "On translation." In *An Anthology of Discourses on Translation: Revised Edition,* edited by Luo Xinzhang, and Chen Yingnian, 491–507. Beijing: The Commercial Press.

Maltby, Matthew. 2010. "Institutional Identities of Interpreters in the Asylum Application Context: A Critical Discourse Analysis of Interpreting Policies in the Voluntary Sector." In *Text and Context: Essays on Translation and Interpreting in Honour of Ian Mason,* edited by Mona Baker, Maeve Olohan and María Calzada Pérez, 209–233. Manchester: St Jerome.

McAlester, Gerard. 2003. "A Comment on Translation Ethics and Education." In *Translation Today: Trends and Perspectives,* edited by Gunilla Anderman, and Margaret Rogers, 225–227. Clevedon: Multilingual Matters.

Mellinger, Christopher D., and Brian James Baer. 2021. "Research Ethics in Translation and Interpreting Studies." In *The Routledge Handbook of Translation and Ethics*, edited by Kaisa Koskinen and Nike Pokorn, 365–382. Abingdon: Routledge.

Moorkens, Joss and David Lewis 2020. "Copyright and the reuse of translation as data." In *The Routledge Handbook of Translation and Technology*, edited by Minako O'Hagan, 469–481. Abingdon: Routledge.

Moorkens, Joss, and Marta Rocchi. 2021. "Ethics in the Translation Industry." In *The Routledge Handbook of Translation and Ethics*, edited by Kaisa Koskinen and Nike Pokorn, 320–337. Abingdon, Routledge. https://doi.org/10.4324/9781003127970-24.

Moorkens, Joss. 2022. "Ethics and machine translation." In *Machine Translation for Everyone: Empowering Users in the Age of Artificial Intelligence*, edited by Dorothy Kenny, 121–140. Berlin: Language Science Press. DOI:10.5281/zenodo.6759984.

Nozick, Robert. 1974. "The Rationality of Side Constraints." In *Ethical Theory: An Anthology*, edited by Russ Shafer-Landau, 521–523. Oxford: John Wiley.

Pokorn, Nike K., and Kaisa Koskinen. 2021. "The ethics of linguistic hospitality and untranslatability in Derrida and Ricœur." In *The Routledge Handbook of Translation and Ethics*, 87–98. London: Routledge.

Pöllabauer, Sonja, and Iris Topolovec. 2020. "Ethics in public service interpreting." In *The Routledge Handbook of Translation and Ethics*, 211–226. London: Routledge.

Prunč, Erich. 2008. "Zur Konstruktion Von Translationskulturen." In *Translationskultur: Ein Innovatives Und Produktives Konzept*, edited by Larisa Schippel, 19–41. Berlin: Frank & Timme.

Pym, Anthony. 1996. "Material Text Transfer as a Key to the Purposes of Translation." In *Basic Issues in Translation Studies*, edited by Albrecht Neubert, Gregory Shreve and Klaus Gommlich, 337–346. Kent OH and Leipzig: Kent State University Institute of Applied Linguistics.

Pym, Anthony. 2011. "Translation Research Terms: A Tentative Glossary for Moments of Perplexity and Dispute." In *Translation Research Projects 3*, edited by Anthony Pym, 75–110. Tarragona: Intercultural Studies Group. www.intercultural.urv.cat/media/upload/domain_317/arxius/TP3/isgbook3_web.pdf.

Pym, Anthony. 2021a. "Translator Ethics." In *The Routledge Handbook of Translation and Ethics*, edited by Kaisa Koskinen and Nike Pokorn, 147–164. Abingdon: Routledge.

Reiss, Katarina. 1977/1989. "Text types, translation types and translation assessment.", translated by Andrew Chesterman. In *Readings in Translation Theory*, edited by Andrew Chesterman, 105–115. Helsinki: Finn Lectura.

Robinson, Douglas. 2021. "The Ethics of Postcolonial Translation." In *The Routledge Handbook of Translation and Ethics*, edited by Kaisa Koskinen and Nike Pokorn, 99–113. Abingdon: Routledge.

Schaffner, Christina. 2020. "Translators' roles and responsibilities." In *The Bloomsbury Companion to Language Industry Studies*, edited by Erik Angelone, Maureen Ehrensberger-Dow, and Gary Massey, 63–90. London: Bloomsbury.

Schleiermacher, Friedrich. 1992. "On the Different Methods of Translating." In *Theories of Translation: An Anthology of Essays from Dryden to Derrida*, edited by John Biguenet and Rainer Schulte, 36–54. Chicago: The University of Chicago Press.

Schleiermacher, Freidrich. 2002a. "Akademievorträge." In *Kritische Gesamtausgabe* 11.1, edited by Martin Rössler. Berlin and New York: Walter de Gruyter.
Schleiermacher, Friedrich. 2002b. *Lectures on Philosophical Ethics.* Trans. Louise Adey Huish. Edited by Robert Louden. Cambridge: Cambridge University Press.
Tate, Granville and Turner, Graham. 2002. "The code and the culture: Sign language interpreting – in search of the new breed's ethics". In *The Interpreting Studies Reader*, edited by Franz Pöchhacker, 372–185. London: Routledge.
Tymoczko, Maria. 2003. "Ideology and the Position of the Translator." In *Apropos of Ideology: Translation Studies on Ideology-Ideologies in Translation Studies*, edited by Maria Calzada Pérez, 182–200. London and New York: Routledge.
Tymoczko, Maria. 2014. "Why Literary Translation is a Good Model for Translation Theory and Practice." In *Literary Translation: Redrawing the Boundaries*, edited by Jean Boase-Beier, Antoinette Fawcett and Philip Wilson, 11–31. London: Palgrave Macmillan.
Van Wyke, Ben. 2013. "Translation and Ethics." In *The Routledge Handbook of Translation Studies*, edited by Carmen Millán, and Francesca Bartrina, 566–578. London: Routledge.
Washbourne, Kelly. 2019. "Ethics." In *The Routledge Handbook of Literary Translation*, edited by Kelly Washbourne and Ben Van Wyke, 399–418. London and New York: Routledge.
Zetzche, Jost. 2020. "Freelance Translators' Perspectives." In *The Routledge Handbook of Translation and Technology*, edited by Minako O'Hagan, 166–182. Abingdon: Routledge.

Books and Reports

Angelelli, Claudia. 2004. *Revisiting the Interpreter's Role: A Study of Conference, Court, and Medical Interpreters in Canada, Mexico, and the United States.* New York: John Benjamin.
Aristotle. [1985] 1999. *Nicomachean Ethics*, Second Edition, translated by Terence Irwin. Indianapolis: Hackett Publishing.
Baker, Mona. 2006. *Translation and Conflict: A Narrative Account.* London: Routledge.
Baker, Mona. 2011. *In Other Words*, Second Edition. London: Routledge.
Baker, Mona. 2014. *Ethics in the Translation and Interpreting Curriculum: Surveying and Rethinking the Pedagogical Landscape.* York: Higher Education Academy.
Berman, Antoine. 1984. *L'épreuve de l'étranger: culture et traduction dans l'Allemagne romantique: Herder, Goethe, Schlegel, Novalis, Humboldt, Schleiermacher, Hölderlin.* Paris: Editions Gallimard.
Berman, Antoine. 1995. *Pour une critique des traductions: John Donne.* Paris: Gallimard.
Berman, Antoine. 1999. *La traduction et la lettre, ou, L'auberge du lointain.* Paris: 7Letras.
Berman, Antoine, Isabelle Berman, Valentina Sommella, and Chantal Wright. 2018. *The Age of Translation: A Commentary on Walter Benjamin's 'The Task of the Translator'.* London: Routledge.
Blackburn, Simon. 2003. *Being Good: A Short Introduction to Ethics.* Oxford: Oxford University Press.

Bowker, Lynne, and Jairo Buitrago Ciro. 2019. *Machine Translation and Global Research: Towards Improved Machine Translation Literacy in the Scholarly Community*. Bingley: Emerald Group Publishing.

Chan, Leo Tak-hung. 2004. *Twentieth-Century Chinese Translation Theory: Modes, Issues and Debates*. Amsterdam: John Benjamins.

Chesterman, Andrew. 2016. *Memes of Translation: The Spread of Ideas in Translation Theory*. Amsterdam and Philadelphia: John Benjamins.

Chesterman, Andrew. 2017. *Reflections on Translation Theory: Selected Papers 1993–2014*. Amsterdam and Philadelphia: John Benjamins.

Cheyfitz, Eric. 1991. *The Poetics of Imperialism: Translation and Colonization from the Tempest to Tarzan*. London: Oxford University Press.

Cronin, Michael. 2017. *Eco-Translation: Translation and Ecology in the Age of the Anthropocene. New Perspective in Translation and Interpreting Studies*. London, New York: Routledge, Taylor & Francis Group

Diriker, Ebru. 2004. *De-/Re-Contextualizing Conference Interpreting: Interpreters in the Ivory Tower?* Amsterdam and Philadelphia: John Benjamins.

Federici, Federico, and Sharon O-Brien. 2019. *Translation in Cascading Crises*. London: Routledge.

Folkart, Barbara. 2006. *Second Finding: A Poetics of Translation*. Ottawa: University of Ottawa Press.

Gouadec, Daniel. 2007. *Translation as a Profession*. Amsterdam: John Benjamins. https://doi.org/10.1075/btl.73.

Gouadec, Daniel. 2009. *Profession Traducteur*. Paris: La Maison du Dictionnaire.

Hale, Sandra. 2007. *Community Interpreting*. New York: Palgrave Macmillan.

Hood, Christopher P. 2001. *Japanese Education Reform: Nakasone's Legacy*. London: Routledge.

Inghilleri, Moira. 2012. *Interpreting Justice: Ethics, Politics and Language*. London: Routledge.

Kelly, Louis. 1979. *The True Interpreter: A History of Translation Theory and Practice in the West*. New York: St Martin's.

Koskinen, Kaisa. 2000. *Beyond Ambivalence: Postmodernity and the Ethics of Translation*. Tampere: University of Tampere.

Lambert, Joseph. (forthcoming). *Ethical Decision-Making*. London: Palgrave.

Lanier, Jaron. 2010. *You Are Not a Gadget: A Manifesto*. New York: Knopf.

Marx, Karl. 1867. *Das Kapital: kritik der politischen Oekonomie*. Hamburg: Verlag von Otto Meissner.

McLaughlin, Martin, and Javier Muñoz-Basols, eds. 2021. *Ideology, Censorship and Translation*. Abingdon and New York: Routledge.

Meschonnic, Henri. 2007/2011. *Éthique et politique du traduire*. Paris: Verdier; translated and edited by Pier-Pascale Boulanger as *Ethics and Politics of Translating*. Amsterdam: John Benjamins.

Munday, Jeremy, Sara Ramos Pinto and Jacob Blakesley. 2022. *Introducing Translation Studies: Theories and Applications*. London and New York: Routledge.

Nord, Christiane. 2018. *Translating as a Purposeful Activity: Functionalist Approaches Explained*. Manchester: St. Jerome.

Phelan, Mary, Mette Rudvin, Hanne Skaaden, and Patrick Kermit. 2020. *Ethics in Public Service Interpreting*. London: Routledge.

Pöchhacker, Franz, ed. 2015. *Routledge Encyclopedia of Interpreting Studies*. London: Routledge.

Prunč, Erich. 2012. *Entwicklungslinien der Translationswissenschaft: Von den Asymmetrien der Sprachen zu den Asymmetrien der Macht*, 3rd edition. TRANSÜD. Berlin: Frank & Timme.

Pym, Anthony. 1997. *Pour une éthique du traducteur*. Ottawa: Artois Presses Université and Presses d'Université d'Ottawa.

Pym, Anthony, François Grin, Claudio Sfreddo, and Andy LJ Chan. 2012. *The Status of the Translation Profession in the European Union*. London and New York: Anthem Press.

Reiß, Katharina, and Hans J. Vermeer. 1984. *Grundlegung einer allgemeinen Translationstheorie*. 2. Aufl. 1991, reprint 2010. Linguistische Arbeiten 147. Tübingen: Max Niemeyer Verlag.

Robinson, Dave. 2012. *Ethics for Everyday Life: A Practical Guide*. London: Icon Books.

Rogers, Margaret. 2015. *Specialised Translation: Shedding the 'Non-literary' Tag*. New York: Springer.

Schleiermacher, Friedrich. 1862. *Psychologie*. Vol. 6. Reimer.

Schleiermacher, Friedrich. 1998. Hermeneutics and Criticism and other Writings." Cambridge: Cambridge University Press.

Shafer-Landau, Russ, ed. 2013. *Ethical Theory: An Anthology*. Oxford: John Wiley.

Skaaden, Hanne. 2013. *Den topartiske tolken: lærebok i tolking*. Oslo: Universitetsforl.

Tymoczko, Maria. 2007. *Enlarging Translation: Empowering Translators*. London and New York: Routledge.

Lawrence, Venuti. 1995. *The Translator's Invisibility: A History of Translation*. London and New York: Routledge.

Venuti, Lawrence. 1998. *The Scandals of Translation: Towards an Ethics of Difference*. London: Routledge.

Venuti, Lawrence. 2008. *The Translator's Invisibility: A History of Translation*, revised edition. London and New York: Routledge.

Venuti, Lawrence. 2013. *Translation Changes Everything*. London and New York: Routledge.

Vermeer, Hans J. 1996. *A Skopos Theory of Translation: (Some Arguments for and Against)*. Heidelberg: TextconText-Verlag.

Weaver, Warren. 1947. 'Letter to Norbert Wiener, March 4', Rockefeller Foundation Archives.

Webpage Content

DePalma, Don. 2014. "Free Machine Translation Can Leak Data." *TC World*. Accessed 26 August 2022. www.tcworld.info/e-magazine/translation-and-localization/free-machine-translation-can-leak-data-516/.

Inbox Translation. 2020. "Research Translator Survey 2020." Accessed 2 July 2021. https://inboxtranslation.com/resources/research/freelance-translator-survey-2020/.

Institute of Translation and Interpreting. 2016. "Code of Professional Conduct". Accessed 26 August 2022. www.iti.org.uk/become-a-member/code-of-professional-conduct.

Institute of Translation and Interpreting. 2020. "Spring 2020 Pulse Survey." Accessed 14 July 2021. www.iti.org.uk/resource/spring-2020-pulse-survey.html.

McNicol, Tony. 2022. "In his shoes." Institute of Translation and Interpreting, Bulletin Article. Accessed 26 August 2022. In his shoes (iti.org.uk).

Stansfield, Kate. 2022. "The world we can save." Institute of Translation and Interpreting, Bulletin Article. Accessed 26 August 2022. https://www.iti.org.uk/resource/the-world-we-can-save.html.

UX Content Collective. 2022. "The international guide to gender-inclusive writing." Accessed 26 August 2022. https://uxcontent.com/the-international-guide-to-gender-inclusive-writing/.

Thesis or Dissertation

Asiri, Eisa Ahmad S. 2016. "Developing a Code of Ethics for Professional Translation in Saudi Arabia: A Survey of Translators' Perceptions." MA thesis, Macquarie University, Sydney.

Somers, Margaret R. and Gloria D. Gibson. 1994. "Reclaiming the Epistemological 'Other': Narrative and the Social Constitution of Identity." CSST Working Paper, University of Michigan. https://deepblue.lib.umich.edu/bitstream/handle/2027.42/51265/499.pdf?sequence=1&isAllowed=y.

News Articles

Cohen, Randy. 2010, 2 July. "Properly Speaking the Improper?" The Ethicist Weekly Column, *New York Times Magazine*. www.nytimes.com/2010/07/04/magazine/04FOB-Ethicist-t.html.

Flood, Alison. 2021, 6 March. "Marieke Lucas Rijneveld writes poem about Amanda Gorman furore." *The Guardian*. www.theguardian.com/books/2021/mar/06/marieke-lucas-rijneveld-writes-poem-about-amanda-gorman-furore.

Kelly, Nataly. 2014, 19 June. "Why so many translators hate translation technology." *Huffpost UK*. www.huffingtonpost.com/nataly-kelly/why-so-many-translators-h_b_5506533.html.

Pidd, Helen. 2011, 12 May. "John Demjanjuk, the 'littlest of little fish', convicted for Nazi atrocities." *The Guardian*. www.theguardian.com/world/2011/may/12/john-demjanjuk-guilty-nazi-killings.

Smith, David. 2013. 12 December. "Mandela memorial interpreter says he has schizophrenia." *The Guardian*. www.theguardian.com/world/2013/dec/12/mandela-memorial-interpreter-schizophrenia-sign-language.

Index

Note: Page numbers in *italics* indicate figures on the corresponding pages.

Abdallah, K. 129, 136, 170–171
accessibility 162
accountability 104–106; case study on 106–107; *telos* and 109–110
accuracy in codes of ethics 122
act consequentialism 22
activism: to accountability 104–106; from advocacy to 101–103; case study on 106–107
advocacy 98–101, *99*; to activism 101–103
Alive 25–26
American Translator's Association (ATA) Code of Ethics 119
Angelelli, C. V. 89–90
Annas, J. 25
applied ethics 16–19
Aristotle 13–14, 24, 33, 37
Arlt. R. 49
Ars Poetica 33
Asimov, I. 21
Asylum Aid (AA) 132
Australian Institute of Interpreters and Translators (AUSIT) 122, 124, 126, 127

Babych, B. 155
Baixauli-Olmos, L. 118
Baker, M. 1, 96, 99, 102, 113; on accountability 102–106; moral relativism and 111–112
Bancroft, M. A. 120, 143–144
Basalamah, S. 139, 156
Bastos, R. 51
Bauman, Z. 96
Bentham, J. 22

Berman, A. 29, 43, 45, 77–78; on ethical translation 50–51; *The Experience of the Foreign: Culture and Translation in Romantic Germany* 46–47; *La traduction et la lettre* 51–54; on translating idioms 52–53; on trials of the foreign 47–48; on twelve deforming tendencies 48–50; on universalisability of ethics in translation 54–55
Biden, J. 169
Bildung 46–47
Birch, A. 151
Blackburn, S. 127
Boéri, J. 84, 101
Bogopane-Zulu, H. 113
borrowing 45
Bowker, L. 150, 152, 153, 158
Bulut, A. 162
Burgess-Jackson, K. 167
burnout 144

categorical imperative 19
censorship in translation 162
Chamberlain, B. H. 36–37
Charron, M. 55
Chesterman, A. 2–3, 29–33, 58–59, 70, 73, 91, 153, 170; on codes of ethics 126; on ethical domains 30–31; on fidelity 130–131; on loyalty and cooperation 71–72; moral relativism and 112; on neutrality 76; on translational *telos* 94, 107–111; on translator loyalty 68; on virtue ethics 32–33
Cheyfitz, E. 78

child language brokering 162
Chinese tradition 40–41, 163
Christianity 15; metaethics in 17; normative ethics in 17
Cicero 33, 41
clarification 48
codes of ethics 116–134; accuracy guideline in 122; American Translator's Association (ATA) 119; competence guideline in 122–123; confidentiality guideline in 123, 130; conflicts of interest guideline in 123; content of 130–132; continuing professional development (CPD) guideline in 123–124; coverage of 128–129; defined 117–118; effectiveness of 126–132; enforcement of 127–128; guidelines within 120–125; impartiality/neutrality guideline in 124; integrity and professionalism guidelines in 124–125; internal conflicts in 126–127; neutrality of 132; problems of interpretation and application of 129; role boundaries guideline in 125
Cohen, R. 106–107
Cold War espionage 163
commitment 93–114; from activism to accountability 104–106; advocacy and 98–101, 99; from advocacy to activism 101–103; moral relativism and 111–113; personal versus professional ethics and 94–98; translator's *telos* and 107–111
communication, ethics of 31
competence in codes of ethics 122–123
computer-assisted interpreting (CAI) tools 150, 151
conceptual narratives 102
confidentiality: in codes of ethics 123, 130; of translation technology 155
conflicts of interest 106–107; codes of ethics on 123
Confucianism 15, 40
consequentialism 21–23, 77
content of codes of ethics 130–132
continuing professional development (CPD) 123–124
contractarianism 62
cooperation 62–63, 65–68, 66, 71; case study on loyalty and 71–73; with technology tools 156
Costa, B. 144

court interpreting 35
coverage of codes of ethics 128–129
Cronin, M. 141
Crots, E. 94–95
crowd-sourced translation 162
cultural hegemony 156–158, 157
cultural innovation 77–82
cultural mediators 76, 87–90

Dancy, J. 105
Delgado Luchner, C. 84, 101
Demjanjuk, J. 97
Demosthenes 33
Dentro de la tierra 109–110
deontological ethics 19–21
deontology: Berman's 45; romantic roots and underpinnings of 46–47; translation and 44–45
De optimo genere oratorum 33
DePalma, D. 155
Derrida, J. 163
Deul, J. 169
do Carmo, F. 163
Donovan, C. 127, 128
Drugan, J. 8, 128–129, 133, 140, 145, 149, 150, 155, 162
Dyson, S. 152

egoism and self-interest 165–167
emancipatory translation 76–77
enforcement of codes of ethics 127–128
enlightened egoism 165–167
ennoblement 48–49
environmental sustainability 141–142
equivalence 35, 45
ethical copyright 162–163
ethical dilemmas 106–107
ethical stress 142–147
ethics 11–27; approaches to studying 16–19; as branch of Western philosophy 13–14; codes of 117–134; of communication 31; consequentialism and 21–23; of cooperation 65–66, 66; definitions of 12–14; deontological 19–21; fundamental questions in 14–16; gender-inclusive language and 164–165; metaethics, normative, and applied 16–19; norm-based 31; personal versus professional 94–98; of representation 30–31; roots in Western translation studies 33–35; of service 31; subjectivity and 77;

textual 43; universalisability of 44, 54–55; virtue 24–26, 32–33; why study 26–27 *see also* translation ethics
exoticization of vernacular networks 49–50
expansion 48
Experience of the Foreign: Culture and Translation in Romantic Germany, The 46–47
explanation 45
expressions and idioms, destruction of 50

"fake sign language interpreter" 112–113
Fédération Internationale des Traducteurs (FIT) 118
Federici, F. 139
fidelity 33–35; Chinese tradition and 40–41; loyalty from 59–64, *60*; problematising translation and 37–40; with technology tools 156; textual 43
Folkart, B. 80
foreign, trials of the 47–48
foreignisation 78–81; in practice 82–84
functionalism 59–60, *60*

Garcia, I. 152
gender-inclusive language 164–165
gender studies 162
Gibson, G. D. 101–102
God 15, 16; deontological ethics and 20; metaethics and 17–18; normative ethics and 17; virtue ethics and 25
Goethe, J. W. von 46
Google Translate 151, 157, *157*
Gorman, A. 169–170
Gouadec, D. 148
Gouanvic, J.-M. 34–35, 54, 82, 93
Grapes of Wrath, The 34
Greenall, A. K. 162
Gross, M. 67

Haddow, B. 151
Hale, S. 89, 117, 120, 126
Heafield, K. 151
Hebenstreit, G. 62
Hermans, T. 38–39
hermeneutics 37
Heyvaert, S. 46
Hieronymic Oath 32–33

Hitler, A. 23, 71–72
Hölderlin, F. 46
Horace 33
Hubscher-Davidson, S. 142–143

identity 68–69
idioms: destruction of expressions and 50; translating 52–53
Igarashi, H. 97
impartiality 85–87; in codes of ethics 124
Inghilleri, M. 2, 75, 76, 91, 133; on cultural mediators 87–89; on dismantling neutrality and impartiality in interpreting 85–87; on mediation 99; on moving from textual justice to wider justice 84–85; on personal ethics 96; on professional codes 131, 133, 134
In Other Words 104
Institute of Translation and Interpreting (ITI) code 118
integrity in codes of ethics 124–125
interpretation and application of codes of ethics 129
Interpreting Justice 85, 131
irrationality of language 39
ITI Bulletin 141, 169

Jantjie, T. 112–113
Japanese national anthem 36–37
Jemielity, D. 141
Judaism 15; metaethics in 17; normative ethics in 17
justice 75–91; cultural mediators and 87–90; dismantling neutrality and impartiality in interpreting 85–87; foreignisation in practice and 82–84; overturning neutrality and looking to emancipatory translation and 76–77; from textual to wider 84–85; visibility and cultural innovation in 77–82

Kamocki, P. 155
Kant, I. 20, 24
Katan, D. 162
Kelly, N. 152
Kenny, D. 163
Khomeini, R. 97
Kimigayo 36–37
Ko, L. 129
Kopp, R. K. 60

Koskinen, K. 2, 18, 43; on ethics of linguistic hospitality 163; on positioning in intercultural space 69; on Venuti 78, 80, 82; on visibility 91
Kotze, H. 168–169
Kruger, H. 94–95
Kurultay, T. 162

Laaksonen, J. 78, 82
Lambert, J. 121, 127–128, 134, 137–138, 147, 165–166
Lan Hongjun 41
Laozi 15
La traduction et la lettre 51–54
LeBlanc, M. 150, 156
Lenin, V. 34
Leong Ko 117
L'épreuve de l'étranger: Culture et traduction dans l'Allemagne romantique 46
LGBTQ activism 169
linguistic hospitality 163
linguistic patternings, destruction of 49
literal translation 51–54
Lomax, E. 145–147
loyalty: case study on cooperation and 71–73; function and fidelity 59–64, 60; how to achieve 63

Määttä, S. K. 143
machine translation post-editing (MTPE) 152–153
machine translation (MT) tools 151; post editing and professional status and sustainability 152–153
macro-ethical matters 2
Maier, C. 2, 133
Maitland, S. 109–110
Maltby, M. 132
Mandela, N. 112
Martin Ruano, M. R. 129, 131
Marx, K. 34, 147
McAlester, G. 144
McDonough Dolmaya, J. 120, 121, 126, 128–129
McNicol, T. 169
Megone, C. 8, 128–129, 133, 149
metaethics 16–19
meta (master) narratives 103
micro-ethical matters 2–3
Mikkelson, H. 120
Mill, J. S. 22
Monzó-Nebot, E. 162–163

Moorkens, J. 138, 152, 156, 163
moral absolutes 43
moral particularism 105
moral relativism 111–113
Moster, S. 71–72, 110

narrative theory 101–103
National Association of Judiciary Interpreters and Translators (NAJIT) 126
National Council on Interpreting in Health Care (NCIHC) 125
Nazi war crimes 97
NCIHC (National Council on Interpreting in Health Care) 99–100
neural machine translation (NMT) 150, 157
neutrality 76–77, 85–87; in codes of ethics 124; codes of ethics and 132
New York Times Magazine 23
Nicomachean Ethics 24, 37
Nishimura, K. 169
non-professional translation and interpreting 163
Nord, C. 1, 59, 61–64
normative ethics 16–19
norm-based ethics 31
Nouss, A. 46
Nozick, R. 20

Obama, B. 112
O'Brien, S. 139
omission 44
"On the Different Methods of Translating" 37
On Translator Ethics 65
oral interpretation 38
O'Regan, J. 155
Other, the 51, 161

Paasilinna, A. 71
Pammachius 33–34
paraphrasing 44
particularism 105
pay rates and payment practices, translator 147–149
personal/ontological narratives 102
personal versus professional ethics 94–98
Phelan, M. 3, 114, 118; on advocacy 125, 131–132; on codes of ethics 120–121, 127, 133; on professional ethics and commitment 94, 95

Plato 33
Pokorn, N. 18, 163
police investigative interviews 162
Pöllabauer, S. 85, 99
post-colonial translation studies 162
Pour une éthique du traducteur 67
privacy and confidentiality of translation technology 155
professionalism in codes of ethics 124–125
professionals, ethical 136–159; definitions of professions and professionals in translation and 136–139; egoism and self-interest of 165–167; ethical stress and 142–147; rates of pay and ethical payment practices for 147–149; responsibility of (*see* responsibility); social responsibility of 139–142; translation technology and 150–158, *157*
proverbs 51, 53
Prunč, E. 107, 123
public narratives 102
Putin, V. 67
Pym, A. 29, 41–42, 75, 114, 162; on codes of ethics 117, 124; on commitment 94; on cooperation, risk, and trust 65–71, *66*; on ethics as either/or situation 44; on fidelity 81; on translation technology 150; on translator responsibility 45, 59, 97

qualitative impoverishment 49
quantitative impoverishment 49

Railway Man, The 145–147
rationalization 48
Reiss, K. 34, 59
religious perspective on ethics 163
representation, ethics of 30–31, 167–170
representativeness 167–170
research ethics 162
responsibility 58–74, 170–174, *171*; cooperation, risk, and trust 65–71, *66*; from function and fidelity to loyalty 59–64, *60*; social 139–142, 159
rhythms, destruction of 49
Ricoeur, P. 163
Rijneveld, M. L. 169–170
Robinson, D. 77
Rocchi, M. 138

role boundaries in codes of ethics 125
Routledge Handbook of Translation and Ethics 162, 174
Routledge Handbook of Translation Studies 137
rule consequentialism 22
Rushdie, S. 97
Rütter, C. F. 97

Satanic Verses, The 97–98
Scandals of Translation, The 78, 80, 83
Schaffner, C. 137
Schlegel, A. W. 46
Schleiermacher, F. 29, 37–40, 41, 44, 67, 78, 91
Schweda-Nicholson, N. 120–121
self-care 144–145
self-interest and egoism 165–167
Septuagint 33
service, ethics of 31
Shafer-Landau, R. 20
Skaaden, H. 89–90, 120
skopos theory 34, 60–64, 96
socialist translation theories 163
social responsibility 139–142, 159
Socrates 33
Somers, M. R. 101–102
standards *see* codes of ethics
Stansfield, K. 141
Steinbeck, J. 34
St Jerome 33–34
Straniero-Sergio, F. 162
stress, ethical 142–147
Strowe, A. 168–169
subjectivity 77
superimposition of languages, effacement of 50
sustainability: environmental 141–142; in machine translation 163; machine translation post editing and professional status and 152–153

Tack 68
Tate and turner 134
technology, translation 150–158; collaboration, quality, and fidelity with 156; cultural hegemony and 156–158, *157*; machine translation post editing and professional status and sustainability 152–153; money, ethics, and 158; privacy and confidentiality of 155; sharing and commoditisation of translation

resources and 154–155; types of 150–151
telos 94, 107–111; accountability and 109–110
textual ethics 43
Tipton, R. 140, 145, 162
Topolovec, I. 85, 99
Topping 154
Translating as a Purposeful Activity 61
translation: Berman on producing ethical 50–52; deontology and 44–45; emancipatory 76–77; ethical professionals in (*see* professionals, ethical); functionalist models of 59–60, 60; literal 51–54; narrative theory of 101–103; neutrality in 76–77, 85–87; new fields in 162–164; as political act 78; range of options for 44–45; technology tools for 150–158; twelve deforming tendencies in 48–50; universalisability of ethics in 44, 54–55
Translation and Interpreting Studies 162–163
Translation and Interpreting Studies (TIS) 1, 29–30; codes of ethics in (See codes of ethics); egoism and self-interest in 165–167; environmental sustainability in 141–142; future of 162–164; as multi-dimensional, complex, and evolving 161–162; representation and representativeness in 167–170
"Translation and the Trials of the Foreign" 47
translation ethics 1–2, 29–42; case study-based approach to 7–8; in the classroom 8–9; commitment in 93–114; fidelity in 33–35; functionalism in 59; justice in 75–91; key ethical domains in 30–31; levels in 3, 3; macro-ethical matters in 2; micro-ethical matters in 2–3; philosophical foundations of 11–27; problematising translation and fidelity in 37–40; responsibility in 58–74; *skopos* theory in 34, 60–64, 96; standards in 116–134; technology and 150–158; truth in 43–56; *see also* ethics
Translation in Cascading Crises 139
translation memory (TM) tools 150, 151; sharing and commoditisation of 154–155

translation proper 38–39
Translation Spaces 163
Translator, The 45, 162
Translator's Charter 118
Translator's Invisibility, The 46, 78, 81
Trump, D. 67
truth 43–56; Berman's deontology and 46; deontology and translation and 44–45; producing ethical translation 50–54; romantic roots and deontological understanding of 46–47; trials of the foreign and 47–48; twelve deforming tendencies and 48–50; universalisability and 54–55
Tymoczko, M. 55, 90
Tyndale, W. 34

underlying networks of signification, destruction of 49
universalisability of ethics in translation 44, 54–55
utilitarianism 22
UX Content Collective 164–165

van Vogt, A. E. 34
van Wyke, B. 137
Venuti, L. 29, 46, 47, 73, 75, 76, 90; on egoism 165; on visibility and cultural innovation 77–84
Vermeer, H. J. 34, 61
vernacular networks, destruction of 49–50
Vian, B. 34
vicarious trauma (VC) 143
virtue ethics 24–26, 32–33
visibility 77–82
volunteer interpreters 162

Walker, C. 147
Wallace, M. 162–163
war crimes 97
Washbourne, K. 167
Weaver, W. 151
Wecksteen, C. 65
Wilensky, H. L. 117
written translation 38

Xie Tianzhen 41

Yo, El Supremo 51, 55

Zhou, M. 9

For Product Safety Concerns and Information please contact our EU
representative GPSR@taylorandfrancis.com
Taylor & Francis Verlag GmbH, Kaufingerstraße 24, 80331 München, Germany

www.ingramcontent.com/pod-product-compliance
Lightning Source LLC
Chambersburg PA
CBHW051358290426
44108CB00015B/2064